MORDECAI RICHLER'S

TEXTS AND CONTEXTS

A NEW HISTORICIST PERSPECTIVE

MORDECAI RICHLER'S

TEXTS AND CONTEXTS

A NEW HISTORICIST PERSPECTIVE

Dr M. Mary Jayanthi

AUTHORSPRESS

Worldwide Circulation through Authorspress Global Network
First Published in 2022
by
Authorspress
Q-2A Hauz Khas Enclave, New Delhi-110 016 (India)
Phone: (0) 9818049852
E-mail: authorspressgroup@gmail.com
Website: www.authorspressbooks.com

Mordecai Richler's Texts and Contexts: A New Historicist Perspective
ISBN 978-93-5529-312-1

Printed in India at Kensington Press

Foreword

> "Fundamentally, all writing is about the same thing; it's about dying, about the brief flicker of time we have here, and the frustration that it creates."
>
> Mordecai Richler

The literary attainments of the last decades of the 20th century is rooted in Canada's literary past. It is the harvest of many decades of thoughtful creations. Canadian writing began as an imitative colonial literature culture. Later on, it steadily developed its own national self. This was because of the huge immigrations of New England Puritans from 1760 and later of American Loyalists during the revolution, it is often said that Canadian literature followed U.S until the confederation in 1867. The corpus of Canadian literature has great international visibility today. It arrests critical attention of readers all over the reading world. The corpus began in the 17th century, achieved its distinctive character only after Canada gained independence from Britain in 1867. From the beginnings of European colonization in the 1600's until national hood various factors affected cultural development in the territory now known as Canada. From colonial times onwards, European Canadians were divided into two distinct populations. In the year that followed the Second World War and in the post-war period of 1960 s the Canadian women began to assert their feminine sensibility and their resistance to the patriarchal system. The Women's Movement in 1960s served as a catalyst and brought about a greater awareness and contributed to strengthen their quest for cultural identity.

Canada's ethnic and cultural diversity are with many of its most prominent writers focusing on ethnic life and cross-cultural hegemony. The two early important novelists were Morley Callaghan in English and Gabrielle Roy in French. The prominent theme in Canadian literature is the search for identity and survival of the self in a society whose public and personal relationship are characterized by estrangement, exploitation, domination and appropriation. At times, it depicts a woman stripping her of social mask, defenses and ideals to discover her essential. There are Woman's novels. There are also feministic and nationalistic concerns in novels. Politics and economy are two important domains which come again and again in literary productions. The reading market is essentially multicultural. Texts are read differently in different cultures. The literary pot is multi layered.

A committed writer, Richler lived as an expatriate in Europe for more than two decades. However, a large part of his fiction is set within the Jewish section of Montreal where he spent his formative years. Richler's fabric has many hues. Mary Jayanthi's reading of the texts give us an eye to delve into fresh perspectives. This book is a rich reading and resource to understand Mordecai Richler's Montreal novels with ample textual reference. The well-organized chapters and sub-chapters lend to the main argument on the construction of 'self' and 'discernment of choice'. They also individually stand out as a definite study to understand Richler's themes and narrative style.

Mordecai Richler's texts are about the conflicting hyphenated identities. This book titled *Mordecai Richler's Texts and Contexts: A New Historicist Approach* is based on Jayanthi's Ph.D. research titled "Conflicts from Surrounding Spaces of the mid-20th Century Jewish Montreal Ghetto: A New Historicist Approach to Richler's Select Novels". It is an attempt to chart the process of cultural negotiation in a hybrid culture of the Jewish-Canadian identity. No doubt, this enhances insight into the construction of the 'self' graphed in the tension of its surrounding space. Jayanthi tries to understand intellectual history of the time through its cultural contexts delving deep into the social, cultural and religious roots. There is no discourse that is archival. Jayanthi takes the contexts of literary and non-literary, and proves that they are inseparable by category. She has made an in-depth analysis of cultural poetics the ideology of Richler's era. Her every act of unmasking the truth, is in a way, her participation in a network of material practices.

This book will surely entice scholars, researchers and students for a better understanding of Mordecai Richler's texts and the literary perspectives.

A book without an expiry date!

Jaydeep Sarangi
Fellow academic and bilingual poet anchored in Kolkata.

Preface

Canadian Literature is a rich platter of multiple ethnic voices. Jewish Writing in Canada especially post-war and post-holocaust is mainly about the moral dilemma under the steady regulation of tradition and culture. The Jewish-Canadian novel generally focuses on the ethnic life of Jews in Canada and on the survival of identity in a multicultural framework. Mordecai Richler, Jewish-Canadian novelist, satirist, story-teller, critic, essayist, editor, children's writer, journalist, screen-play writer and social commentator is a cultural icon in Canada. A prominent, literary contrarian, Richler was best known for his black comical novels in which he examines such diverse topics as Canadian society, Jewish culture and Quebec nationalism.

Richler's themes include the adverse effects of materialism, relationships between individuals from different socio-economic backgrounds and the constant argument between Jewish Orthodoxy and Secularism both at societal and individual levels. The moral codes of his age, home and exile, familial relationships within a Canadian geographical space and Canadian space outside the national boundaries are also his concerns. He projects the effect of Holocaust, socio-geographical living space of the Jewish ghetto in Montreal, Canada, 'third solitude' and the legroom of a third generation Jewish-Canadian in a crowded multicultural land. A brutally honest writer, Richler lived as an expatriate in Europe for more than twenty years. However, a large part of his fiction is set within the Jewish section of Montreal where he was raised. Kramer notes that if scholars need to understand Canada at mid-century that is between 1940 and 1970 or the secularization of western Jews, they turn to Mordecai Richler.

Mordecai Richler's texts delve into the conflicting hyphenated identities and recreate the surrounding space of his period. This book titled *Mordecai Richler's Texts and Contexts: A New Historicist Approach* is based on my Ph.D. dissertation titled "Conflicts from Surrounding Spaces of the mid-20th Century Jewish Montreal Ghetto: A New Historicist Approach to Richler's Select Novels" submitted to Bharathidasan University, Tamilnadu, India. The book follows the 7th Edition of *MLA Handbook for Writers of Research Papers* for documentation.

This work is an attempt to map the 'contexts' and 'co-texts' that had been 'exchanged' and 'negotiated' in a hybrid culture of the Jewish-Canadian identity. I've closely juxtaposed the select literary texts with select non-literary texts to validate the work by applying the New Historicist textual practice to reconstruct the ideology of Richler's age. This could possibly enhance insight into the construction of the 'self' caught in the tension of its surrounding space.

Six out of Richler's ten novels which have a Jewish-Canadian Surrounding Space and Montreal as its social geography are chosen for the present study. According to PC Kar, Surrounding Space refers to Greenblatt's idea of *circumambient space* to suggest that a work of art draws its creative energy from the surrounding space as a cultural artifact. The select novels include *Son of a Smaller Hero* (1955), *The Apprenticeship of Duddy Kravitz* (1959), *St. Urbain's Horseman* (1971), *Joshua Then and Now* (1980), *Solomon Gursky was Here* (1989) and *Barney's Version* (1997). The scope of this work is limited to these novels of Richler as representative of texts written in mid and later half of twentieth century and set primarily in the Jewish Montreal ghetto.

A serious study of Richler leads to the research question, 'What makes Richler's protagonists have such a moral dilemma that it inevitably results in criminal transgression?' The aim of the research is to draw new attention to Richler's texts from a New Historicist perspective "in which literature reflects not only the intentions of its creators as self-conscious respondents to their time periods but also the ways in which a variety of systems and responses to power are reflected in a given text" (Hall 301). Are these, indications of an intrinsic thematic pattern of moral conflict and transgression that suggests itself in Richler's novels, which may throw more light on the research question, point at answers or new directions and raise debates? The hypothesis is that, Surrounding Spaces affect Richler's protagonists who indulge in criminal transgressions and possibly in moral policing others they expose hypocritical families and societies. All this in turn may affect or change them. The study also works on Richler's insights into how people's lives are a reflection of their time, place, race, gender, sexuality and economic situation and how these factors contribute to the moral vision of the protagonists.

The methodology adopted for the study includes a non-linear New Historicist perspective of the intricately styled Richler's novels along with a parallel reading of select non-literary texts to see whether a thematic pattern evolves from this. Greenblatt in *Towards a Poetics of Culture* defines a work of art as "The product of a negotiation between a creator or class of creators, equipped with a complex, communally shared repertoire of conventions, and the institutions and practices of society" (158). The study plan is to apply Greenblatt's concepts of New Historicist practice to the select novels. Richler's novels are interlaced with the Jewish tradition and milieu in a Canadian context. These highlight Jewish inclinations and deviations in working out their identity. He explicates the conflicts and moral issues that arise in a multicultural set up. His novels also resonate with 'wonder' of his time and place and can be studied as cultural texts with a symbolic dimension of social action. Application of the New Historicism practice shows how the present work latches on to that dimension of religious and familial representation seen in the works of the author. This entails a historical research of the culture and tradition of the mid-20th century Montreal ghetto which may throw further light on the thematic pattern of the select novels. These in turn focus on the conflicts that arise from the 'circumambient space' and again in Greenblatt's term the *improvisation* the characters make to tune in or out of their cultural constraints.

The present focus on texts and contexts of Mordecai Richler's select works can be explained. The Jews came to Canada, around two-and-a-half centuries ago, and as Joe King historicizes, "...brought with them their history, their traditions and their culture. They also brought with them memories of hate and hostility, of abandoned homes and ancestral graves" (xix). In Montreal, the wandering Jews finally found a new home and as King records, "... their lives centered on the "lower Main," the southern-most portion of St. Lawrence Boulevard" which developed into a Jewish Quarter or ghetto in downtown Montreal (102). But these settlers were subjugated to anti-Semitic prejudice and inequality in a Christian-Canadian context. So, conflicts in living styles were obvious outcomes and it is these surrounding spaces and disturbances that constitute life in the 20th Century Montreal ghetto. These conflicts influence the cultural context of Richler's setting, theme and characterization and lead to the present analysis. The pattern also traces how conflicts arising from cultural contexts affect the protagonist and indicates whether the Canadian-Jews conform to or deviate from power and conflict.

Greenblatt's 'Self-Fashioning' argues that the self is a social-construct. He asserts that "social and ideological forces prevail over individual desires" and "the fiction of autonomous selfhood remains" (Robson 64). This is debatable. Fashioning the Self, according to the social and cultural aspects is unidimensional where the self is superficially or outwardly modelled and the self may become stagnant. It creates an internal void where the person is condensed to puppet-forms of survival and gives no room for the individual's choice. The present work aims to show that a self, although caught in the mire of cultural definitions and distractions, finds meaning from within through discernment of choice with reference to Richler's protagonists.

Human beings are in a constant state of flux. The definition of the Self is dynamic. The ideas that people are culture-sculpted or capable of making their own choice has been a field for the creation and rewriting of theories. The present study evolved as part of the universal quest to understand the conflicting definitions of the Self by writers and philosophers. Similar patterns of conflicts are recognized in the novelist Mordecai Richler's Jewish protagonists who are fashioned and redesigned by their surrounding spaces and selves. Are they just by-products of conflicting spaces, their troubled selves or both or do they evolve into a proactive self with awareness and purpose are questions that need to be examined. Richler true to his age and period astringently looked out of the less-chosen window, sharply rebuked, laughed and tirelessly chronicled the Jewish-Montreal life and experience. This made him at once an ingenuous storyteller and acidic reprover of his times. Richler's works lend a powerful voice of truth with his artistic literary techniques. Kramer calls the works as "important relics of contemporary secular culture" (7) set in the mid-twentieth century Jewish Montreal ghetto. Richler states, "I'm trying to tell the truth, I don't think it's something that has to be in season, like hockey or hay fever. I think you should be able to tell the truth any time" (Posner 281). Richler's truthful literary recreation of his times can examine the question on the Self on an objective plane.

The book is divided into 5 Chapters and each chapter is further divided into sub-sections. It also contains three appendixes which include a glossary of Yiddish words used in the book, a page of important photographs and photocopies of E-communication with Richler's biographer Charles Foran and daughter Emma Richler.

Chapter I entitled *In the Beginning* elucidates the Canadian literary mosaic, identity and image. It introduces the Jewish Tessera of writing, focuses on Richler's works and maps the evolution of New Historicism as a textual practice. It explicates Stephen Greenblatt's major concepts and terms to support the present work's focus and assertion and explains why it differs with his model of 'Self-fashioning'. It explains why New Historicism has been chosen as a textual approach and details the literature review done and expounds the scope and hypothesis of the present argument. It shows that Canadian Literature is a much-sought destination for scholarship and Richler's works stand out as signature texts for its authentic voice and literary excellence.

Chapter II entitled *Surrounding Spaces* is on the application of New Historicism as a textual practice to Richler's select novels. It explains how Richler's novels absorb the surrounding space of the mid-twentieth century Jewish Montreal ghetto throwing light on the Jewish race, Montreal space, Orthodox Judaism, effect of Holocaust and the Jew-Gentile divide. It aims to explain the New Historicist practice, that context and text are inseparable and the text cannot be an isolated entity. The intention is to analyze the surrounding spaces of the mid-twentieth century Montreal life and tradition and how it fashions individuals.

Chapter III on *'Self-Fashioning' – Confronting Conflicting Conflicts and Moral Policing* is directed on how the surrounding space constructs a socially-conditioned self. Questions arise. How do Duddy, Noah, Jake, Joshua, Moses, Solomon and Barney confront conflicts and moral dilemma? Do the protagonists conform to or rebel against the social-given self? These questions are analyzed by studying the constraints imposed by the 'circumambient space' and the various forms of 'improvisations that the protagonists' resort to. It discusses the individual versus power structures built on religion and tradition. It outlines the conflicts, moral issues and discernment of choices of Richler's protagonists. It also traces the model of human personality the novels imply or construct and the type of a historically specific representation of truth and authority they reveal. This chapter examines the importance of the knots and ties of families and man-woman relationship, deliberates on gender-roles and explains the "third solitude" of the Jewish-Canadian. It brings out some of the driving forces governing the moral policing of hypocritical families and societies.

Chapter IV on *Textual Relics* analyzes the formal aspects of narratives which Greenblatt calls as 'cultural poetics'. Richler's texts are literary artifacts that resonate with Greenblatt's 'wonder' of the 1940's and 50's Jewish Montreal Ghetto. It explores how Richler recreates it through narratives, language, imagery, parody and satire.

The final chapter on *The Promised Land* analyzes the roads taken by various protagonists and how the tradition, culture and the towering ghetto wall affect the social formation of the characters and the choices they make. Do the protagonists reach their Promised Land and are their lands the same are discussed. Do the routes they opt in turn affect the family and there by the society are also examined.

The present study is truly original from a perspective of an Indian's understanding of the Jewish-Canadian culture and social living of the mid-twentieth century Montreal based on the written word in Richler's select novels. The book studies the select novels of Richler a world class writer and hopes to popularize his works in India so that it may bring in more debates and scholars interested in his works.

"The LORD is my strength and my shield; my heart trusted in Him, and I am helped; therefore, my heart greatly rejoiceth; and with my song will I praise Him" (Psalm 28:7). I praise God for the grace to develop my Self from within and for steering a spiritual journey into the intellectual realm of letters and revelations.

It is with a warm heart and a grateful spirit that I thank my Research Supervisor, Dr. Cheryl Quental Mary, whose innate graciousness, deep concern and counsel had ingrained clarity and precision in the work done. I praise and thank God for the treasure trove of teachers, friends, colleagues, well-wishers whose steady support and ready help and prayers has brought me this far. I would love to thank my students whose spirits and moments of questioning have made the teacher in me grow into a better scholar every time.

I sincerely thank Stephen Greenblatt for his encouraging line, Emma Richler and Charles Foran for their responses to my queries on Richler. I owe my beginning interests on New Historicism to Prof. Prafulla Kar, Director, Centre for Contemporary Theory, MS University of Baroda, for his talk and e-communications.

I am grateful to Holy Cross College Library, Tiruchirappalli, for the extensive resource support and for making available books in Jewish-Canadian literature and New Historicism. A special note of gratitude to the library and centre in charge of The Centre for Canadian Studies and Central Library, Bharathidasan University,

Tiruchirappalli, The Indo-Shastri Canadian Institute, Delhi, The Centre for Canadian Studies at the SNDT Women's University, Mumbai and Jadavpur University, Kolkatta, The Osmania Centre for International Programmes, The Ramesh Mohan Library, EFL University and The Indira Gandhi Memorial Library, Hyderabad for allowing easy access, immediate responses and liberal use of resources.

With immense love, I thank my parents, my moral strength, who let me see the different paths of life and allowed the discernment of choice, to let me be and become a finer version, day by day. I owe it to my parents-in-law, for all the time and health I had to write and also for help extended to balance my study and home.

I thank my husband G. Manoj Kumar, my entire energy system who gave me the luxury of 'A Room of One's Own' space to progress as a 'thinking woman' with the choices I made not only to work the thesis/book but also in life. I affectionately thank my sister Mary Priya Michael for her soulful encouragement at every stage of my development of ideas. My special words of gratitude to my spiritual sister M. Gayathri whose selfless concern to help me out in small and great ways expedited the completion of my work. A loving note of thanks to my little princess Juanne Jananee Manoj, who evolved into her own independent self and made life beautiful throughout the scholarly journey. I fondly remember my mentor and spiritual mother Dr. Shanti Baliah who taught me literature and life with proficiency, passion and zeal.

Mary Jayanthi

Contents

A Note on Documentation

The following editions of the primary sources have been used:

Richler, Mordecai. *The Apprenticeship of Duddy Kravitz.* Ontario: Penguin Books Ltd., 1959. Print.

.......*Barney's Version.* Canada: Alfred A Knopf. 1997. Print.

.......*Joshua Then and Now.* Ontario: McClelland & Stewart Inc. 1980. Print.

........*Son of a Smaller Hero.* Toronto: McClelland and Stewart Limited, 1955. Print.

.......*Solomon Gursky Was Here.* Ontario: Penguin. 1990. Print.

.......*St. Urbain's Horseman.* Toronto: McClelland & Stewart Inc. 1989. Print

The following shortened forms have been used in this book for the works printed against them when they form part of the study:

Smaller Hero – Son of a Smaller Hero

Solomon Gursky – Solomon Gursky Was Here

Duddy Kravitz – The Apprenticeship of Duddy Kravitz

The following abbreviations have been used in this book for the works printed against them in citing parenthetical references:

BV *Barney's Version*

CJW *Contemporary Jewish Writing in Canada*

GRY *Every Goy's Guide to Richler: Yiddish phrases & Jewish cultural references in The Apprenticeship of Duddy Kravitz*

GJ *"Glossary of Judaism"*

HSH *Home Sweet Home: My Canadian Album*

IDK *Introducing Mordecai Richler's The Apprenticeship of Duddy Kravitz*

JGV *"Jewish Glossary" Jewish Virtual Library*

JTN	*Joshua Then and Now*
LC	*Learning To Curse: Essays in Early Modern Culture*
MP	*Marvellous Possessions*
RSF	*Renaissance Self-Fashioning: From More to Shakespeare*
SG	*Solomon Gursky Was Here*
SH	*Son of a Smaller Hero*
SUH	*St. Urbain's Horseman*
DK	*The Apprenticeship of Duddy Kravitz*
TS	*Third Solitudes: Tradition and Discontinuity in Jewish-Canadian Literature*

Use of Greenblatt's expressions/ conceptual phrases/ ideas for the first time is in Bold. The repeated use of Greenblatt's concept and language is marked in single quotes to indicate that they are used in the Greenblattian sense.

Yiddish words and references that connote Jewish tradition are marked in italics within single quotes.

Courtesy Credits

The following papers have been published previously and are related to this work.

The figure a Jew makes in Mordecai Richler's select novels – *Academia and Society, International Journal of Education Society* Vol 2, No. 2, (ISSN 2393-9419) Vol 2, Number 2, (Pgs 42-46), pub by Academia and Society, Come Alive Centre, HCC campus, Tiruchirappalli-2, February 2016

Textual Relics of 'Wonder and Resonance' in the select novels of Mordecai Richler. Gandhigram Literary Review, Vol 6, *Peer-reviewed Journal of Literary Studies*, Gandhigram Rural Institute, Tamilnadu, summer 2017

Dilemma and Deviance in the Select Novels of Mordecai Richler-*Contemporary Contemplations on Diasporic Literature*, ISBN 978-93-88008-58-7, Page Numbers 9-38, Editors Dr. Suresh Frederick and Dr. Samuel Rufus, Authorspress, New Delhi, 2018

Silhouettes, Silences and Voices of Women in Mordecai Richler's Select Novels – *Contemporary Contemplations on New Literatures in English*, ISBN 978-93-89615-61-6, Page Numbers 58-71, Editors Dr. Suresh Frederick and Dr. Samuel Rufus, Authorspress, New Delhi, 2020

1

In the Beginning

> It (Canada's) is a literature that, compulsively seeking its own story, ... comes compulsively to a genealogy that refuses origin, to a genealogy that speaks instead, and anxiously, and with a generous reticence, the nightmare and the welcome dream of Babel.
>
> (Robert Kroetsch, "Beyond Nationalism: A Prologue" 71)

Canadian Literature is a rich platter of multiple ethnic voices. Officially bilingual, its literature branches off into three primary divisions which include The English, The French and the Aboriginal Writings. Although early Canadian writing began as a replication of colonial texts, which Frye calls "formula-writing", it has devised distinctive nationalistic themes, patterns, characteristics and has risen from its provincial status to a universal stature. Before the Confederation of 1867, myriad accounts, images, visions and creations of Canada as a nation have been argued and contested. The granular beginning of a nation and a national literature began to take shape after 1867 and crystallized during Canada's participation in World War I.

1.1 The Canadian Literary Mosaic

The Canadian novel came into existence with the pioneering work of John Richardson, who's *Wacousta* (1832) popularized the genre of the national historical novel. However John Moss traces *The History of Emily Montague* (1769) by Frances Brooke as the earliest entry into the Canadian tradition (7). *The Clockmaker* (1836) by T. C. Haliburton and the historical novels of William Kirby, author of *The Golden Dog* (1877), and Sir Gilbert Parker, author of *The Seats of the Mighty* (1896), Jeannette Duncan's A *Social Departure* (1890), Rev. C. W. Gordon's (Ralph Connor) *Black Rock* (1898) marked the beginnings of the Canadian novel.

The early-twentieth century Canadian novels intended towards stricter realism and have remained predominantly regional. William H. New traces that, "The 1950's expressed the liberal views of English and Scots Canada, affirming as ideals an international social identity and an image of the nation as a cultural mosaic" (234). Claude Bissell writes that the new political agenda of the 1960's harbingered the rise of Literature in Canada which achieved a new self-consciousness as a force within society and edged slowly upward in the list of national priorities. New, views this period especially between 1960 and 1973 as continuity with the past which tends to reflect something about the Canadian character. Works of writers who put forth their voices in 1940s and 1950s marked the literary output of the age. Michael Cross states that, the controlling concept of the "Laurentian orthodoxy" began to break up during this period. Appearance of small presses and literary magazines encouraged writing. Works of MacLennan, Atwood and Purdy responded to the political theme as quoted by Bissell, "(what is the nature of the Canadian place and how does its definition relate to our well-being?)" (10). By the end of the 1960's both English and French Canadian Literature constituted the double heritage of the mainstream literature.

Literature in Canada gained status as late as the early sixties with exemplary works from writers like Morley Callaghan, Hugh MacLennan, Ernest Buckler, Robertson Davies, Brian Moore, Robert Kroetsch, Timothy Findlay, Rudy Wiebe, Michael Ondaatje, Neil Bissoondath, M. G. Vassanji and Mordecai Richler. Profound women writers include Sheila Watson, Mavis Gallant, Sara Jeanette Duncan, Ethel Wilson, Gwethalyn Graham, Margaret Laurence, Margaret Atwood and Alice Munro.

According to Linda Hutcheon, the palpable effect of the decade of 1960's continued to be felt in the novels of the 1970s and 80s which reflected the ideological climate of the sixties in their broad political orientation. New observed that by the 1970s, realism was losing ground to improvisational modes and the voices of ethnic minorities began to be heard. He notes it to be a time full of paradoxes and difficult decisions and literature more often expressed disappointment and anger than joy.

Following the Canadian tradition of the novels, other genres of writing began to surface. Northrop Frye made original contribution to criticism through his archetypal theory. Humourist and essayist Stephen Leacock's fine scholarship and essays of Sir Andrew Macphail, Archibald MacMechan and Lorne Pierce are notable for their ideas and style. Plays of James Reaney and George Ryga brought alive the theatre of Canada. Canadian poetry, despite late development, began to flourish with the works of Charles Sangster, Charles Heavysege, C.G.D. Roberts, Archibald Lampman, Bliss Carman and Duncan Campbell Scott. Outstanding poets in the E.J. Pratt tradition include Earle Birney, W. W. E. Ross and Dorothy Livesay. F. R. Scott, Irving Layton, Phyllis Webb and Leonard Cohen are other prominent poets.

The tessellated literary canon of Canada began to be noticed globally, slowly but steadily from the late fifties and early sixties onwards. The post-1960's period has come to be known as the Canadian "renaissance" because it marked the "new beginnings" in Canadian writings as opined by Salat. Marta Dvorak observes that, Canada like many postcolonial societies began her literature with "an initial period of imitation or emulation of metropolitan norms, then a configuration or shift towards assimilation, and finally – in a desire to forge a distinctive national culture – a reconfiguration or revaluation of that which has been considered marginal" (155).

The Canadian identity and image

"Nations," wrote Aldous Huxley in *Texts and Pretexts,* "are to a large extent invented by their poets and novelists" (qtd. in Salat 1). With a land of striking physical contrasts and survival-conscious people, the vexed question of a Canadian identity is an unrequited puzzle. Germaine Warkentin's question "With what are we to identify ourselves" in his *An Image in a Mirror* and Northrop Frye's riddle on "Where is here?" in *The Bush Garden* are inquiries of a Canadian mind to find "What is Canadian about Canadian Literature"? (Atwood 9-11). It is not only a literary question but a national enigma. Hutcheon observes, "Canada can in some ways be defined as a country whose articulation of its *national* identity has sprung from regionalistic impulses: the ex-centric forces of Quebec, the Maritimes, the west. Its history is one of defining itself against centres" (4). As examined by many the nature and definition of the country, its literature and identity constitute philosophical, psychological, political and cultural debates which often find literary expression. "For the members of a country or a culture, shared knowledge of their place, their here, is not a luxury but a necessity. Without that knowledge we will not survive" (Atwood 19). As the "island" and "frontier" connote the British and American identities, Atwood recognizes "survival" as the Canadian identity. "A national literature is an essential element in the formation of national character. It is not merely the record of a country's mental progress: it is the expression of its intellectual life, the bond of national unity, and the guide of national energy" (Waterston 79). The Canadian identity of survival survived self-deprecating questions and armoured against the colonial effect of the British and frontier influence of the American nation and literature. This led to a Canadian multicultural pattern and mosaic of varied voices.

The Multicultural Mosaic

> Consider a mosaic: it consists of an arrangement of individual tiles with distinctive shapes, colours, and textures. These tiles are aligned in a unified and coherent pattern whose overall image is one of unity and coherence. The overall effect transcends the individual tiles, although all continue to retain their integrity and distinctiveness. (Fleras and Elliott 65)

The Canadian Rockies, Tundra, Prairies, Great lakes, maple leaf, fur trade, Canada Goose, Common Loon and Inuksuk are symbols synonymous to Canada and its existence. Canada is more than spreadsheets of ice and mountains topped with snow, with beaver on the rivers and stories of frozen deserts. Ranking second as largest country in area next to Russia, Canada is a cultural mosaic, populated with a global presence of a broad assortment of ethnic, regional and aboriginal origin and strives to sustain its theory of a multicultural mosaic. The mosaic image provides an intriguing metaphor to describe the ideal of Canadian multiculturalism. "The emergence of multiculturalism as a formal instrument in managing diversity is widely recognized as Canada's outstanding contribution to the field of race and ethnic relations" (Fleras and Elliott 2). Multiculturalism is a "distinctive way of thinking" about ethnicity, which welcomes the "mosaic" culture as opposed to the American "melting pot" culture. The mosaic culture is an attempt to make visible the minorities. Lipset notes that the Canadian Jewish Community is much better organized than its American counterpart because of the Cultural Pluralism.

From a struggle to "surface" and "survive", Canadian Literature has grown into an appreciative, universal literature not only for its English and French material, but for its thick, variant, cultural fabric which includes the work of ethnic writers. The Canadian literary history is a mosaic of settlers and ethnic imprints. Mordecai Richler is a profound ethnic writer who has carved a niche for himself in the realm of Jewish-Canadian Literature with his creative and critical writings. According to Moss, Richler along with Robertson Davies, Alice Munro and Rudy Wiebe marked the Canadian tradition with a rather wishful optimism, "(whose troubled visions of loss include the possibility of redemption)" (10).

1.2 The Jewish Tessera

> "Breaking and joining with tradition, Jewish Canadian memory rises out of lost homes and voices to populate a no-man's land with figures of the imagination" (Greenstein, *TS* 17).

Jewish Writing in Canada especially post-war and post-holocaust is mainly about the moral dilemma under the steady regulation of tradition and culture. Similar to the mainstream writers, preoccupation of identity constitutes the thematic structures of the writings of A.M. Klein, Mordecai Richler, Henry Kriesel, Adele Wiseman, Jack Ludwig, Norman Levine, Naim Kattan, Monique Bosco, Leonard Cohen and Matt Cohen. The works of these writers build up a respectable corpus of Jewish-Canadian writing and these ethnic voices in print began to grow up in bulk and stature. In *Contemporary Jewish Writing in Canada,* Greenstein traces that at the confluence of Frye's image of the bush garden with the Laurentian shield and the St. Lawrence River lies the island of Montreal, which is the birthplace of Jewish Canadian literature. He notes Klein's idea that Montreal Jewry had flesh and blood ties with many parts of Eastern and Central Europe and also a strong Yiddish influence. The Jewish-Canadian novel generally focuses on the ethnic life of Jews in Canada and on the survival of identity in a multicultural framework. As observed by Salat, the writers like their mainstream counterparts are engaged in the Jungian internal quest and the search for modes of relating oneself to the community and the communal heritage.

A.M. Klein is the father of Jewish-Canadian literature. *The Second Scroll* (1951) his seminal novel, "acts as a point of departure for short stories and novels" by the other writers and the works "mediate between tradition and modernism, home and exile, Jewish-Canadian particularism and universal significance" (Greenstein, *TS* 3). Jewish-Canadian fiction deals with the quests of anti-heroes, orphans, adolescents, immigrants for their parents, their homeland and a meaningful tradition. Greenstein notes that *The Second Scroll* breaks with earlier sacred texts in its attempt to stake out new territory and to discover new directions for Jewish-Canadian literature.

Jewish literature thrives both in America and Canada. The Jewish-American writers, Saul Bellow, Bernard Malamud and Philip Roth as well as their Canadian counterparts that include Klein, Richler and their clan, explore what Maurice Wohlgelernter discusses as the ambivalences of assimilation with encroachments of a provincial past and dissatisfactions with mainstream culture.

George Woodcock in his introduction to *Smaller Hero* credits the Jewish writers in Canada with a peculiar force, sensitivity and genuine artistry, that specially created the Canadian urban life. Themes of complex heritage of experience, isolation and division, which are truly Canadian and the invisible ghettos being a land of minorities, are the major themes of Jewish-Canadian writing. Greenstein observes that Jewish-Canadian Literature although caught between a conservative British tradition and an aggressive American influence with a long immigrant history has charted a unique, intermediate course with an all-encompassing centre. He calls it to be "doubly ghettoized and regionalized" between Montreal and the prairies and "internalizes the ghetto-garrison mentality as each writer seeks a means of escaping the ghetto while adhering to its traditions" (*CJW* xii). It has traditionally been a tale of two ghettos – Montreal's Main, or St. Lawrence area and the north end of Winnipeg. While A.M. Klein, Mordecai Richler, Leonard Cohen and Irving Layton mint the Montreal ore, Miriam Waddington, Jack Ludwig and Adele Wiseman absorb their material from the Winnipeg ghettos. Other writers who explored the theme of the hybrid identity through varied genres include Coleman J. Newman, Eli Mandel, Monique Bosco, Phyllis Gotlieb, Ted Allen, Shirley Faessler and Seymour Blicker. Norman Levine consciously questioned his childhood Judaism faith in his works. The model of immigrant settlement especially Jewish and the trials and feats of these communities were written and documented widely.

Apart from literary interests, works on Jewish settlements in Canada such as Kastus Akula's *Tomorrow is Yesterday* (1968), Hilda Shubert's *They Came from Kernitza* (1969) and Phyllis Gotlieb's *Why Should I Have All the Grief?* have sociological value to their works. With mass immigration, generations of younger writers, have shifted from the earlier centers to Toronto, becoming a part of a multicultural mosaic, blending Jewish, Canadian and cosmopolitan values. From Anne Michaels's *Greek Island* to Aryeh Lev Stollman's *Berlin* and Michael Redhill's *Irish synagogue*, Jewish-Canadian literature engages exile, both "at home abroad and abroad at home". Norman Ravvin states that "Jewish Writing since the Second World War has been burdened – or one might say, inspired – by the past" (3). Greenstein traces, "Out of the prophetic tradition and Klein's polished lens, Layton's improved binoculars and Richler's and Cohen's wrong-ended telescopes aim their satiric vision at the immortality of Jews and Gentiles alike in modern society" (*TS* 203).

1.3 Mordecai Richler-The Honest Voice

> "Mordecai would never bow his head to him, which made him (Haman) wonder about his muscle" (*JTN* 290).

Mordecai Richler (1931-2001), Jewish-Canadian novelist, satirist, story-teller, critic, essayist, editor, children's writer, journalist, screen-play writer and social commentator is a cultural icon in Canada. A prominent literary contrarian, Richler was best known for his black comical novels in which he examines such diverse topics as Canadian society, Jewish culture and Quebec nationalism. His themes include the adverse effects of materialism, relationships between individuals from different socio-economic backgrounds and the constant argument between Jewish Orthodoxy and Secularism both at the societal and individual levels. The moral codes of his age, home and exile, familial relationships within a Canadian geographical space and a Canadian space outside the national boundaries are also his concerns. He projects the effect of Holocaust, the socio-geographical living space of the Jewish ghetto in Montreal, Canada, the "third solitude" and the leg room of a third generation Jewish-Canadian in a crowded multicultural land. A brutally honest writer, Richler lived as an expatriate in Europe for more than twenty years. However, a large part of his fiction is set within the Jewish section of Montreal where he was raised and explores the characteristics of the Jewish-Canadian identity in his works.

Critical reception for Richler's undaunted writing, at least during his time was ambivalent. As Charles Foran examines, he was a man of mixed-reputation among many Jews, being "the self-hating Jew, the anti-Semitic Semite" (x). Named after the teacher of his maternal grandfather Hassidic Rabbi Yudel Rosenberg, the honest Mordecai, was angry with the meanness and self-pity in the ghettoed Jewish minds and not with the Jews as such. An undercurrent of hypocrisy is what he abhorred not only in the Jewish tradition but in the human nature as a whole.

Although Richler's writing instinct could be attributed to the Rosenberg's lettering roots, the Hebrew scholar, author, teacher and mystic *'zeyda'*, couldn't fully convince the grandchild of his rich religious tradition. Richler inherited the fearless mind of his Biblical namesake Mordecai from the *Book of Esther*, which is reflected in his acerbic tone. His paternal grandfather Shmarya Richler, whose family name Mordecai has immortalized, has also been a large influence in shaping the young boy's morale. Living a life of materialistic values except on the day of *shabbus,* Shmarya Richler's hypocritical moral-code in his scrap yard business and "tyrannical orthodoxy", made young Mordecai question the whole practice of Jewry. This misplacement of moral compass encased in strict adherence to religious strictures and the double standards of living is what Mordecai repeatedly questions, mocks and jests in his writing.

Richler was born on 27th January 1931, just in time to give his mother Leah Rosenberg a reason to hold on to the already cracking marriage and another occasion of excuse for the father Moses Richler. Richler's parents never had a common referral point either in their upbringing, tastes, ambitions, interests or living. Sarah-Gittel Rosenberg, Lily's mother tried cheering up Leah, "When a child is born, he brings with him his own destiny, his own ability and his own luck," (Foran 9). But Mordecai could not do more than a temporal plastering of the relationship, as the crack was already deep, wide with multiple fractures.

Raised in a community dominated by the first large wave of Jewish immigrants who fled from Russia during the massacres that followed the Russo-Japanese War and a traditional Jewish upbringing in Canada, Richler could never settle with a custom or society that lacked the spirit of the idea. It is the same force of non-conformism he had towards his education at Sir George Williams University in 1949. He dropped out of it two years later, believing that the spiritless academia would distort and devitalize his creativity. In 1951 Richler left Canada for the literary capitals of England, Paris and Spain. But for a brief return to Montreal in 1952, Richler settled in England, where he lived until 1972. His first marriage with Cathy Boudreau was mutually defunct and in 1960 he married Florence Wood, "his heart's desire" and "the Miriam" of his life. In 1972 Richler moved back to Montreal permanently, by then having established himself as a hard-core ethnic voice having already written seven novels and numerous essays and other writings. His criticism of often-taboo political issues, both in the oral and written word made Richler a Canadian national celebrity with a strong-say in magazines and television. His literary influences include American writers Dos Passos, Hemingway, Fitzgerald, Faulkner and black humourists Terry Southern, Mason Hoffenberg, Nathanael West, Celine and Evelyn Waugh. Richler died of complications from cancer on 3rd July 2001, in Montreal. Richler's five children have made successful creative imprints. Daniel, Emma, Noah, Jacob and Martha have all written books and Martha is also a leading political cartoonist.

Richler is a complex mosaic of a character. Foran sums up that he was for his admirers, courageous and honest and for his detractors, abrasive and aggressive. To his friends he was the *'mensch'*, to his children a tender, loving father and to his wife a deeply sensitive and devoted man. An unmasked public figure, comfortable with contradictions, he blatantly challenged hypocrisy through his works "asserting real values" and constructed "the humane, the real, the civilized" realm in his novels (xv). Foran quotes Richler's speech to a group of Jewish students at Niagara Falls to introduce the reader, to a slice of Richler's barbs hurled at empty rituals. Richler bluntly criticized the students when they raised an agitation to pressure the University to alter the date of a dance programme scheduled on a Sabbath. He rebuked them for letting pass a whole lot of non-Jewish concerns that were less intellectual and unimportant to them and that they continue to overlook injustice, insult and depravity of mankind at large and are obsessed with trivia as bigots.

Richler is naturally a Montreal writer who when away and back home, interlaced Montrealism, Jewishness and Canadianism in his writings. Joe King quotes Richler's statement, "coming from Canada, being a writer and Jewish as well, I have impeccable paranoia credentials" (292). His deca-novels are a decahedron of his time, space and ideology. He donned the cap of a novelist with the publication of *The Acrobats* (1954) which Kramer calls as a "...young man's book, simplifying communism, capitalism, the bourgeoisie, and God" (99).

Following what was criticized to be a maiden and less mature work, Richler's next two novels, *A Son of a Smaller Hero* (1955) and *A Choice of Enemies* (1957) signal a progression toward a more satirically humorous tone. In *Smaller Hero,* Richler recreates the Jewish community of his childhood, with stark, unsympathetic depiction of Jewish culture which drew charges of anti-Semitism, a common response to several of his consequent works.

Richler's *The Apprenticeship of Duddy Kravitz* (1959) is marked for the "remarkable authenticity of voice", with an infectious humour narrating the experience of growing up in a working-class Jewish neighbourhood in Montreal (Dvorak 162). Richler was nominated for the Academy and Screenwriters Guild of America awards for his screenplay adaptation of the novel.

Richler's ace novel was followed by two caustic satires, *The Incomparable Atuk* (1963) and *Cocksure* (1968). He vehemently scoffs at the society's penchant for materialistic values through the life, travel and experience of an Innuit poet who accumulates wealth and popularity in *The Incomparable Atuk. Cocksure,* which won the Governor General's literary award, is a black comedy that ridicules popular culture and the entertainment industry, details an unscrupulous movie of a mogul's takeover of a British publishing company. Dvorak observes that in his three novels *A Choice of Enemies, The Incomparable Atuk* and *Cocksure,* "he delighted in debunking the myths of his time" (162).

His later novels *St. Urbain's Horseman* (1971) *Joshua Then and Now* (1980) interested readers with "labyrinthine narrative lines interwoven with virtuosity" (Dvorak 162). In *St. Urbain's Horseman,* Richler returns with a parade of secondary characters, focusing on the life of Jake Hersh, his sense of disillusionment and remorse with his fantasies of the Horseman. Richler's next novel, *Joshua Then and Now* (1980), a full-time family drama is composed of extensive flashbacks describing the prominent events and personal crisis of Joshua Shapiro.

Solomon Gursky Was Here (1989) is a mordantly hilarious, multiplexed work of diligence, intensity and extravagance. The Richler map is an intricate fictional landscape that moves beyond the Montreal boundaries, linking Canada to the Gursky power, moving far, far north and countries across the globe. Richler dexterously knits a four generational history of the family and the country, expansive geography, religious traditions and treads the path of a mystery novel with vicious satire. It bagged the Commonwealth Writers' Prize and was shortlisted for the Man Booker Prize. The eponymous novel *Barney's Version* (1997) is a "hilarious and heart wrenching" fictional memoir of Barney a TV producer and writer in Montreal heralding the pangs of old-age, "wasted life" and a decaying memory. It won the Giller Prize, Stephen Leacock Memorial Medal for Humour.

The typical Richler protagonist is an alienated, morally disillusioned, ill-bred individual who finds stability and inner-knowledge difficult to attain. Driven by greed, guilt and ambition, they are prone to acquire their space in terms of money, land, power, fame or even an empire through ruthless and exploitative ways. In doing so, Richler depicts the Montreal society as an equal victim of moral dilemma.

Richler's world is big and complex. The novels as Richler in his Author's note states are generously spurred with the "seasons, tempers and moods" of mid-twentieth century Montreal (*SH* xii). It was an age of mimeograph and gramophones. A first time Oriental reader has to unlock his world with key reading on Jewish tradition and culture and be acquainted with the Canadian land. Inside are the realistic streets, living people, dominant heroes, aggressive voices, ruthless actions, rich rituals, sardonic humour and black laughter. Below the conundrum of life is the hunt to find their identity, self and truth. Richler may never be forgiven for bringing forth the Duddy Kravitz prototype and his vicious kind, for poking enough laughter on his own people whom he lovingly never spares and for daring to rip open the masked faces of hypocrisy. As it is noted he told uncomfortable truths in a comfortable style.

The Jews in Richler's novel are obsessed with their cultural memory and traditional Jewish ways in a Canadian space. From an Orthodox Smicha, Melech and comical Reuben Shapiro to the protagonists of the third generation Canadian Jewry, the characters forever keep binding and unwinding tradition in their lives. As the milkman Reb Tevye in the movie *Fiddler on the Roof* [1] says: "Tradition, Tradition, Tradition. Without it we are shaky like a Fiddler on the roof."

Richler's critical works attracted considerable attention for his themes on Canada and the Canadian identity. He won the Governor General's Literary Award for *Hunting Tiger under Glass: Essays and Reports* (1969). *Home Sweet Home: My Canadian Album* (1984), explores the defining elements of Jewish-Canadian culture. In the controversial polemic work, *Oh Canada! Oh Quebec! : Requiem for a Divided Country* (1992), Richler provoked a virulent national debate in Canada with regard to the self-sovereignty of Quebec. In *This Year in Jerusalem* (1994), he blends his remembrances of growing up in the Montreal Jewish community with descriptions of his visits to Israel, where he questions a few Western Jews' decision to immigrate to the Zionist state. In both *This year in Jerusalem* and *Home Sweet Home,* Richler experiments personal narratives and the genre of Life writing. Richler's final two essay collections, *Dispatches from the Sporting Life* (2001) and *On Snooker: The Game and the Characters Who Play It* (2001), recount the author's reflections on such sports as ice hockey, fishing, bodybuilding and pocket billiards.

Richler's three hilarious works for children include *Jacob Two-Two Meets the Hooded Fang* (1975) which won the Canadian Library Association Book of the Year Award, *Jacob Two-Two and the Dinosaur* (1987) and *Jacob Two-Two's First Spy Case* (1995). *The Street* (1969) is an interesting collection of short stories of autobiographical sketches. *Shovelling Trouble, (*1972), *Notes on an Endangered Species and Others, (*1974) are his other works of interest.

On Being Canadian

Richler today is Canada's authority on Canadians. It is to be noted that Canada as a nation and its literature in the mid-twentieth century, were in its nascent stage. The rest of the world could never imagine a routine beyond what Barney wittily tells Clara "Snow-shoe. Hunt beaver. Boil maple syrup in the spring" (*BV 139).* It was a retreat for retirement where the West could not actually guess that there could be real-time progress. Richler quotes Dr. Johnson who dismissed Canada as "a region from which nothing but furs and fish were to be had" (*SUH* 197). Richler as a young writer shared the same idea of Canada being a cultural desert. He notes that the negligible interest in Canadian writings attracted only rejection-slips. In most of his novels he touches on the difficulty of establishing oneself as a Canadian writer. Morrie notices, "that art isn't the fast-moving commodity in this country" (*SG 214*). Morrie's son Barney who had a bad luck in many of the business ventures had decided to become a writer to try his luck in the new trade. Jake Hersh, the hero of *St. Urbain's Horseman* (1971), tells the story of a New York publisher who amused himself by drawing up a list of ten books for a new firm that were bound to fail. Leading the list of unreadables was a book titled *Canada, Our Good Neighbor to the North*.

In a CBC Television interview in 1961, Richler is taken to task for an editorial in the *Spectator,* London in which he described Canada as a boring and apathetic country. He offers no apologies and is blunt in his assertions. Like Atwood and Frye, Richler questioned the Canadian soul in literature. One of his characters Mrs. Ogilvy in *Barney's Version* calls Canada as a "copycat" and "callow" dominion. Though he questions the Canadianess of the New World literature he never complains or rejects. Richler later admitted that he had mistakenly blamed "all things boring on Canada". But in *Coming Home Again* a 1975 CBC documentary he explained that he eventually came to realize that he would find the boring and the absurd wherever he settled. His reasons for returning were as mixed as his reasons for leaving eighteen years earlier. They involved, as he has mentioned on different occasions, a certain nostalgia for the seasons, the Laurentians and hockey; an odd fascination with Montreal; a realization that Canada was no longer a cultural backwater; an acknowledgement that Canada in recent years has been kind to him as a novelist; and a need to return to the wellsprings of his creative imagination. He soon discovers "Canada's no joke. We're the world's leading producer of uranium. Walter Pidgeon was born in this country" (*SUH* 122).

In the 1961 CBC interview, Richler says that his writings were rooted in the Montreal experience. He genuinely asserts that yet years away, he intimately felt Canadian and could never Europeanize his novels. This truth he kept for life and remained a Montreal storyteller true to his time and place. In his ardent exploration to retrieve the Canadian voice he left behind a tradition of Canadian experience in his writings. Although in his early career he opined that Canada had less cultural capital than Europe, one evidently finds that his material is Montreal-grown. Richler in "Why I write" states that its sheer egoism, aesthetic enthusiasm, historical impulse and political purpose that urges him to write. He strongly feels, "... I do feel forever rooted in Montreal's St. Urbain Street. That was my time, my place, and I have elected myself to get it right" (231).

Richler in another CBC Radio interview in 1965 tells that the purpose of a novelist is to give particularly his viewpoint and honestly speak about his time and place. It is as personal as looking out of the window and giving his point of view. From his literary window he looked at the Montreal Jewish ghetto, sporting life, Quebec Nationalism, hypocritical families and society, moral rectitude of human values, a distracted world with ambivalence, foreshadowing absence and exile with black humour and caustic satire.

Richler with his Montreal stories has surpassed Robert Kroetsch's question in his essay *On Being an Alberta Writer*, "How do we lift an environment to expression? How do we write in a new country?" (75). In his interview with Graeme Gibson in the 70's, Richler found virgin Canada as a Bonanza country for a writer who could mine the ore for the first time. From a doubting-Thomas period of being a Canadian writer, Richler established himself as the most caustic satirist of his generation. The maturing of the self from a morose intellectual, to the experimentation of success, settling as a family man and unsettling with umpteenth questions of a Jew in a '*Goy*' world, his own dreams and nightmares, his stinging fangs of disapproval of the society and his barbed wires on his own people recreate the fictional world of his Jewish men in a Canadian space.

A writer on a portable typewriter, typing in as a social commentator, an individual thinker and a cultural analyst, Richler is what as Foran states, "As a writer and public figure, he was singular-his own club, in effect" (ix). A writer with a high home profile and an international visibility, he was an unquestioned Canadian literary figure. Foran in an E-mail communication opines:

> Richler is best compared with the American-Jewish writers of his generation – Saul Bellow, Philip Roth, Joseph Heller. The influence of British satirists like Waugh is evident in a couple of his middle period books, and he was always trying to emulate the sensibility of Isaac Babel. That said, like all major writers, his voice, is work, was entirely his own – a unique vision.

Gurevich prefers Richler to his American counterpart Philip Roth. He observes that although they are equally brilliant they differ in tone. He prefers Richler's mature and social observance in writing to Roth's analyst's couch and blaming tone. A documentary film *Mordecai Richler: Last of the Wild Jews* fixes Richler in the context of a particular North American Jewish identity, one that emerged from the immigrant ghettos of Montreal, New York and

Chicago in the 1930s and 40s and burst onto the literary and cultural scene in the 1950s and 60s. Finding himself a place Richler was "The Last of the Wild Jews" who believed that Jews should no longer be timid little *'shtetl' people,* riding the horse in the *'shtetl'* but needed to gallop out into the world. The last in the trail of the wild Jew writers of Philp Roth, George Carlin, Lenny Bruce, Woody Allen, Norman Mailer, Allen King, Groucho Marx, Saul Bellow, Jimmy Durante is Mordecai Richler, a polarizing figure.

Richler in *Barney's Version,* sketches one of the CBC interviews of a Toronto writer who complains that his books were not accepted even for a window display in stores "because he wasn't American or British" (*BV 289).* But Richler as his character Pamela said, "the sterner the trials of creation. The finer that which is created" (*SUH* 189) excelled as a writer above the geographical discrimination and along with the literary faculty of Godfrey, Atwood, Davies, Laurence, Butler, Kroetsch, Wiebe, Munro and Cohen, contributed and enhanced Canadian fiction from 1950 onwards and positioned a distinct status in the literary world map. Thus, Canadian Literature has become a destination for scholarship and study in recent days for its varied voices, witty, laconic and ethically committed and a concern for language and form with its innovative artifice and Richler is a golden-signpost to it.

1.4 Evolution of New Historicism as a Textual Practice

New historicism evolved as a literary critical phenomenon and textual practice in 1980 with the publication of Stephen Greenblatt's *Renaissance Self-Fashioning,* "a work that drew new attention to the ways in which literature reflects not only the intentions of its creators as self-conscious respondents to their time periods but also the ways in which a variety of systems and responses to power are reflected in a given text (Hall 301). It is a "synthetic methodology" developed out of contemporary theory, drawing on several of the forms of analysis. The method is based on the "parallel reading of literary and non-literary texts, usually of the same historical period" (Barry 172). Hence, a new historicist notion is that "literature is related to other practices, behaviour and values, and that literature is thus always in relation to the non-literary (Robson 18).

New historicism was a reaction to the "text only" approach of Formalism. In a critical essay entitled *The New Historicism in Literary Study* D.G. Myers observes: "The eighties witnessed the emergence of a new movement in Anglo-American literary scholarship which, in methodological sophistication, theoretical all-inclusiveness, and classroom appeal, bid fair to rival anything from Germany and France" (27). Largely as a result of post-Structuralism, this new movement of historical approach proved to be a return to historical scholarship in the academic study of Literature. Bijay Das advocates that this practice was neglected over the past half century of Anglo-American criticism, with focus of New Criticism being a narrowly "text-centered" approach, followed by the Structuralist's announcement of the death of the author, next came the Deconstruction free-play of signifiers without a centre and then the spot-light was on the reader with the advent of the Reader-Response theory. New Historicism is a call to return to the "context" which includes the social and political conditions of the period of literary evolution of the text or in other words to "re-historicize" the literary texts. "The New Historicist tries to negotiate between the extreme positions of New Critics and Deconstructionists in order to find out if a common ground could be created between them" (Das 217).

Chris Baldick states that a new-historicist's reading involves reference to non-literary texts, "demonstrating the presence of a similar governing discourse" (187). The literary text is juxtaposed with co-texts which could include published historical data, analysis, reports, write ups, news reportage, social and political history, travelogues, letters, diaries, audio, video, interviews, films and other popular sources of information to advance insight and enrich analysis. Donald E. Hall explains: "All these allow access into many ways in which people expressed their beliefs, hopes, and fears, and all are equally valid sources of data for understanding the diversity of human perception and experience" (301).

The Old and the New Word: Historicism

It is necessary to state the differences between the traditional and new practice of Historicism to understand what is "new" about Historicism.

> "History is not linearly progressive and is not reducible to the activities of prominent individuals" (Hall 302).

New Historicism rejects power narration. History of World War II is Nazi dictated. The discovery of America is Columbus' version. As Hall explains, the discovery of America or Columbus' arrival hardly signaled progress for the native people who already knew the existence of the land below their feet. It was discovery for Spain and "a slow process of cultural decimation" for the indigenous people. New Historicists are concerned with the ignored parts of history of marginalized people, as in this example the victims of Nazi power and the native inhabitants of the New World at the time of discovery and focus on these forgotten or neglected versions. Unlike traditional Historicism, New Historicism states that power which was once the only reliable source of narrating history is never confined to a single person or single level of society. It moves through culture by exchange of ideas between the members of society as well as exchange of goods over a period of time and it keeps changing.

Brizee and Tompkins quote Tyson's explanation of retelling history itself: "...questions asked by traditional historians and by new historicists are quite different ... traditional historians ask, 'What happened?' and 'What does the event tell us about history?' In contrast, new historicists ask, 'How has the event been interpreted?' and 'What do the interpretations tell us about the interpreters?'". New Historicism resists the notion that "...history is a series of events that have a linear, causal relationship: event A caused event B; event B caused event C; and so on" (Tyson 278 qtd. in Purdue OWL). Old Historicism believes History is an accurate view of what really has occurred and serves as a background to literature. New Historicists believe history is subjective: one of many discourses. History is shaped by the people who lived it.

> "... that literary and non-literary "texts" circulate inseparably" (Vesser 1989: xi).

Peter Barry notes that the practice of New Historicism, giving "equal weighting" to literary and non-literary texts is the major variation between the two. Mark Robson explains Greenblatt's attempt to differentiate between the two forms. In Old Historicism "...history as the 'explanation' of a text...the text is read off against a context...", thus placing the historical text in the background and placing it as secondarily important because the text mirrors the history of its time (9).

For new historicists literary texts cannot be isolated as entities that exist outside the realm of history, nor do the political and social concerns serve as a backdrop. Rather, as in Greenblatt's practice, "there is a relationship between art and other elements within a culture, and it is for the new historicist to work out what that relationship might be. It is also necessary to take account of how artistic texts contribute to the production of that culture" (Robson 9). Louis Montrose terms this double sense of relationship as "The Historicity of Texts and Textuality of History". Hence a new historical essay or thesis will place the literary text of study within the "frame" of non-literary texts.

> "New historicism accepts Derrida's view that there is nothing outside the text, ...it is 'thrice processed'..." (Barry 175).

An old historicist critic believes that the historical context of the texts formulate a more accurate interpretation of texts than if one did not know such historical context. A new historicist states that everything about the past is only available in textualised form. The critic follows Derrida's view of the text as "thrice-processed...first through the ideology, or outlook, or discursive practices of its own time, then through those of ours, and finally through the distorting web of language itself" (Barry 175).

Brizee and Tompkins accept the practice of New Historicism that assumes every text and work is an outcome, a product of the historic moment that created it. They quote David Richter to validate their stand: New Historicism is "...a practice that has developed out of contemporary theory, particularly the structuralist realization that all human systems are symbolic and subject to the rules of language, and the deconstructive realization that there is no way of positioning oneself as an observer outside the closed circle of textuality" (1205-qtd. in Purdue OWL). Whatever is represented in the text is thereby remade by the interaction between the historic context of the work and the critic or reader's interpretation and understanding. A new historicist reading juxtaposes a text with a chosen document to remake another permutation of the past and thereby a new entity is formed. As Barry points out, "the aim is not to represent the past as it really was, but to present a new reality by re-situating it" (175).

The historical criticism practiced in the 1980s differs in practice from the historical criticism of the 1930s and 1940s. New Historicists believe that criticism should incorporate diverse discourses; new historicism is informed by poststructuralist theory and deconstructive way of thinking, as well as feminist, cultural and Marxist criticism.

The New Historicists: Influence and Impact

D.G. Myers notes that the doctrine of historicity is a Heideggerian motif that came to the movement via the writings of German hermeneutical philosopher Hans-Georg Gadamer. Greenblatt develops his new historicist approach by taking into consideration the works of Mikhail Bakhtin, Clifford Geertz and Michel Foucault.

"New Historicism" as Myers states "appeared to offer a distinctive approach, a rigorous method, along "with the opportunity to salvage one's political commitments". Indeed, at times New Historicism seemed almost designed to methodize the political interpretation of literature. As Ryan notes:

> The new historicists were primarily influenced by the analysis of power and the historical studies of Michael Foucault, whose work shifted critical interest away from the macronarratives of politics and

> economics and toward the micrological discursive practices and knowledge/ power regimes that construct different forms of domination. (129)

New Historicism, informed by Foucault's "discursive practices" is a less rigid institution than the "repressive structures" also focuses on "the way power is internalized by those whom it disempowers, so that it does not have to be constantly enforced externally" (Barry 177). "New historicism tends to be thought as a practice rather than a theory … To some extent, new historicism has revived the traditional split between 'theory' and 'practice'…" (Robson 4-5). Greenblatt along with Jonathan Goldberg, Louis Montrose, Catherine Gallaghar, sincerely declined declaring a new theory or doctrine and considered New Historicism more of a practice. Edward Pechter, Jane Tompkins, Don E. Wayne, Walter Benn Michaels, Arthur F. Marotti, Jean E. Howard, Stephen Orgel, Annabel Patterson and Peter Stallybrass practiced it in England and America. This textual practice had some methodological principles and terms that fashioned a new-historicist reading of a text.

Conception of Ideology

D.G. Myers elucidates Greenblatt's 'enabling presumptions' to insist that a new-historicist reading unlike the traditional approach does not attempt "a recovery of the original meaning of the literary text" but "a recovery of the original ideology which gave birth to the text, and which the text in turn helped to disseminate throughout a culture".

> The movement establishes itself upon four main contentions. (l) Literature is historical, which means (in this exhibition) that a literary work is not primarily the record of one mind's attempt to solve certain formal problems and the need to find something to say; it is a social and cultural construct shaped by more than one consciousness. The proper way to understand it, therefore, is through the culture and society that produced it. (2) Literature, then, is not a distinct category of human activity. It must be assimilated to history, which means a particular vision of history. (3) Like works of literature, man himself is a social construct, the sloppy composition

> of social and political forces—there is no such thing as a human nature that transcends history. Renaissance man belongs inescapably and irretrievably to the Renaissance. There is no continuity between him and us; history is a series of "ruptures" between ages and men. (4) As a consequence, the historian/ critic is trapped in his own "historicity." No one can rise above his own social formations, his own ideological upbringing, in order to understand the past on its terms. A modern reader can never experience a text as its contemporaries experienced it. Given this fact, the best a modern historicist approach to literature can hope to accomplish, according to Catherine Belsey, is "to use the text as a basis for the reconstruction of an ideology."

From Culture to Poetics of Culture

Hayden White talks about the "metahistorical" element in historiography. He explains that in writing history there is always a philosophy in the ways in which histories get written. Robson explains, "For White, historians work by *representing* the past, and these representations open up an awareness of what he calls the 'poetics' of history" (10). Greenblatt agrees with White on the formal aspects of narratives and shares the view that historical and formal concerns are inseparable in the writing of history. Robson notes that this formal aspect has given rise to the use of the term cultural poetics to describe his work. He further explicates that New Historicism is by itself a part of a formalist practice with the inclusion of the term 'poetics' to focus on the formal aspect, avoiding the New Critics opposition to historicism.

Defining the concept of culture, Greenblatt refers to two contradictory ideas called constraint and mobility. 'Constraint' refers to the boundaries, limits or rules in culture which people may try to break, or gesture signs of disapproval or adhere to it. A positive reinforcement could result in reward or the vice-versa may attract punishment. But the instances of reward or punishment according to Greenblatt are not necessarily any direct sense of a disciplining power at work, nor a matter of policing or reinforcement. Instead as Robson explains, he suggests that people at any level of society may play an active part in exercising control over others within the same society. Greenblatt links this idea of 'constraint' to Literature.

> Literature, he proposes is part of this cultural reinforcement of boundaries between that which is approved and not, that which is legitimate and not, that which is legal and not. This is most obviously apparent in the praise and blame that is to be found in literary genres such as satire and panegyric. (Robson 20)

Alongside the reinforcement of boundaries, Greenblatt suggests that culture is also what gives structure to movement. 'Mobility; is the movement of crossing the borders of 'constraint'. Robson explains that "Boundaries only become meaningful if there is also mobility, if there is a possibility of their being crossed..." (20). Thus, this dualistic sense of culture in terms of 'constraint' and 'mobility' brings in another Greenblatt's term called *improvisation.*

'Improvisation' as explained by Robson "refers to the ways in which individuals accommodate themselves to their cultural constraints" (22). One of the functions of literature is to present improvisation as something to be learned or as a process of being 'cultured' and offer a clear example of how it works.

Robson states, "The artwork draws from the culture in which it emerges, but it also reproduces that culture in a modified form that can travel, across the boundaries within a culture, between cultures and across times" (24). The works of art are structures for the 'accumulation, transformation, representation and communication' of the 'social energies' of the surrounding spaces.

In the essay *Towards a Poetics of Culture,* a lecture given by Greenblatt at the University of Western Australia in 1986, he establishes the idea that, though New Historicism is influenced by both Marxist thought and post-structuralism, 'cultural poetics' is ultimately neither of these things. 'Cultural poetics' combines a historically specific attention to the shifting senses of the critical terminology with sensitivity to aesthetic considerations which will be able to map the negotiations, circulations and exchanges. "In order to achieve the negotiation, artists need to create a currency that is valid for a meaningful, mutually profitable exchange" (158). By *currency* Greenblatt metaphorically designates the systematic adjustments, symbolizations and lines of credit necessary to enable the exchange. In the 'mutually profitable exchange' the return is in terms of pleasure and interests. Robson explains that, "The cultural aspect of cultural poetics allows for a recognition of the specific location of a given artwork in space and time; the poetic element opens up the possibility of seeing what the artwork makes happen in that location" (32). So the critic apart from focusing on the historical context that shapes the work must be drawn towards the literary conversion of the materials into a work of art by the writer and be perceptive of the transformations of the context of the work of art. Greenblatt in *Towards a Poetics of Culture* constructs 'an interpretative model' which would account for the 'unsettling circulation of materials' and establishes a practice of perceiving the 'hidden places of negotiation and exchange' (*LC 159*). Thus, as Robson summarizes a sense of culture must be complemented and enhanced by an attention to poetics, and the terms of poetics are always cited and found in culture.

Surrounding Spaces

A New Historicist practice argues that a work of literature does not exist devoid of its conditions or circumstances and literary works are as much a product of the author's mindset as well as the conditions that surround it. Michael Ryan observes, "Greenblatt's approach destabilizes the text and argues for a focus on its margins, the borders where it connects through complicated exchanges with other representations in the culture" (129).

Veeser notes, "Circulation, negotiation, exchange" and other marketplace and trade-related metaphors characterize New Historicists' working vocabulary. Many or some factors influence the small fraction of 'space' and 'time' in which the text is created. This constitutes the surrounding space which is absorbed into a text. In the circulation in space, the culture of a space is formed by the previous spaces in time. The writer is one of the connections to its space. 'Social currency' represents the connection of the author to other people, classes, groups, etc.

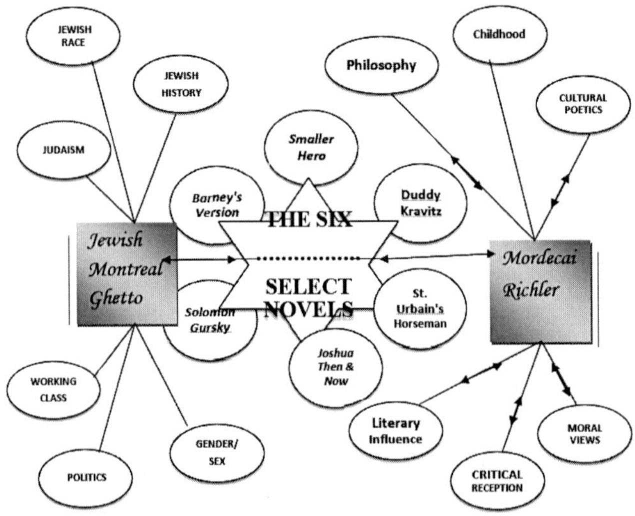

Figure 1. Surrounding Spaces (SS) of Richler's Select Novels based on New Historicist Practice

In Circulation in Time, 'time' is the order of spaces in which texts are created. There are multiple interconnections of spaces. No process is unidirectional and transfer of material from one discourse to another occurs in oscillation. Negotiations in time include tradition, inheritance, transmission, alteration, modification and reproduction. The recursive character of social life and language point out that art, history, and literature are always repetitive. 'Social energy' is a part of circles in time.

Social Energy

Robson explicates that 'social energy' is a term derived by Greenblatt from the term *energia.*

> It is manifested in the capacity of certain verbal, aural, and visual traces to produce, shape, and organize collective physical and mental experiences… it is associated with repeatable forms of pleasure and interest, with the capacity to arouse disquiet, pain, fear, the beating

> of the heart, pity, laughter, tension, relief, wonder. (qtd. in Robson 69)

Texts charged with social energy produce resonance with their cultural environment and a text is embedded in a network of social circulation. Robson states that 'social energy' is the force that a text takes on and its capacity to have an effect on the mind of the reader. Greenblatt focuses on those moments within works which retain the force, energy or power to move someone, to laughter or tears, anger or anxiety, moving the text beyond the confines of a given cultural moment, allowing the texts to be effective in other places and times. Greenblatt attributes this power to a series of "negotiations, exchanges and movements". He discusses the central issue of 'exchange' focusing on theatre scripts and performances. This can be true of writers too. Writers freely take objects, ideas and narratives that already exist and transfer it to their texts. Such exchanges in the early modern period take various forms such as, *Appropriation*, *Purchase* and *Symbolic acquisition.* Hence a relationship between the aesthetic practices of literary texts and other social practices is established indicating:

Mimesis involves negotiation and exchange.

Negotiation and exchange involve more than one kind and is not limited to money.

The agents may appear to be individuals, but are themselves the products of collective exchange.

To use Robson's explanation: "This relationship is seen to be dynamic" in which the literary text not only borrows or buys objects from the wider culture, "but in doing so also allows for a re-conception of the objects or practices presented" (70). Thus, Greenblatt insists on a collective nature of aesthetic production and stresses that:

1. There can be no appeals to genius as the sole origin of the energies of great art.
2. There can be no motiveless creation.

3. There can be no transcendent or timeless or unchanging representation.
4. There can be no autonomous artifacts.
5. There can be no expression without an origin and an object, a from and a for.
6. There can be no art without social energy.
7. There can be no spontaneous generation of social energy. (qtd. in Robson 70)

Symbolic Economy

Literature is a cultural product. Robson explains Greenblatt's description of the power of language and the writer's use of it to appeal to the reader's most fundamental emotions. Greenblatt claims that in any culture there exists a general 'symbolic economy' that is constituted of myriad signs that stimulate 'human desire, fear and aggression'. A literary artist is skilled in manipulating this economy with an ability to 'construct resonant stories', create effective imagery and their 'sensitivity to the greatest collective creation of any culture-language'.

Robson explains Greenblatt's 'symbolic economy' through an example of how representation of Queen Elizabeth II image although the same would mean something different when used in bank notes, postage stamps, semi-fictional character in drama, television and films in modern culture. Thus "Thinking about the symbolic in terms of economy allows us to see how images, objects, narratives and representations are produced, reproduced, consumed, traded and circulated, and how they change value as they move from one area of a culture to another" (Robson 3).

Self-Fashioning

In Renaissance Self-Fashioning Greenblatt writes, "fashioning may suggest the achievement of a less tangible shape: a distinctive personality, a characteristic address to the world, a consistent mode of perceiving and behaving" (2). Robson explains that fashioning is a part of the practices of a culture, which also includes educational modes, its rules of behaviour, its rituals and representations. Likewise, literature and the structures of social life are rooted in culture. He also explicates that according to Greenblatt; human beings are also constructions like works of art and the acts of creating and fashioning take place within symbolic structures. Greenblatt proposes an approach to literature in the light of the dialectical sense of production: "Literature functions within this system in three interlocking ways: as a manifestation of the concrete behaviour of its particular author, as itself the expression of the codes by which behaviour is shaped, and as a reflection upon these codes" (*RSF* 4). "Fiction" as D.G. Myers explains is the lens through which a certain portrait of the human experience is brought into focus. Mediation, not imitation of social practices, that shape rather than to reflect an age and understand the human experience.

Greenblatt's idea of 'Self-Fashioning' suggests that cultural negotiation is necessary to fashion identity. Robson explains that, "Identity is culturally constructed..." and states that Greenblatt rejects the ideas of an innate natural definition of the self and the existentialist freedom to choose (63). "Self-Fashioning" for Greenblatt involves, "submission to an absolute power or authority situated at least partially outside the self – God, a sacred book, an institution such as church, court or military administration" (*RSF* 9). As a historicist, he sees that it is achieved in relation to the outside as something perceived as alien, strange, or hostile that threatens the self. Greenblatt says that it is fictitious to believe that individuals have the power to shape their own selves, but people continue to live in this illusion.

At this point, the researcher differs from Greenblatt. It is easy to agree with the idea of a culturally constructed self, but difficult to accept that societal and ideological force prevails over personal desires and that human choice is non-existent. While a total existentialistic mode of being is hardly acceptable, at the same time it is difficult to accept a socially-constructed identity completely. This raises a series of questions:

1. Is there no place for individual choice or freedom in designing one's life? How are the children born into the same family, bred in the same surrounding space, different from each other? What is responsible for this difference?
2. Is the individual's yearning to connect with a higher power or providence a mere social-construct?

There is certainly a difference between an Indian, American, English or Spanish. If we claim that each group of people is a social-construct what makes two individuals, say Indians different from each other. If we are to focus on a particular Indian family, how are children born to the same parents, studying at the same period of time in the same institutions, celebrating the same festivals, mourning the same losses, accessing the same resources or facing the same rejections, different from each other in behaviour and response? Possibly each one has a different experience in living in the same space and the choices they make are their own individual choices.

It is an individual's conscious effort to root oneself in what could be a morally right or wrong decision. The cultural and social ideologies no doubt prescribe a pattern of living. But how far can it enforce the individual's choice? Is the choice not based on the moral standards, values and ideals negotiated with culture? Culture by itself has evolved out of a system of beliefs and faiths directed at a higher power and morality. This discernment of choice is often attributed to God, fate, one's religious upbringing and the dictates of the conscience and they do not exist outside the self. Hence, there exists the innate definition of the self and freedom of one's choice which would be influenced by the surrounding space. Seeing the cultural construction as a pressure applied or limitation on the person and an individual's freedom lies in the choice to yield or find alternatives. The circumstances or situations are cultural demands of the period whereas the response to it lies in the value of an individual's freedom. Thus, a mid-way between a culturally-constructed ideology and an existentialist choice of freedom needs to be considered. Although the choice itself would be an influence of the social-construct, there is an inner or higher power of the spiritual being which rises above the social ideology and culturally-constructed self that affects largely or minimally the choices that one has to make.

Wonder and Resonance

Stephen Greenblatt's concept of 'Wonder and Resonance' is one of the most important aspects of New Historicism which he elaborates in his acclaimed essay Resonance and Wonder and central to his book Marvelous Possessions. His critical interest is historical and he opines, "If I do not approach works of art in a spirit of veneration, I do approach them in a spirit that is best described as wonder" (*LC* 170). Robson traces Greenblatt's sense of Wonder and Resonance to German romanticism, especially in the work of Johann Gottfried von Herder. He claims that the emphasis on a historicized sense of culture related to language and national identity is also seen in a Kantian way, in which wonder can be seen as a property of both an object and the experience of the subject who perceives it.

"By wonder I mean the power of the object displayed to stop the viewer in his tracks, to convey an arresting sense of uniqueness, to evoke an exalted attention" (*LC* 170). Wonder in something or someone, which or who causes admiration or spontaneous overflow of powerfully fresh feeling of delight or horror between the reader, writer and text. The power of wonder affected by past artifact or moment is a present disturbance as manifested in Greenblatt's historical analysis. In simple words objects that strike one with wonder encapsulate a sense of surprise that is produced by encountering it.

Greenblatt refers to Albert the Great's passage to explain that wonder occurs at two levels, one at the physical level and secondly at the mental level. Wonder when it strikes at the first level causes a disturbance in the rhythm of the heart. The mental process is the experience of wonder which precedes knowledge of what has caused it. Wonder is one of the effects of art, of literature, and of theatrical presentation. It is the element of pleasure and of emotional response that is aroused by literature. What an artistic work possesses is the power to arouse wonder, and that power, in the dominant aesthetic ideology of the West, has been negotiated by the artist. In Greenblatt's example of the State Jewish Museum at Prague, he discusses that this power seems to be possessed by the work itself, so that the art-object appears to escape possession even by the museum that displays it. He says that the works of art are characterized by wonder extends to the sense of objects that normally lie beyond the boundaries of art. According to Gallagher and Greenblatt, Wonder is 'democratized' and is found in a wide variety of objects, as characteristic of new historicism. Greenblatt explains,

> By Resonance I means the power of the object displayed to reach out beyond its formal boundaries to a larger world, to evoke in the viewer the complex, dynamic cultural forces from which it has emerged and for which as metaphors or more simply as metonymy it may be taken by a viewer to stand. (*LC* 170)

"Resonance" as Robson explains "lacks the immediacy of wonder demanding an explanation of its context and of the life to which it is, or was, connected" (99). New Historicism has distinct affinities with resonance. It analyzes a literary text to recover as far as possible historical circumstances of original creation, consumption and to examine the relationship between these circumstances and our own.

> New Historicist critics have tried to understand the intersecting circumstances not as a stable, prefabricated background against which the literary texts can be placed, but as dense network of evolving and often contradictory social forces. The idea is not to find outside the work of art some rock onto which literary interpretation can be securely chained but rather to situate the work in relation to other representational practices operative in the culture at a given moment in both history and our own. (*LC* 170)

New historicism through the power of resonance seeks to locate the traces of the world that an object bears. The use of the terms 'wonder' and 'resonance' for representation is both productive and reflective of power. One differentiates 'wonder' from 'resonance' by the practice that the experience of 'wonder' does not require the knowledge of it. The movement from 'wonder' to 'resonance' occurs when 'wonder' leads to a desire to know what it is that has aroused this effect.

Greenblatt in *Marvelous Possessions* discusses the nature of wonder in terms of a connection between the one who interprets and that which is interpreted takes on a particular resonance in the context of colonial encounters. Finally, Greenblatt discusses that an effective work of art would be one if the impact of it leads one easier from 'wonder' to 'resonance' than 'resonance' to 'wonder'. Thus, this gives rise to a "meaningful desire for cultural resonance" and requires a new historicist "continually renew the marvelous at the heart of the resonant" (*LC* 181).

Use of Anecdotes

Anecdotes are real stories that are small, self-contained and has something useful. Robson quotes Fineman who proposes that "the anecdote determines the destiny of a specifically historiographic integration of event and context" (40). He continues to remark that an anecdote is the narration of singular event, the literary form or genre that perforates or punctures the grand narrative into which it is inserted. Gallagher and Greenblatt claim inspite of the interruption "at the anecdote's rim, one encounters a difference in the texture of the narrative, an interruption that lets one sense that there is something – the "real" outside of the historical narrative. The narrative thereby exposes history" (50). An anecdote provides one of the most subtle attempts to link new historicist practice at the level of style to its intellectual impact. Thus for a new-historicist according to Gallagher and Greenblatt an anecdote:

> could be conceived as a tool with which to rub literary texts against the grain of received notions about their determinants, revealing the fingerprints of the accidental, suppressed, defeated, uncanny, abjected, or exotic-in short, the non-surviving-even if only fleetingly. (52)

For this purpose, the two critics claimed that, "The desired anecdotes would not, as in the old historicism, epitomize epochal truths, but would instead undermine them" (51). Through anecdotal stories, Greenblatt lends a happening feel to his ideas. He makes criticism appeal to the mind as human and not as a string of abstract sentences understood through labourious reading. The 'desired anecdotes' create a visual effect on the reader and hence help him to ascertain the purpose of his argument. He makes the whole practice of New Historicism experiential and practical and this contemporary style makes the ideas interesting to the modern critic.

Thick Description

Robson's account of Greenblatt's interest in Geertz is fairly from the fact that both literary criticism and anthropology share a common concern with meaning and the cultural transactions that occur in the mutual exchange. Geertz's "native informant's tale" turns to the "empirical" evidence and distinguishes itself from the borrowed notion of Gilbert Ryle's "philosopher's tale" which is comparatively artificial. For Geertz culture is primarily "semiotic" which is based on the use and interpretations of signs. "Thick description attempts to take into account the conflicting and shifting structures through which meaning is generated, moving beyond the 'thinness' of a simple enumeration of events and actions or a catalogue of uninterpreted data" (Robson 43). Gallagher and Greenblatt prescribe application of "ethnographic realism" for purposes of literary study.

Theory of Subversion and Containment

Greenblatt discusses 'Subversion' and 'Containment' in *Invisible Bullets.* He refers to the way the English colonists duped the natives of North America into believing that the natives who were dying of diseases had been shot by the English God with invisible bullets. "This subterfuge had the effect of augmenting the natives awe at the power of the colonists" (Notes 799). To subvert is to undermine or weaken the power and authority of an established institution.

Containment in its simple sense is the action of keeping something harmful under control. Hence 'Subversion' and 'Containment' are a means of control. At its simplest level this is achieved by manipulating the fact that the other power or party has doubt in their belief system. The doubt is dubbed 'Subversion' and control of this is 'Containment'. 'Subversion' is created by the party that wishes to contain it.

Cultural Mobility

Greenblatt's *The Cardenio Project* is based on his theory of 'cultural mobility'. Cultural mobility talks about the movement of traded sources, images and ideologies rooted in localness. So, the much-researched lost play of Shakespeare's *Cardenio* has drawn the main plot from the story of the "Curious Impertinent" recounted in the Cardenio section of *Don Quixote.* This lost play is retrieved by the acclaimed Shakespearian Lewis Theobald and improved as *Double Falsehood* in the eighteenth-century which becomes an Indian Sukanta Chaudhuri's *Jaha Chai* in the twenty-first century, expanding into the various global languages which include Japanese, Brazilian, Croatian, Egyptian, Polish, Spanish and American. Greenblatt outlines the following characteristics of 'cultural mobility'.

> *First,* mobility must be taken in a highly literal sense
>
> *Second*, mobility studies should shed light on hidden as well as conspicuous movements of peoples, objects, images, texts, and ideas.
>
> *Third*, mobility studies should identify and analyze the "contact zones" where cultural goods are exchanged.
>
> *Fourth*, mobility studies should account in new ways for the tension between individual agency and structural constraint.
>
> *Fifth*, mobility studies should analyze the sensation of rootedness.
>
> (http://www.fas.harvard.edu/~cardenio/mobility.html)

Hence 'cultural mobility' refers to the model of understanding the patterns of meaning that human societies create. It refers to Greenblatt's conviction that even traditional cultures are rarely stable and how literature written at various periods of time get absorbed with specific themes, plots, images and assists in the new *avatar* of these artifacts renovated by its 'contact zones' and developed out of new tension and mobility between the individual and cultural constraint. The researcher calls it as the phoenix effect that resurrects the spirit of the text and can be read separate from its sources since they are rooted in different ideologies and localness.

In defense of New Historicism

New Historicism has been subjected to questions as to why there is no single method, no overall picture, no exhaustive and definite cultural politics. D.G. Myers explains that the movement is not an effort to discover what it means for a literary work to be historical; it is really little more than an attempt to get literary works to conform to a particular vision of History. The whole point is to grasp the terms of the discourse which made it possible for contemporaries to see the "facts" of their time in a particular way – indeed, made it possible to use certain phenomena as facts at all. Veeser opines, "...New Historicism has given scholars new opportunities to cross the boundaries separating history, anthropology, art, politics, literature, and economics... The New Historicists combat empty formalism by pulling historical considerations to the centre stage of literary analysis" (Introduction ix-xi). Hence New Historicists are agents of ideology.

Why New Historicism?

New Historicism acknowledges that any criticism of a work is coloured by the critic's beliefs, social status and other factors. It represents a significant change from critical theories like New Criticism, because its main focus is to look at many elements outside of the work, instead of reading the text in isolation. New Historicism focuses on how the History of the literary text participates in the development and construction and comes to conclusion on the pattern of events. It states that history is a story narrated and is not objective as believed by traditional historicists. Life of people cannot be documented on empirical evidence. The history of Taj Mahal is power narrated. It is a record of the King's achievement and architecture and not of the 21 years of hard work by the untiring workers and builders. History is subjective and a study of literature of that period of time can give clues to unheard voices. New Historicism looks out for these gaps to be filled in by texts, both literary and non-literary, that voices the voice of the voiceless. One of the key perspectives of New Historicism is to critically evaluate mainstream and marginalized populations as well as traditional and subversive discourses of the era when interpreting a text.

Richler's novels focus on the marginalized Jews. He records the ordinary language of the common man. The study, applies the practice of New Historicism and analyzes the select works of Richler, focusing on his point of view of time, space, race, religion and history as lived and perceived by the author and the episodes and incidents of his childhood and youth. This analysis makes a study through an intense perception of the author's period of how people indulged in transgression and moral policing to expose hypocritical societies and families.

New Historicists as quoted by Ryan, "... conceived of literature as one among many discourses or systems of representation that exist in dynamic interchange at a particular historical moment" (129). He further explains that, "the relationship between literature and history is one of circulation, exchange and negotiation rather than of reference and reflection" (130). For New Historicism, a piece of Literature is shaped by the time period in which it is written and hence must be viewed, examined and interpreted in the context of that time period. This textual practice attempts to bind the themes, characters, events and language of pieces of literary work to the happenings from the time period in which it has been written. It also takes into account, political and cultural events that marked the time of the author.

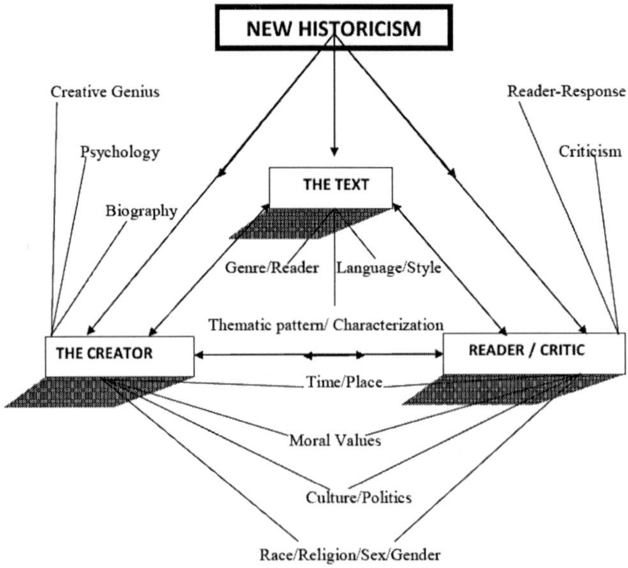

Figure 2: A New Historicist Analysis

New Historicism has an all-inclusive formula that focuses on all three aspects of reading a literary work – the author, text and critic. To evaluate the multi-faceted writer-hero, Mordecai Richler and his works, a rich textual practice such as New Historicism may do great justice. Barney in *Barney's Version* writes that it delights him to read a biography of writers to understand their writings to reveal the real sense of it (276). The present study takes into consideration a three-dimensional view from a New Historicist perspective. This view is of the space and turbulent times that nurtured the writer in a social, historical and political context, his moral standards and attitudes that have been absorbed into his texts. It also analyzes his talented literary skill that enables him to craft his age and finally responds to the text from the reader's point of view. All this builds a comprehensive analysis of his monumental works.

1.5 The Scope of the Study

A serious study of Richler leads to the research question, "What makes Richler's protagonists have such a moral dilemma that it inevitably results in criminal transgression?" The aim of the research is to draw "new attention" to Richler's texts from a New-Historicist perspective "in which literature reflects not only the intentions of its creators as self-conscious respondents to their time periods but also the ways in which a variety of systems and responses to power are reflected in a given text" (Hall 301). Are these indications of an intrinsic thematic pattern of moral conflict and transgression that suggests itself in Richler's novels, which may throw more light on the research question, point at answers or directions or raise debates?

The hypothesis is that, Surrounding Spaces affect Richler's protagonists who indulge in criminal transgressions and possibly in moral policing others they expose hypocritical families and societies. All this in turn may affect or change them. The study also works on Richler's insights into how people's lives are a reflection of their time, place, race, gender, sexuality and economic situation and how these factors contribute to the moral vision of the protagonists.

The Literature survey conducted shows a sustained research interest in Mordecai Richler's themes and stylistics. His works have been conversed widely by a number of critics, writers and scholars through books, journal articles, interviews, newspaper items and films. The chronology of *The Cambridge Companion to Canadian Literature* records *Duddy Kravitz*, *Solomon Gursky* and *Barney's Version* as significant publications in the literary history of Canada (xxi, xxv, xxvi). Richler's novels are discussed under Regionalism and Urbanism focusing on "working life of a city, with an even stronger focus on class and ethnic topography" and emerge as a record of Jewish-Canadian hyphenated communities (Fiamengo 256-257). John Moss in his Introduction to *The Canadian Novel-Beginnings* talks on how Richler's troubled vision of loss, (along with Davies, Munro and Wiebe), "include the possibility of redemption" (10). William H. New discusses how the works reflect the tension between being a "committed artist and accomplished public entertainer" (241-242).

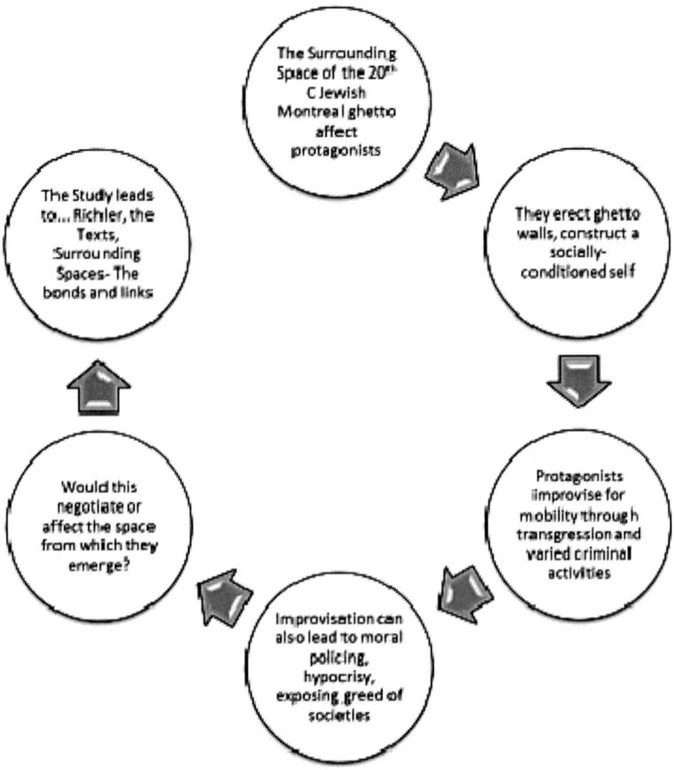

Figure 3. Flow chart of the Hypothesis

The books of Arnold E. Davidson and Victor J. Ramraj, both titled *Mordecai Richler* are a useful resource for a Richler beginner. George Woodcock's *Introducing Mordecai Richler's The Apprenticeship of Duddy Kravitz* is one of the early critical commentaries on the seminal novel. Michael Greenstein's introduction to *Contemporary Jewish Writing in Canada* and the concept of *Third Solitudes* critically place Richler's works in the context of the Jewish Canadian literature. Tom Marshall elaborates on the concept of "Third Solitude: Canadian as Jew" (147-155) with reference to Richler's works. Michael Darling's *Mordecai Richler: An Annotated Bibliography* gives a comprehensive review of work done on the writer between 1960s and 1980s.

There are many articles of academic interest on Mordecai Richler and his works. Articles that analyze Richler's works appear in *Ariel:* A Review of International English Literature, as early as 1970s focusing on Jewish themes of exile, landscapes and satire. D.J. Dooley's, "Mordecai Richler and Duddy Kravitz: A Moral Apprenticeship" (93-107) spotlights Richler as a moral precipitate. John Moss' "Richler's Horseman" (156-165) also elaborates on the writer's moral conviction. Daniel Golden's "Mystical Musing and Comic Confrontations: The Fiction of Saul Bellow and Mordecai Richler" (62-85) compares and contrasts the writings of the two. Another essay of rich interpretation on Richler's form, context and development is Kerry McSweeney's "Mordecai Richler" (129-179). While Irving Howe gives a broad view of "The Nature of Jewish Laughter" (16-24), Greenstein's essay on "Mordecai Richler and Jewish-Canadian Humor" (196-215) brings out Richler as a satirist. Graeme Gibson's interview brings the writer face to face in print and Robert Fulford's CBC interviews are valuable media records for a Richler scholar. Newspaper articles by Sian Griffiths' "Mordecai Richler's Montreal" and David Gurevich's "St. Urbain Revisited" in the *Guardian* and *New Criterion* re-examine Richler's Montreal in present day context.

Although his works received mixed criticism for his satirical teeth, posthumously an enormous interest has been on the rise. An exclusive international conference on "The Richler Challenge" conducted by McGill's Institute in 2004 plat formed fresh thoughts and analysis. *Canadian Literature,* A Quarterly of Criticism and Review brought out an issue dedicated to Richler in 2010. Critical writings of Glenn Deer, Brian Johnson, Robin Nobel, Melina Baum Singer focused on the journal's theme of critical relationships of Richler's heroes with all forms of established identity. Richler's works also inspired the silver screens. Movie adaptations of Richler's *Duddy Kravitz* and *Barney's Version* and Television drama based on *St. Urbain's Horseman* and *Joshua Then and Now* have recreated Richler's neighbourhood, dramatic storylines and wit on visual media. Francine Pelletier's *Mordecai Richler: The Last of the*

Wild Jews is a documentary that traces Richler as the last in the track of wild Jew writers.

While his works draw a lot of critical attention, writers have been drawn towards Richler the man. Although he vehemently denied being autobiographical, Richler apparently mined a lot of material from his life. Ada Craniford's *Mordecai Richler: A life in ten novels* (2005) analyzes his life and works in entirety, centering on parody and thrust. Michael Posner's *The Last Honest Man* (2004) is an oral biography. Reinhold Kramer's *Mordecai Richler Leaving St Urbain* (2008) is a highly researched biography that demonstrates with insight, how the artist's life is certainly a point of reference for shaping his artistic works. The latest of Richler's life story is *Mordecai: The Life and Times* (2011) by Charles Foran. This is voluminous with an epic touch. Glenn Deer in his "Review Essay: Richler's Biographers" notes Vassanji's *Mordecai Richler* (2009) uses Richlerian "gruff caricature" and anecdotes with caution to use "memory to embellish, reinvent, settle scores" (103). Joey Yanofsky in *Mordecai and Me: An Appreciation of a Kind* (2003) writes on Richler through obsession and admiration. While Posner harnesses the Richler associates' commentary, Kramer's book has extensive archival research done and Foran brings to the reader the man through remarkable interviews with the Richler family unit.

Studies are also conducted through the literary walking-tours to St. Urbain to revisit Richler's Montreal which is the locale of his fiction. Thesis submissions both at M.A. and Ph.D. degree level focusing on the Duddy prototype have been done as early as 1970s at the University of Calgary, Canada. The Proquest Dissertations and Theses for Calgary, as well as the Library and Archives Canada Theses collection feature around 20 to 30 Research titles that focus on or refer to Mordecai Richler's fiction and non-fiction. Rachael Feldhay Brenner's published dissertation entitled *Assimilation and Assertion: The Response to the Holocaust in Mordecai Richler's Writing* (1989) is a valuable thesis that examines how the effect of the World War II genocide crippled the cultural memory of the Jewish protagonists.

These works along with primary and secondary sources on New Historicism and select non-literary texts have been used as reference points in the present study. Although a lot of critical commentary has been done on the prolific writer particularly in Canada, yet Richler is an unexhausted research subject. Nathalie Cooke and Norman Ravvin, guest editors of the Mordecai Richler issue in *Canadian Literature* observe that the writer has been "lightly served by the Canadian scholarly community" (9) in comparison to the research reception for Margaret Atwood and Margaret Laurence. While Canadian Literature has become a much-pursued research area in India, reception for Richler is in a nascent stage. Publications and paper presentations on the writer including comparative studies with Indian authors indicate the growing interest. Two Ph.D. dissertations by Prof. S. Lakshmi, "A Thematic Study of Search for Identity in the novels of Mordecai Richler" (2003) and Prof. S. Ganesan, "Quest for values in the novels of Mordecai Richler" (2006) have been done at Bharathidasan University, Tiruchirappalli. However, it has to be noted that there have been no significant published books on Mordecai Richler in India. The present study examines Richler's texts as textual relics of the conflicting hyphenated identities of the protagonists from a New Historicist perspective.

Methodology Adopted

The methodology adopted for the study blends Michael Ryan's historical research using archival material and focussing on a few dimensions of the text with readings in the historical materials available on the select issues (131). The present research employs a non-linear New Historicist perspective of the intricately styled Richler's novels along with a parallel reading of non-literary texts to see whether a thematic pattern evolves from this. Non-literary texts based on study of archival material on Richler, Montreal and Jews, e-mail communications audio, video interviews and relevant movies are referred to analyze the 'circumambient space' represented by race, space, time, tradition, religion, gender and culture of the mid-twentieth Jewish Montreal.

Greenblatt in his essay *Towards a Poetics of Culture* defines a work of art as "The product of a negotiation between a creator or class of creators, equipped with a complex, communally shared repertoire of conventions, and the institutions and practices of society" (*LC* 158). The study plan is to apply Greenblatt's concepts of New Historicist practice to the select novels. Richler's novels are interlaced with the Jewish tradition and milieu in a Canadian context. These highlight Jewish inclinations and deviations in working out their identity. He explicates the conflicts and moral issues that arise in a multicultural set up. His novels also resonate with 'wonder' of his time and place and can be studied as cultural texts with a symbolic dimension of social action. This entails historical research of the culture and tradition of the mid-twentieth century Montreal ghetto which may throw further light on the thematic pattern of the select novels.

This book is based on my Ph.D. thesis titled *Conflicts from Surrounding Spaces of the mid-20th Century Jewish Montreal Ghetto*[2]*: A New Historicist Approach to Mordecai Richler's Select Novels.* Six out of Richler's ten novels which have a Jewish-Canadian surrounding space and Montreal as its social geography are chosen for the study. The select novels include *Son of a Smaller Hero* (1955), *The Apprenticeship of Duddy Kravitz* (1959), *St. Urbain's Horseman* (1971), *Joshua Then and Now* (1980), *Solomon Gursky was Here* (1989) and *Barney's Version* (1997). The scope of the present study is limited to these novels of Richler as representative of texts written in mid and later half of twentieth century, set primarily in the Jewish Montreal ghetto with Jewish protagonists. The six novels are juxtaposed with non-literary texts related to Jewish, Montreal and Holocaust histories, tradition and religious practices of Judaism and the Jew-Gentile divide in a Canadian context. This is to explain how Richler's novels absorb the surrounding space of the mid-twentieth century Jewish Montreal ghetto. Some of the co-texts are Joe King's *From the Ghetto to the Main: The Story of the Jews of Montreal*, Lawrence E. Sullivan's *The Religious Tradition of Judaism*, William Weintraub's *City Unique: Montreal Days and Nights in the 1940s and '50s.*

The topic chosen can be applied to many texts, writers and backgrounds of severe physical and mental ghetto-mindedness. Some path-breaking, original contributions in this work can be summed up in these points. First the present finding is based on a new-historic analysis of 'circulation, exchange, and negotiation' between literature and history in the select novels of Richler in relation to select non-literary texts of the age. The idea is to focus on the 'circumambient space' that includes the representation of Religion, Politics, Family, Gender and Social issues of the mid-twentieth century Montreal Jewish ghetto life. Secondly the study analyzes the pattern of 'improvisation' as part of Richler's literary creations with Greenblatt's dualistic sense of culture as both 'constraint and mobility'. Thirdly it studies Richler's delineation of female characters. Fourthly it examines the 'Wonder' and 'Resonance' movement that is embedded in the literary creation. Finally, although Greenblatt talks about culture-sculpted selves, this work through a study of Richler's characters aims to show that 'self-fashioning' cannot be devoid of discernment of choice.

The following chapter II discusses the first part of the proposed analysis focusing on the surrounding spaces or the 'circumambient space' that are absorbed into the select novels of Richler.

End Notes

1. Fiddler on the Roof (1971) is a poignant movie of a Jewish father of five daughters, Reb Tevye who holds on to tradition against the raging currents of an ever-changing society. The "fiddler on the roof" metaphorically is the balancing of life amidst survival and tradition.
2. A ghetto is a part of a city in which members of a minority group live, especially because of social, legal or economic pressure. The Holocaust Encyclopedia records that, "The term "ghetto" originated from the name of the Jewish quarter in Venice, established in 1516, in which the Venetian authorities compelled the city's Jews to live". Ghettos were created for Jews in Frankfurt, Rome, Prague and other cities in the 16th and 17th centuries and during World War II. Ghettos isolated Jews from the non-Jewish population and they lived under miserable conditions. The St. Urbain ghetto in Montreal, Canada was the home of Jewish immigrants in the mid-twentieth century.

2

Surrounding Spaces

> "Culture" according to Geertz is "not a power that can be seen as the cause of events, but rather the context in which those events happen and become meaningful" (Robson 43).

Robson explains that, "Cultural contexts are not outside the text, but are absorbed into it and it is this process of absorption that explains the persistence of works of art outside of the contexts in which they are originally produced" (22). Prafulla Kar in an E-mail writes "the phrase "surrounding spaces" is not used by any specific critic; Greenblatt used the phrase "circumambient" space (*LTC* 176) to suggest that a work of art draws its creative energy from the surrounding space as a cultural artifact".

Vesser states, "That literary and non-literary "texts" circulate inseparably;" (xi). This chapter is on the application of New Historicism as a textual practice to Richler's works and placing it in the context of select non-literary texts. Gallagher and Greenblatt note that "... in making the literary and non-literary seem to be each other's thick description" to facilitate ethnographic realism for literary purposes (31). Richler's novels have a thick cultural fabric with threads drawn from religion, history, politics and literature that are collective representational systems that work in the reproduction and contestation of social power.

Veeser affirms that, new historicists have evolved a method of describing culture in action. This chapter focuses on the context-text relationship through the dynamics of their 'negotiation and exchange', to use Greenblatt's phrase. It also studies the minute details of the Jewish behavioural codes. These are religious and cultural logics informed by sociological factors that constitute the 'circumambient space' of the Jews and non-Jews and the motive forces that control the whole society that in which Richler sets his works. To discuss the present idea in detail, the chapter is divided into five sub-divisions. The six novels are juxtaposed with non-literary texts related to Jewish, Montreal and Holocaust histories along with tradition and religious practices of Judaism and the Jew-Gentile divide in a Canadian context. This is to explain how Richler's novels absorb the surrounding space of the mid-twentieth century Montreal ghetto.

2.1 The Figure a Jew Makes

> "To be a Jew" is something that cannot be defined for the cultured, assimilated Jew, except paradoxically and circuitously: by the *mere* fact of always being susceptible to gratuitous murder "because of being Jewish". Robert Mirashi (qtd. in Greenstein *TS 54*)

The image of a Jew in literature as in history is ambivalent. The *Encyclopedia Judaica* traces the figure of the Jew in English literature as one that varied from the evil stereotypes and unfavourable portraits as in Marlowe's Barbara, Shakespeare's Shylock, Dickens' Fagin to Charles Kingsley's good Jew in *Hypatia.* Considerate treatments of Jews are in the Romantic poetry of Coleridge, Byron, Shelley and Browning. The twentieth-century writers return to a portraiture of the black, dark Jew as in Eliot's *Gerontion* and Catholic writers such as Belloc, Chesterton and Greene. Shaw brought back the Jew-Devil stage tradition in burlesque form. Galsworthy's *Loyalties* and Joyce's *Ulysses* is an attempt to abandon the old stereotype and depict Jews in natural, human terms. Whatever may be the image sketched, the figure of the Jew has been prominently noticed with frequent tagging and untagging of stereotypes based on prejudice and idealization. The Jew not only provoked fear and hatred but also awe and admiration for wisdom, experience and survival.

In Richler's select novels the figure the Jew makes is also a dual image. Richler's use of the Jew-image as a 'symbolic economy' marks his diverse tone. This tone as Victor Ramraj observes in his Bio critical essay, varies from being a "loser's advocate" to the most condemned satirical one. In Richler's novels, the Jews are repeatedly referred to as a "law-abiding bunch" by the non-Jews, especially the Senator, Joshua's father-in-law and repeated by O'Hearne to Barney (*JTN 132*) (*BV 331).* Richler's tone like the Jew-image is dual. While he voices out for the minority, he never fails to target their hypocritical ways. When Wolf remarks that he'd worked like a nigger, Leah immediately says, "Don't say 'nigger'. Noah wouldn't like it. He recognizes the niggers!" (*SH* 31). Virgil, an epileptic, says that they were a persecuted minority – the Jews, Negroes and epileptics. Irony continues. Jews also have the famous tags attached to themselves as tax-collectors from the Bible to fleecing money-lenders and the "Jumpy Jews" (*SG 351*) as someone "who wears a yarmulke, accepts bribes..." (*BV 125).* Duddy's ruthless play games leave an Irwin Shubert remarking, "It's the cretinous little money-grubbers like Kravitz that cause anti-Semitism" pointing out to the Jewish stereotype of money-makers (*DK 68).* Sister Octavia campaigned in 1937 to her people as not to purchase from Jew shopkeepers "who had cheating in their blood" (*BV 72).*

Anti-Semitism moves beyond Canada and the World War era. Richler notes the social tone with regards to Jews in the Newgate Calendar which was recorded around the mid-eighteenth century, "negroes, Jews, gypsies, and vagabonds of every description" as the very "refuse of the society" and a Montagu memoir around 1880 which complained about "shabby Jews with anxious faces" (*SUH* 48-49).

Joshua asks his father, "Why aren't we popular?" Reuben replies "Go know" (*JTN* 168). This question possibly finds an answer in Moses' attempt to trace the Jews in Canada through various accounts of the tribe. He quotes one Mayhew who deplored the prejudice against Jews as "misers, usurers, extortionists, receivers of stolen goods, cheats, and brothel-keepers" (*SG 412*). But Mayhew allowed some foundation for many of these allegations. He states that gambling was their chief vice, just as the excessive love of money was the main characteristic. He also wrote that the Jews were also known for their communal spirit who contributed generously to Jewish charities, so that no Jew ever had to die in a parish workhouse. It is an ambivalent characteristic considering their undeniable greed for money.

Uncle Oscar in *Joshua Then and Now* is another money-making think-tank. He cracked his head for the money-making ideas that would lift him out of his dreaded yard into the splendor of Outremont. In order to move beyond the ghetto, he educated himself, wrote letters for *The Star* to imprint his views on the plight of the Jews in Europe. As an enterprising Jew he conceived a new form of crossword puzzle, hurried to Ottawa to offer his war plan to the ministry of Defense and also invited one ingenious ratio game after another. Richler sharply questions "but would the CBC buy from a Jew?" (*JTN 51*).

Minting money is repeatedly attributed to the Jews. It is a skill to claim material success and to escalate the ghettoed environment. Barney claims to be a "natural-born entrepreneur" (*BV* 2). Clara predicts that "when you go home, it will be to make money, which is inevitable, given your character..." (*BV 187)* which Barney disliked himself. From the ghetto, Barney emerges as a successful money-making producer after many experimental stints from selling ice cream, chocolate bars, peanuts in the Gayety Theatre, dealing in cheese, olive oil, stolen Egyptian artifacts and finally ends churning out crap for his totally unnecessary productions. At an advanced age he regrets his morally weak money-making skills and preferred to have lived a *'mensch'*. His son Michael Panofsky notes, "I am the beneficiary of Barney's gift for money-making. Alas, it is an attribute he always deplored in himself, which is why, I suppose, I was his least favourite of the children, the one who bore the brunt of his sarcasm" (*BV 413).*

Prejudice and anti-Semitism made the Jews an unwanted tribe and Prohibition was also felt in Canada. When Solomon meets MacIntyre, the deputy minister of immigration, to consider placing more Jews in the province of Quebec, the latter tells:

> Let's not hide behind euphemisms, Mr. Gursky. By refugees you mean Jews… Jews are to be classified as 'non-preferred immigrants' not because of their race, which prejudice I would find repugnant, but because they consider work in agriculture or mining beneath their dignity… It is because your people are such confirmed city-dwellers, and would usurp positions that could be filled by the native-born, or immigrants from the Mother Country, that we simply cannot open the flood gates. (*SG 375)*

Solomon defends his tribe and tells MacIntyre that his grandfather was a coal miner and his father a farmer. The deputy minister gleefully points out that the Gursky brothers since then have found the booze dynasty. MacIntyre makes it clear that this endless agitation to flood the country with Jewish relatives and so-called farmers must stop. He shows a clipping from *Le Devoir*: "The Jewish shopkeeper on St. Lawrence Boulevard does nothing to increase our natural resources" (*SG 379*). He informs Solomon that a petition signed by more than 1, 20,000 members of the St. Jean Baptiste Society opposed "all immigration and especially Jewish immigration" to Quebec, had been delivered to the parliament. He tells Solomon, "Yours is a race apart with… an exasperating penchant for organizing their affairs better than other people" (*SG 379).* The Jews communal spirit excluded others. Just as they failed to be inclusive of other people, the world found reasons to exclude them.

Jews also take an ambivalent position that constitutes the eternal Jewish dilemma. Jews themselves thought of Canada as a country of exile and then it is difficult to be recognized as mainstream Canadians. Grandfather Ephraim's escapades into the Arctic provided the entire Gursky clan with Canadian credentials. Bernard, the brother of Solomon says that they didn't come to Canada fleeing from some dirty village. Their family was established much before Canada became a country. A sense of being rooted in a home is a recurrent argument and motif.

Ironically threat was on both sides. The threatened Jews in turn threatened all to exist. McMaster the sergeant speaks about how a Canadian feels about the Jews who elbowed ahead of them.

"A Jew elbows ahead of you in a line-up outside a movie and you shove him back a little, just to keep him honest, and right off he's hollering about the six million" (*JTN 16*). A totally frustrated MacPherson tells Duddy, "The trouble with you Jews, is that you're always walking around with a chip on your shoulder" (*DK* 34). Mariano of Ibiza tells Joshua about the Jews, "They are very clever and it is better not to mess with them. But, man, you certainly come from a difficult people" and Joshua replies "Stiff-necked" (*JTN 336).* Pauline a gentile in *Joshua Now and Then* at McGill University talks about how Kevin discovered the Jews to be pushy, rude and impolite forever jutting into the other person's space. The following textual quotation explicates a non-Jew's understanding of the Jews:

> And, suddenly, there were all those fierce, driving Jews, who didn't play by their rules, each one hollering "me, me, me." My God they demanded space, lots of space, but they didn't even know where their grandfathers came from. They interrupted you in mid-sentence. They grabbed seats in the front row in lecture rooms. They wore diamond socks. They didn't give a shit about football. Clearly, no matter how dazzling their marks, they would never be accepted into the right law firms, but they could argue rings around most of the law professors and they were not going to be denied. They had already taken over the *McGill Daily*, raging at each other in the columns, arguing about beasties Kevin and Pauline had never heard of. Trotsky. Brecht. The Rosenbergs. With their stinging wit, they drove Kevin out of the mock parliament. (*JTN 177-178*)

On the other side of the line, the non-Jews like Pauline and Jane giggled at being called gentiles and '*shiksas*'. Pauline recalls how they were scared by the pushy Jews, invading their space. The Jews wanted to frighten the world that had scared them continuously. Once when Pauline had invited a few Jews for a party they were abrasive and made deprecating remarks about the tasteless food. They never felt odd about being inquisitive, "One of them stepped right up to my father and asked him how much he had paid for our house" (*JTN* 178).

Atwood on Victim Positions writes, "Position One: To deny the fact that you are a victim" (36). This position is taken by people who deny their identity as victims for the fear of losing the benefits they possess. People like Lennie, Clara and Joshua denied their identity as a Jew and did not want to be recognized with their tribe. While Duddy invented a brother Bradley in Arizona to claim a wealthy and adventurous connection, Lennie never told that he had a brother in St. Urbain to deny his Street roots. One of his friend's say, "He wasn't a St. Urbain Street boy either. He lived on Cote St Catherine Road. That was Uncle Benjy's address" (*DK 165).* It was difficult for the Jewish boys to keep up with the rest of the crowd. It was pretty expensive. Riva on Lennie says, "Jewish boys and girls aren't good enough for him. It's a disgrace honestly" (*DK 168).* Usually the Jewish boys were rarely noticed. But Lennie got mixed up with the non-Jewish and finally becomes an assimilationist.

As a non-observant Jew, Joshua feels that his identity as a Jew was a burden and its didactic law, a pain. At Ibiza he dreads to be recognized as a Jew. When Juanito identifies him as a Jew, Joshua thinks "Jews, Jews, Joshua thought, everywhere I go there are other Jews to advice me. Clutching. Claiming. I probably wouldn't be safe in Senegal" (*JTN* 166).

Clara said to Barney, "My mother would suffer a stroke if she knew I was living with a Jew," *(BV 63).*She added that the Jews were the poison contaminating America's blood stream. But the irony is she had lied about being a non-Jew. "Clara's father asks Barney, "But you're not ashamed of being Jewish… Like Clara" (*BV 150).* Many of the Charnofskys regarded Clara's father "… an embarrassment. An atavism. A ghetto Jew" although he was instrumental in bringing them to America from Poland (*BV 156).* They considered him awkward when he put on his *'tallis'* and *'davening'* in their living room and giggled when he wore his *'yarmulke'*. These people abhorred Hebraic connections lest they be isolated from the melting pot culture. When registering for a camp, Boogie's mother instructs him to fill in "atheist" under religious denomination. The camp commander winked, crossed it out, and wrote "Jewish." Being denied and unaccepted historically and universally, many of the Jewish Diaspora decide to deny their Jewish origin. Barney tells Mike that they rather restricted their identity to be "of Jewish descent" rather than to be called Jews. Though the challenge is socially-constructed, the choice is individual.

Unbecoming the Lesser being

Race is forever a question for the Jew. Persecution has been their way of life. In spite of rejection and denial there is an earnest desire to prove something to the world as a Jew. Max echoes this aspiration for a Jew to be somebody known to others. He dreams that Lennie the medical student would become another Pasteur, "That would be a big thing for the Jews. One of ours finding the cancer-cure. Aw, they'd still make us trouble" (*DK 173).* This is the yearning that all Richler's Jew men seek to fulfill. The dispersed Jews have amazing resilience. With the longest-tortured history, they survived on all lands, be it sand or ice across the globe. Henry tells a surprised pilot to see a Jew living in the Eskimo region: "We're an astonishing people. Dandelions, my father used to say. Dig us out here and riding the wind and the rain we take root there" (*SG 95).* Thus, the figure that a Jew makes and the 'symbolic economy' of the Jew image in Richler's select novels have an inherent ambivalence, they struggle and threaten, oblige and question tradition, fear and terrorize, transgress or transform to survive.

2.2 Space and 'Social Energy'

> "It is, so to speak, not the tradition and milieu which Richler chose, but the tradition and milieu which chose him" (McSweeney 137).

Richler's texts charged with 'social energy' of Montreal produce resonance with their cultural environment. They are embedded in a network of social circulation of post-World War II and Jewish Immigrant living in a Canadian space of the mid-twentieth century. It also traces the presence of the psychological ghetto wall which has an impact on the hyphenated identity and the dividing lines in the geographical streets of the Montreal ghetto.

George Woodcock calls Montreal as a great frontier city, where various traditions intermingled and reacted upon each other. He claimed it to be a "natural laboratory" for examining fears and fascinations that flow between various communities particularly of the Jews in a Canadian land. Richler's Montreal based novels 'recover its histories', the urban texts are entrenched in the small fraction of space and time of Montreal set in the hollow of the great depression and mature with the aging characters to the latter half of the century. Thus, the texts chronicle the ideology of the mid-twentieth century Jewish-Canadian mindscape.

The Historical Context – History of Jews in Canada

The Jewish community of Canada is a rich, diverse and significant ethnic group of multicultural Canada. Their minority status has its effect on the community and this in turn creates an ongoing discourse concerning what this means for them.

James March records that the first significant wave of Jewish immigrants to Canada arrived with General Jeffery Amherst in 1760. Most of these Jewish settlers emigrated from the United States and settled in urban centres, the majority in Montreal. "The 1831 census recorded 197 Jewish residents in Upper and Lower Canada. By 1851 the number had increased to 451. Most were middle class and well educated; they were involved in trade and contributed to the economic growth of the country. (7) Louis Rosenberg statistically proves that Canada has led the world with a nine fold increase in its Jewish population within a period of 35 years at the beginning of the twentieth century and stood thirteenth in size of Jewish Population in 1931 (5).

Michael Greenstein notes that Richler's writing in 1968 described Canada as the ghetto of the north. "Canada's vast distances, natural barriers, diverse patterns of settlement and locally specific histories have led many commentators to see regionalism as a defining feature of Canadian culture" (Fiamengo 241). Regionalism and Urbanism constitute Richler's literary space.

The Ghetto Wall

> "the ghetto of Montreal has no real walls and no true dimensions. The walls are the habits of atavism and the dimensions are an illusion. But the ghetto exists all the same" (*SH 14*).

The Jewish Montreal ghetto plays a definite role in Richler's works. Richler uses the details of the real-world geography and examines what Fiamengo opines as the impact of a distinctive terrain, topography along with the social, economic and cultural dynamics of the period. The tradition and cultural psyche of the Jewish ghetto of Montreal in the early-twentieth century are also woven into the story-telling.

> Out of the ghetto streets where a Jewboy
> Dreamed pavement into pleasant Bible-land,
> Out of the Yiddish slums where childhood met
> The friendly beard, the loutish *Sabbath*-goy,
> Or followed, proud, the *Torah*-escorting band,
> Out of the jargoning city I regret,
> Rise memories... (A.M.Klein, *Gloss Aleph*)

Michael Greenstein observes Klein's use of "Out of" as a phrase with three-fold connotations of space, time and transformation (*TS* 20). Similarly In *Hunting Tigers Under Glass* Richler states the challenge of double emergence, "To be a Jew and a Canadian is to emerge from the ghetto twice" (9). Richler's protagonists are engaged in the spatial interpretation of the mid-twentieth century ghetto, where a wandering Jew boy travels out of Montreal's ghetto to a Diaspora space, beyond the walls, sometimes back and forth. They work to set up a home beyond the boundaries of St. Urbain Street and alike, force themselves into self-imposed exile between the Canadian and European space, roping in their Jewish tradition and visiting their St. Urbain roots through childhood memory. Thus home and exile is a strong theme in the select novels.

The ghetto wall was both a social construction and a self-imposed one. Noah flees home, Duddy socially strives to escalate, Jake, Joshua and Barney venture past Canadian borders throwing light on transnational and individual meanings of identity and Solomon globe trots. These flights beyond the ghetto wall and the restrictions of the community indicate the impulse in the characters to venture beyond the boundary.

The Orthodox like the Adlers considered the ghetto as a safety and "a kind of felicity" and did not mind the faults. They couldn't imagine that they could exist beyond it. But for people like Noah it was a cage. "He flung open the door to that cage, and said, in effect, follow me to freedom" *(SH 36)*.

Montreal Ghetto of the 1940's and 50's was clawed around with effects of the Depression. Charles Foran notes the rectangular "ghetto," as it was then called, ran from the eastern slope of Mount Royal to a few streets beyond St. Lawrence, a.k.a. "The Main," and from Sherbrooke Street north to Bernard. A city unto itself, it was entirely immigrant and mostly poor (2). William Weintraub in a historical account of the city Montreal in the 1940s and '50s notes that problems in paying rents, savouring the habit of thrift by walking distances to save on carfare were common. The cold-water flats, "heated by a single coal stove in the kitchen," the never warmed houses in winter and clothes warmed on stoves constituted a typical poor Jew home on the streets east of the Main (185). These sordid economic conditions of living widened the Jew-Gentile social divide. The baiting Outremont and Westmount "mansion" living and a free gentile-world compelled many of the third generation Jews to move beyond the ghetto walls and traditional strictures of Orthodox Judaism as envisaged in Richler's literary men. Jake said to his relatives that Montreal, "was a cultural desert, a colonial pimple, and he was off to nourish himself at the imperialist fountainhead…" London (*SUH* 193).

Optimism and idealism were rife in 1940s. Unlike their parents, the frivolous generation saw a world beyond boundaries and increasing possibilities on education including attending Universities and venturing less traditional fields for the Jews, which was not a phenomenon of the past. Parochial curriculum in schools was gaining importance. Yiddish became Montreal's third language in the mid-twentieth century, a status that was never before and that could not survive after being termed as "the "old country" language of their parents" (Weintraub 189). Richler's Montreal rooted novels absorb these contexts into the texts.

The Streets of Jewish-Montreal Ghetto

> Street life in the Jewish streets was lively and noisy. The milkman, the breadman and the iceman, with their horses and wagons, all made a hearty clatter as they plied their trade... For young mothers, the centres of their social life were those long outdoor staircases, so peculiar to Montreal. They would sit there on hot summer days, feeding their babies, scolding the older children for getting dirty on the street, and – above all – gossiping with the neighbours. (Weintraub 187)

Richler captures the buzzes of Montreal life extensively from cluttered living conditions to the conundrum of the mundane life. The reader can blink at the neon signs of beer houses and listen to the cacophony on these streets. Noah's room on Dorchester Street was just a block away from St. Catherine Street of the down town. Life on Dorchester Street was simple and unassuming. Summer evenings found men and women sitting on the steps of the "long outdoor staircases" of houses helping themselves with beer and smoke, music from gramophone, tuning on to the CBC and listening to radio plays. Drug trade, suicides and police raids punctuated their lives.

Montreal streets are a character by themselves. The description of the ghetto projects a dilapidated structure of living. Imposing and strangling, the ghetto is criss-crossed with divisions and ambiguity. The streets are more than streets.

> If the poorest Jews lived in the streets just east of St. Lawrence Main, their somewhat more affluent cousins lived in streets to the west like St. Urbain and Waverly. There were not only working-class people here, but also small merchants and the owners of corner candy stores. (Weintraub 192)

True to Weintraub's historical account, Richler immortalizes the St. Urbain ghetto in his works. Joe King traces the history of new waves of immigrants to Montreal, in the first and second decade of the 1900s. He writes that at the time of the Second Settlement of Jewish immigrants (C. 1921 – C.1940), "St. Urbain Street was almost 100 percent Jewish. The area became known locally as the St. Urbain Ghetto" (104). He refers to Richler's *The Street* to describe the ghetto as a self-contained world made of five streets; Clark, St. Urbain, Waverly, Esplanade and Jeanne Mance, bounded by "The Main" on one side and Park Avenue on the other. Richler notes that St. Urbain Street next to the bottom rung on a ladder which in their days were all hot to climb (*HSH* 107-108). The youthful days of Richler's protagonists recreate the everyday life on the streets of the Jewish ghetto in Montreal. Duddy, Jake and Joshua are grown on St. Urbain, Moses and Barney on Jeanne Mance Street and Noah on St. Laurence Bouleward.

> Most of the Jews who live at the diminishing end of the ghetto, on streets named St. Urbain, St. Dominique, Rachel, and City Hall, work in textile or garment factories. Some are orthodox, others are communist. But all of them do their buying and their praying and their agitating and most of their sinning on St. Lawrence Boulevard, which is the aorta of the ghetto, ... All day long St. Lawrence Boulevard, or Main Street, is a frenzy of poor Jews, who gather there to buy groceries, furniture, clothing and meat. Most walls are plastered with fraying election bills, in Yiddish, French, and English. The street reeks of garlic and quarrels and bill collectors... *(SH 15)*

Children grew up gobbling pilfered plums and the gutter loaded with dead rats, rotten apples, cigar butts and horse manure flowed slowly, racing with a terrifying zigzag of flies. In *St. Urbain's Horseman* Nancy talks of greenhouse and raspberry picking in the backyard garden of a *goysy* Ontario childhood. Jake admits that these were alien to him because he had been raised on St. Urbain's urban backyard dumped with punctured tires, cracked sinks, watermelon husks and rotting mattresses. Squalid living conditions and reeking atmosphere made up the 'circumambient space' of the Jewish ghetto.

Social status was marked on the roads. The well-to-do-Jews walked on Queen Mary's road, the middle class on Park Avenue and the poor and the elderly walked on St. Lawrence Boulevard. It was restrictions within restriction. As a social commentator, Richler records the walking gestures of people signaling their class. "Each street had its own technique of walking, a technique so finely developed that you could always tell a man off his own street" (*SH 16*). The Queen Mary Road Jews walked prosperous with a rich grin banking on the money they possessed. The wives exchanged small flatteries. The aspiring Park Avenue Jews walked without certainty, pompous and ingratiating by turns. The bearded poor on St Lawrence Boulevard walked with their heads bent and their hands clasped behind their backs. They walked with bowed heads with looks rooted on the pavement or high up at the sky, rarely did they risk looking straight ahead. Leah Adler in one of her conversations with Wolf yearns to walk on Park Avenue with her head high up, if he could leave his father's scrap yard and begin like a man on his own.

Duddy Kravitz with its lucid, graphic portrait of the Streets of Richler's youth, permanently carved a niche for itself on the literary map of Canada.

> To a middle-class stranger, it's true, one street would have seemed as squalid as the next. On each corner a cigar store, a grocery, and a fruit man. Outside staircases everywhere. Winding ones, wooden ones, rusty and risky ones. Here a prized plot of grass splendidly barbered, there a spitefully weedy patch. An endless repetition of precious peeling balconies and waste lots making the occasional gap here and there. But, as the boys knew, each street between St. Dominique and Park Avenue represented subtle differences of income. No two cold water flats were alike … No two stores were the same, either. Best Fruit gypped on the scales, but Smiley's didn't give credit. (13)

The descriptions were not restricted to the landscapes, but were commentaries on the mindscape and lifestyle of people lodged in the St. Urbain ghetto.

L.B. Berger and his bunch in *Solomon Gursky* represent the literate section of the ghetto. Their cold-water flat on Jeanne Mance Street had loquacious Russian Jews, Yiddish poets and other artists visit day and night. The whole lot was "Washed on the shores of a cold country that was as indifferent to them as they were to it" *(SG 12).* Sitting around a dining table with a crocheted tablecloth they would discuss the latest turn of events in Russia or the political developments in Poland or Palestine. They would go to USA to meet their Jewish friends and relatives on holidays. For them Canada was not yet a country but the next door place. It was a rough and new land. Richler notes that they feared and scorned gentiles, seldom touched anything but apricot brandy, dreamed of owning their own duplex in Outremont, paid Kronitz 50 cents a week for insurance policies from the Pru, and were constant husbands and loving parents *(SG 14).* L.B.Berger found himself welcome as an exotic garlicky pirate, a living proof of the ethnic riches that weave the Canadian cultural tapestry. Richler's true to life accounts won literary acclaim and Jewish discontent. He blatantly sketched their cluttered living space and zoomed into their cheating scales, scrap yards deceiving peddlers and war-time profits which tainted the "chosen" tribe.

Dividing Lines

Louis Rosenberg notes that Westmount and Outremont, the suburbs of Montreal record the highest increase of Jewish population between 1921 and 1931. This led to the formation of two distinct Jewish communities. The uptown Jews in the suburbs were the rich and anglicized old guard and the downtowners were the recent arrivals who lived in the area along St. Laurent Boulevard, called "The Main". "The street forms the east–west dividing line in the city. The area around this street north of the downtown core was the Jewish area of Montreal from the turn of the century to the 1950s" (King 102). This social demarcation is immersed in the surrounding space of Richler's novels.

Montreal in the 1940s and 50's was Canada's largest and multihued city. Jews fleeing European oppression immigrated to

Montreal and by 1941 they numbered to sixty-four thousand. The shabby streets on either side of St. Lawrence Main were fully Jewish. "These were mostly working-class Jew-toilers in the sweatshops of the garment industry, fabricators of fur coats and handbags, shoe makers, deliverymen, mechanics" (Weintraub 184). Prosperity of the 1940's and '50s brought opportunities for the working-class Jews who could start afresh a new factory of their own, braving "the tyrannical boss". Their new affluence encouraged determination to move towards westward homes in the new suburbs abandoning the dingy old dwelling.

> Going farther west, one came to Park Avenue, an economic dividing line, for beyond that, again to the west, was Outremont, abode of Jews with healthy bank accounts, proprietors of clothing factories. It was to Outremont that ghetto boys from St. Dominique Street went in spring to steal lilacs from the gardens of prosperous Jews. This posh precinct was a different world where, the boys had heard, there was a synagogue whose rabbi didn't have a beard and who spoke with a British accent. (Weintraub 192)

Richler writes, "Outremont, our heart's desire, was amazing" (*HSH* 108). Weintraub also records Outremont might be "comfortable," but Westmount was rich, very rich" (193). Westmount was the "abode of much of the city's wealth...home of bankers, financiers, company presidents and tycoons of every stripe. They lived in grand houses built in a great...styles – Gothic Revival, French Provincial..." (11).

Richler plaits the geographical distinction of status between the land of the rich and poor in the descriptions of Westmount, Outremont and St. Urbain Street which classified identity in the novels. "Westmount was where the truly rich lived in stone mansions driven like stakes into the shoulder of the mountain. The higher you climbed up splendid tree-lined streets the thicker the ivy, the more massive the mansion, and more important the men inside" (*DK 170).* In *Smaller Hero,* Richler notes that the employer and professional Jews owned duplexes in Outremont and their sons studied at McGill. Barney in *Barney's Version* points out that St. Urbain Street was a neighbourhood that had elected the only

Communist (Fred rose) ever to serve as a member of Parliament, produced a couple of decent club fighters (Louis Alter, Maxie Berger), the obligatory number of doctors and dentists, a celebrated gambler-cum-casino owner, more cutthroat lawyers than needed, sundry school teachers and shmata millionaires, a few rabbis, and at least one suspected murderer. Based on Richler's accounts, St. Urbain Street was crowded with promising thieves, clattering women, dusty dames and criminal fathers.

While the poor people of the Montreal Streets were into needle trade of scrap or bootlegging or prizefighting the Westmount was rich and cultivated. Each house had a maid, some even a butler and a buzzer in the dining room to bring them what they wanted. "This is Westmount. Mothers didn't bargain here, or fathers cheat at pinochle. The daughters were blonde and leggy, they were taught horseback-riding…and the sons didn't collect butcher bills on Sunday mornings to earn enough to buy their own two-wheel bikes but instead were given sports cars. British. The Best" (*JTN 92)*. Joshua observes the Westmount children to be prissy and neat.

Many wealthy Jews had their Westmount address including the domain of the Gurskys in *Solomon Gursky.* The Gurskys based on the real-life Bronfmans did everything from bootlegging to philanthropy by establishing themselves as kings of legal booze, thereby dictating politics, patronizing arts and expanding trade. Children like Moses Berger from Jeanne Mance Street are awe struck with the "undreamed-of splendour" by the Fieldstone mansions of the Gurskys on the Montreal mountainside. "All of the Gursky children, secure behind the tall stone walls of the estate, had been munificently provided for" (*SG 24*). An enormous swimming pool, a heated multi-level tree house, a miniature railway, a hockey rink, a musical merry-go-round and much more were part of the rich Jewry mansions of the Gursky lineage. Lionel's extravagant birthday party included a little circus jalopy, jugglers, dancers, magician flown in from New York and an Indian war dance. Bernard's seventy fifth birthday was charged with the Gursky grandeur with red roses flown in and festooned at every table and take away gifts of one-ounce bottles of perfumes for the ladies and slim gold cigarette lighter for the men and a specially commissioned birthday film. Ice sculptures of Gursky endowed university buildings, hospitals, museums and concert halls were set everywhere to testify Mr. Bernard's largesse. While gutter and clutter marked Street living, finery, grandeur and magnificence marked Outremont and Westmount living.

Smaller Hero, Duddy Kravitz, St. Urbain's Horseman, Joshua Then and Now and *Barney's Version* chronicle the lives of middle-class working Jews in Montreal who forever try to cross the lines of demarcations between the streets in and around "The Main" and Outremont and Westmont. *Solomon Gursky* records the province of the wealthy Jews, who have established themselves as Montreal ambassadors, forever trading and expanding the Gursky Empire.

The Real in the Literary

> *"The mundane activities and conditions of daily life can tell us much about the belief systems of a time period"* (Hall 302).

A New Historicist considers relatively mundane, but extremely essential daily aspects of common people important to delineate the ideology of the age. Hall writes, "The bulk of people's lives, their degree of happiness, and their goals and desires are hardly reducible to or understandable through the activities of their political or military leaders (303). Richler's select novels add to the 'thick description' of his age.

Richler skillfully absorbs what Greenblatt would call, 'seemingly insignificant occurrences' to show how individuals socialized or resisted particular forms of socialization to a greater or lesser degree. His narratives reveal the ghetto man's life that includes mundane activities such as employment conditions, education, recreation and other interests. A ghetto boy from "The Main" played snooker, sneaked to watch Lili St. Cyr (*BV 161)*, studied in Fletcher's Field, learnt '*Torah*', ate '*Kosher*' food, aimed Mc Gill education, aspired Medicine or squeezed into dentistry or else experimented writing. These traits are found in the select novels. Richler's places are real, seasons' actual and people's moods and tempers authentic which fashioned the ideology and living designs of the Jewish-Montreal ghetto.

The Richler landscape and seasons

John Moss defies the idea that land predominates Canadian writing. "If the Canadian imagination is in fact preoccupied with geophysical conditions, it is so on a nearly subliminal basis" (9). Richler's novels are urban in style and do not confirm much to the myth that Canadian Literature is predominantly on nature. Although Richler does not indulge much in privilege descriptions of an icy wintery landscape or verdant scenes of spring, he focuses on an exploited and degenerating Canadian environment. Blair in *Barney's Version* is an environmentalist and he rings in the global warming alarm. Blair campaigns for Save-the-Whales, Stop-the-Seal-Hunt and Recycled-Paper. Terry declares "Biodiversity is our living legacy" (*BV 168)* and opposes clear-cut logging which even his foe-friend Barney acknowledges. Henry's plan to build a modern "Noah's ark" is based on his predictions of the ensuing Ice Age, a punishment for the New Age with strong hints on global climatic changes that echo the theme of Al Gore's, highly researched, documented movie entitled *An Inconvenient Truth*[1]. Canada a land lapped by nature sends signals of global warming and climatic changes from its Arctic territories.

True to Richler's claim *Smaller Hero* is about the seasons of Montreal. Richler's graphic description of the urban landscape breaks the myth that Canada is a mass of ice. Apart from the iced wintry ghetto streets, he verbally illustrates how hot days created heat rumours of old men going crazy and women swooning on streets and babies born prematurely. "The sun swelled in the sky and stillness gripped the ghetto. When the heat was about two days old everyone seemed to have forgotten that there had been a time of no heat" (*SH 16).* Rains were paltry and were soon replaced by heat again bringing back the flies and odours of the heated ghetto.

The seasons have their utmost effect on the daily lives, at least for the middle-class Jews. They are not mere climatic conditions but also are a narrative tool to explain the social ambience. Business was slow in autumn but they knew it would pick up in winter. "Autumn is stingy" (*SH 49*) thinks Noah. An autumn cold night sets each building and tree a separate shivering entity. Richler characteristically states that it's autumn in Montreal when whores no longer stroll on St Lawrence Boulevard, but call out of sheltered doorways. Richler also uses the withering image of autumn. Noah recollects that all the threats and laws of Melech withered away when he decides not to go to class once in school and indulges in a long walk discovering beauty. Duddy against all odds hints on a prosperous winter. That was when everything was cold around him and a frostiness of relationship developed, he prospered focusing more in business. For the prosperous Outremont people, the "red and yellow" falling leaves season was the time to bring their families back from their Laurentian summer homes. Emma Richler in an E-message wrote, "I loved Montreal in the keen autumn colours with its blazing blue sky and I thought it spectacular in the snow". For the graduated children it was time for pipes, party dresses and engagement rings. Jake in *St. Urbain's Horseman* recalled when the trees on the mountain went crimson and yellow and curling brown and the streets were strewn with swirling leaves, the synagogue advertised seats available for the High Holidays and sports' page would be filled with speculation of young hockey champs.

A frozen St Lawrence Canadian climate winter hosts chill grey mornings and darkening skies. When the snows came, the earth froze, bed sheets hung stiff as glass on the ghetto backyard clothesline (*SUH* 125). Burning children's cheeks, old men blowing on their wrinkled hands, boys with blue lips and women with running nose, long waits for liquor commissions, late dates and streetcars mark the wintry days of the ghetto.

> I remember snow banks five feet high, winding outside staircases that had to be shoveled in the sub-zero cold, and, in days long before snow tires, the rattle of passing cars and trucks, their wheels encased in chains. Sheets frozen rock-hard on backyard clotheslines. In my bedroom, where the radiator sizzled and knocked through expatriate adventures. (*BV* 3)

Richler employs the image of icy winter to communicate the frozen lives of the near-grave aging flesh. "We know the winter in our souls. We know its blustery days, its solitude, its false eternity, and its apparent deaths. We know what it is to be bitten by the winter cold" (*BV 81).* Winter is doubly cruel to the poor in Canada. The cold-water flats of the Jewish ghetto in Montreal and sheets of frozen eyes cutting through everyday living harden their everyday survival. Frozen lakes wait to be relieved by spring.

"That first thaw is a glory" *(SH 107).* Spring is welcomed by giant sweepers on foot, redeeming iced streets of frozen flakes, sprouts of yellow grass grasping a glimpse of the sun, gurgling gutters in noon and the "impolite smell" back on the streets. White turns green slowly, opening up the gates of the parks, ports and flower shows. People sprout in thickets on streets, children wander and "Everybody is full" (*SH 108*). The lilac trees were in full bloom in the backyard. Richler ingrained into his writing in the seasons of urban Canada, recreating the "sights, smells and temper" of the Jewish-Montreal ghetto that had an effect on the working-class lives.

Landmarks

Richler recreates the academic atmosphere of his Baron Byng School in *Smaller Hero* under same name and as the five-storey Fletcher's Field High School (FFHS) in his select novels. The Baron Byng High school was on the St Urbain Street, a shapeless brown brick building surrounded by tenements. The first few chapters of *Duddy Kravitz* are set in the FFHS campus punctuated with the pranks of students spearheaded by Duddy of the terror Room No: 41. Duddy Kravitz, Jake Hersh, Joshua Shapiro and Barney Panofsky are all alumnae of the Jewish institution. In spite of the school being entrenched in a parochial curriculum and a platform for its students to pursue medicine, politics and business, unsavory reputation and seedy behaviour were common among the boys who hailed from the streets of Montreal. Ironic to its Jewish moral instruction and scholastic system, an air of disrespect and scandalous activities had to be continuously checked by the school teachers like Jacksons, Mac and Feeney. Richler records the notorious acts of Duddy that even ended the life of Mrs. MacPherson and the most badly behaved Jerry Dingleman who put an end to the merit card system with his tomfoolery. Like Duddy, Barney in *Barney's Version* also an FFHS student of Room 43 escaped punishments while innocent students were reprimanded for his offensive behaviour. But boys like Jake Hersh were focused and took after-school jobs.

Richler also records that once the FFHS students graduated from the cold-water flats that enclosed the school to own duplexes in the tree-lined streets of Outremont they opted to send their children to better schools than FFHS. Duddy also notes that with the trickling in of gentile students he foresees that in ten years' time there would no longer be a Jewish high school. Joshua and his friends of Room 42 frequently had get-togethers in Outremont and Westmount. FFHS is a Jewish forte. Handing out New Testaments outside the school and anything Christian was a taboo. Although it's a Jewish school, denigration abounded. Fighting against the onus of shame of being a Jew is recreated at various points of time and Richler's Jew-men fight it in various ways. Thus, FFHS is a repeated landmark in Richler's select novels which shapes the formative years of the protagonists and echoes the Street boys growing-up pranks and their precocious learning of what Greenstein notes as "comic tactics to rebel against authority of the right side of the tracks" (*TS* 159).

Apart from FFHS, Richler repeats his Dink's Bar, Wilensky's restaurant and Eaton's, a downtown Montreal department store, the landmarks of his childhood neighbourhood to authenticate and immortalize a life that duly belonged to his age. Bars continue to be a place where people come searching for things and happiness they'd lost elsewhere. Izzy drinks when he loses his wife and Barney's act post-bar hangover makes him lose his wife. Margo Mac Gilivery of Richler's youth is the inspiration behind the bartender in the movie *Barney's Version*[2].

Everyday Life

Richler reveals in his works what Hall explains as "values and valuations, through an understanding of common daily activities and material struggles" (303). He chooses to set his narrative in the common man's daily routine giving insight into the life of the working-class of the Jewish-Montreal ghetto. His select works project vivid sketches of the everyday life which included partying, holidaying, eating, furnishing, reading and recreational activities.

Richler satirically sketches the everyday life of the middle-class Jewish population who raced for education, economic status and socialization. They are a bunch of naïve people, less pruned by etiquette. On the graduation day of class of '49, the parents "arrived too soon and thirsty and proud, and immediately shamed their sons and daughters by waving and whistling at them" *(DK 63).* Richler ridicules their quest to socialize on par with the elite, create material reserves and claim sophisticated holiday homes. Enjoying the newly acquired resorts in Ste Agathe, families clowned with, "The short husbands with their outrageously patterned sports shirts arm in arm with purring wives too obviously full for slacks, the bawling kids with triple decker ice cream cones, the squealing teenagers, and the trailing grandfather with his beard and black hat" *(DK 71).* This complete family picture of the middle-class Jewish immigrants portrays the process of modernizing everyday activities and apes the gestures of the upper-class. The bourgeois life of Barney Panofsky included "Country club. Cartoons scissored out of *The New Yorker* pasted up on my bathroom walls. *Time* magazine subscription. American Express card. Synagogue membership. Attache case with combination lock" *(BV 187).* People retreated to cottages in the country side for weekends in the European style.

Richler pans his camera three sixty degrees to draw differences between St. Urbain Street food limited to chopped liver and gefilte fish in Duddy's home and treating Montreal as hub of "continuing devotion to pleasure" which signals salvation to the troubled city. He amusingly celebrates his favourite restaurant Le Mas des Oliviers as the nucleus of everyday luxurious luncheon of the affluent and political people who frequent to settle business deals, treat mistresses than wives and indulge in salacious gossips. He wittily claims, "In Montreal they do not jog or nibble a quick salad after their noon-day squash game, a disease money-driven Toronto suffers from", rather indulge in elaborate "three-hour lunches" (*BV 106).*

Through living space and furnishing homes Richler gives insight to the concept of dwelling in *Smaller Hero.* How people maintained homes reflect their attitude and mind. Theo's and Miriam's furniture were functional. The hall was spilled over with books and walls hosted paintings. Wolf always felt relieved whenever he was in his "den". Whenever he retired to the den an undisturbed territory, he knew that "The den was his", and not that of his father. His room was clean and well-ordered and a corner was devoted to his hobby, woodwork. Leah Adler loved to furnish and she was particularly proud of the parlour. Noah was simple and didn't much like his mother fussing with the furnishing of his room. Leah Adler's furnishing was cheap. She never-ever felt settled. She always thought if trouble broke and they had to flee, investing on such things would be a waste. Thus, Leah's fear reiterates that fleeing and running in search of a stable land is a strong cultural memory.

An interesting feature of Richler's characterization is the reference to the magazines and journals that one subscribed. Characters who intended social advancement read magazines. Subscriptions to the magazines indicated the choices, tastes and political inclinations of the individuals. Barney's "ugly competitive nature" and initial hiccups to the habit of reading, got him subscribed to old *Liberty* magazine, "which prefaced each of its articles with a headnote saying how long it would take to read..." and then advanced on to read John Marquand's "Mr. Moto" novel (*BV* 2). While Miriam read *The Economist*, Mrs. Second Panofsky read *The New York Book Review*. Barney had a collection of books which he waited to bequeath to his children. *Time* Magazine represented the bourgeois life and a number of characters subscribed to it. The *Reader's Digest* was enormously popular. Duddy in one of his examples of "big idea" talks about the profound success of the Wallaces. When he grows prosperous, he is found with a lot of magazines and books and treasures *God's Own Acre*. He also reads *Fortune, Time and Life.* Duddy asks Yvette to subscribe for Irwin the *Tribune* and other commie papers to prove him a communist. In one of his efforts to tarnish Blair, Barney gets him a subscription for *Boy Toy Monthly,* a playboy magazine. The "smaller hero" Wolf Adler silenced and tamed by the king Melech stocked traces of his intellectual quest. He shelved scrap yard books and copies of *Life, Popular Mechanics, Reader's Digest* and *True Crime* while Melech was spotted with a *Jewish Star.* Noah too read a lot. Young Joshua's father bought the *The Mirror, Life, The News, New York* newspapers and *Action* comics from the junkyards. Joshua's favourite read was Isaac Babel's short stories. Jake recollects that the St. Urbain Street children gobbled comics. To keep up with the elite life Mr. Trimble subscribed to *Punch* and *Country Life.* Jake had his loads of books cratered and uncratered every time and subscribed to the *Guardian* and *Times*. Greenstein observes that Jake's relationship to literary history is far more complex as he "struggles to overcome the burden of the past" and combated anxiety of influence to emerge as a renowned writer. "Literature, once his consolation, was no longer enough" (*SUH* 301). Other magazines of socialite interest included the *Observer* and *Vogue.* Living in a young country with writing and journalism at its nascent stage, the mid-twentieth century Canadians fed themselves on the American and British magazines.

People's love for music is forever young. On the busy streets of Dorchester, members of the family listened to gramophones or portable radios outside their home. Theo and Miriam listened to Beethovan symphonies. Out of the ghetto, music for Noah becomes a discovery of beauty. He became aware of booths at music stores to try records. He kept coming back to Vivaldi. Duddy increases his collection on Mozart and Beethovan for social gatherings in his apartment on Tupper Street.

Nothing like a game of snooker or hockey got the Canadian men and boys more engrossed, not even one's own marriage as in the case of Barney. Richler's son Noah recollects, "Richler looked at sports as a way out of the ghetto" to get ahead and your way in the world (Kramer 30). Playing pinballs were popular and Duddy prospered on pinball business for some time. Hanging out in pool rooms, playing squash and cards were other past times. Reuben adds on an eleventh commandment to suit his age and people. "Thou shalt pay thy gambling debts" (*JTN 69).* People luxuriously entertained themselves with reckless gambling.

Duddy exploits the movie industry to make quick money. His idea of the offbeat *'Bar mitzvah'* movies clicked. Shlomie in *Smaller Hero* is also a movie buff. Shlomie is reprimanded for being in the pool room instead of the synagogue.

Philanthropic activities claimed attention. Mel West mentions Duddy Kravitz in "AND MONTREALERS WITH A HEART" advertising his claim to show movies free, anytime, anywhere, if it was for a worthy cause. He claims Duddy's success to be the rags to riches story in the country and another Boy Wonder from the St. Urbain Street. Charity balls and fund-raising dinners constituted a rich Jew's altruistic activity and added a signature status to the opulent. A wealthy Jew was recognized with the Charity club he was associated with. Duddy asks Calder to name his favourite charity so that he could send a check as a gift to honour the latter. Fighting against anti-Semitism becomes more an occasion for money laundering, expansion of status symbol and a conversation feed for a tete-a-tete at High Tea parties. Raising flags against anti-Semitic activities, Irv embarks on feel-good tours to Israel and for official agenda coddled in expensive hotels. A B'nai Brith-type fund raiser prays for anti-Semitic incidents like racial slurs on media and swastikas on synagogue walls which become fodder for fund-raising activities. Once back in Montreal, Barney infiltrates into the Jewish establishment and volunteers to work as a fund-raiser with a hidden agenda to search for a wife "...the missing piece in my spiteful middle class equation, the jewel in Reb Barney's crown, so to speak" (*BV 187).* They advertise Israel as an insurance policy for promoting donations.

The Boy Wonder with his expanded business connections received supplicants from his kind on '*Schnorrers'* day'. This ritual begins in *Duddy Kravitz* and continues

> in *Barney's Version* where Izzy goes to meet him. "The Boy Wonder was only a St. Urbain Street boy to begin with, he remembered well his own early hardships, and he liked to lend a helping hand" (*DK 131*).

Donations were partly out of charity and partly to trade status symbol as in Duddy's reappearance in *Barney's Version.* He demands Dr. Morty to name a disease neglected by charitable trusts so that he could become its Founding father. He believed that, setting up such a trust would help him crack the Westmount society to his wife's satisfaction. Duddy goes on to set a trust for a not so common Crohn's disease which around two hundred thousand Canadians suffer.

While the young aimed Medicine or squeezed into Dentistry "a predictable ghetto syndrome" (*SUH* 148), artistic persuasion and escape to European literary capitals of London, Paris and Spain was the activity of the creative minds of Richler's varied fictional crowd. Canadian literature gains a footing in the late fifties and early sixties. Just as the ghetto had raised literary figures such as A.M. Klein and Saul Bellow, Richler also adds a lot of St. Urbain Street manufactured creative minds in his novels. A Richler protagonist is destined to be a writer like Joshua and Moses Berger, a film screenplay writer like Jake Hersh and a TV show producer like Barney. Richler himself was engaged in varied creative genres contributing to the period of literary renaissance. He also records the ordeals of a Canadian writer to establish his voice. *Barney's Version* teams with names of writers who belong to both Barney's and Richler's time, signaling the rise and growth of the literary output in Canada. He notes that Terry, but for his Canadian origin would have become an acclaimed international writer instead of being "overlooked by the cultural imperialists in New York and the snobs who rule the London literary roost" (*BV 167).* Through Terry, Richler brings to light the Canadian writers' struggle to surface.

While the ghetto boys tried their hand in a writing career, the rich Jew patronized Arts and savoured vanity claims. Mike Panofsky in London owned an art gallery of works by unknown painters and sculptors. Bernard bought paintings of Jacques Martineau. In his later appearances, Duddy buys paintings to furnish his Westmount manse and Harvey Schwartz owns a "rising in value" paintings of Jackson Pollock and Leo Bishinsky. The St. Urbain Street Yossel turned Dr. Jonathan Cole in *Joshua Then and Now,* who was a collector of street junk graduated to Canadiana arts of Pellan and William Ronald. Lucy, daughter of Solomon Gursky, amassed paintings that looked like blow-ups from comic books. These textual references record the rising interests of the people in creative and artistic activities during the period.

Ghetto Behaviour

Terry writes of Barney, "Since he sprung from the ghetto's mean streets vulgarity comes naturally to him, but he is inclined to both drunkenness and fisticuffs, which is surprising, considering his Jewish origins. A denial? Possibly" (*BV 98).* This also reflects how the WASPS viewed Richler's street grown boys. Instances of speaking about sewer rats at the dining table and whistling marked the lack of table manners. Smoking, yawning and snoozing through literate conversations on killing of animals, ills of segregation and Mc Carthyism are unavoidable gestures of the street-grown Barney. Jake Hersh finds himself comfortably belching at the Blitz table in London. As a St. Urbain Street boy, he was ashamed of his parent's Yiddish accent. Miriam was the first modern, sophisticated woman Noah had ever met. He is totally lost in front of Miriam. He tries to hide his dirty nails and corrects saying "Yeah" by saying "Yes". He is highly tensed and asks for the toilet and considers a plan to escape through the window from a totally nerve-racking environment. Coming from the ghetto, Noah felt insufficiently bred in front of a refined Miriam. An irritated Hersh complains about Duddy's foul comments on Mrs. Cox "You have to make everything dirty. Nothing's good for you, unless you can make it dirty" (*DK 21).* Although Duddy preferred marrying into a rich Outremont family, he knew only Yvette wouldn't mind his less groomed, vulgar ways. He scratched his head and bit his nails and had a crude body language. Singer explicates Duddy's acquaintance with Mr. Calder. "Duddy knows his lack of "civility" or whiteness structures his difference. Mr. Calder may entertain himself with Duddy in the privacy of his home, but their relationship has no real place in his larger life" (16). She explains that Duddy is not introduced to any of Mr. Calder's mainstream society because he has not yet internalized the etiquette of the white world and hence the relationship is superficial.

For Joshua his father was a big embarrassment, snoring away with wide open mouth and clipping toe-nails at the kitchen table. The respectable Leventhals looked down on their ghetto connection because of Joshua's father. But Pauline compliments Joshua. She tells Reuben that his son had become a *mensh,* "She said he never entered her boudoir without folding his trousers neat and washing up good, even if he no longer kept his wallet under his pillow. She also allowed that he had yet to hit her" (*JTN 223).* Barney as an "unredeemed sadist" ridicules people and is a petty thief which is recurrent ghetto behaviour. Izzy's crass conversation on opium and girls troubled The Second Mrs. Panofsky's parents, traumatized the rabbi's wife and shell-shocked the elite guests at the wedding table. The need for better grooming is repeatedly hinted.

Greenstein observes, "Agricultural sterility determines the character of the ghetto's inhabitants, because from where Duddy sprung boys grew up dirty, sad, and spiky like grass beside the railroad tracks" (*TS* 148). Richler also writes about how Smicha persistently planted radishes, peas and carrots inspite of poor harvests. Petty crimes such as shoplifting and pilfering are recurrent characteristics of ghetto living as depicted in the novels. Arty, Jake and Duddy regularly shoplifted at the Eaton's. Mostly the major characters as young boys have their moments of stealing and running. Some outgrow as they mature, but a lot like Duddy, Joshua and in a sense Barney have it in the "unconscious", in their "id" which they consciously employ at times to climb social status. Minor characters such as Gitel Kugelmass in *Solomon Gursky* shoplift and Moses reflects that pilfering was common at Holt Renfrew, Miracle Mart and Eaton. Richler's ghetto-grown characters are caught in recurrent acts of petty crimes.

Changing Times

Every age wonders at the changes of its period. Richler's characters are at awe of the changing phase of their time. Wolf in *Smaller Hero* registers the shifting ways of the new age. He is shocked with non-Yiddish names, no more Sunday family visits, children chaperoned by nurses and kissing grandchildren was no longer hygienic. Max tells Duddy, "Montreal wasn't what it is now, you know. For kids these days everything's a breeze. I remember when the snow in winter was piled higher than a man on the streets. There was a time back there when they had to pull the streetcars" (*DK 130).* Max goes on with his lists of have-nots and don'ts where he was not given a bicycle while Duddy drove a car. '*Zeyda'* would have belted Max if he had brought in even half the trouble that of Duddy from school. For the fathers, physical hardships, adversity and stringent rules constituted life in early-twentieth century while the sons were born into freedom, better living and free thinking of the mid-twentieth century Montreal.

Further in *Barney's Version,* Richler summarizes the changes in Montreal of the 1950s and 1980s bringing in a complete picture of the twentieth century life. Keeping pace with the changing times from a "carbon paper, portable typewriter" world to a "remote-controlled, voicemail message" communication, Richler records the Montreal of his youth and old age. Barney fondly recalls:

> Why, in those days we not only used carbon paper, but when you phoned somebody you actually got an answer from a human being on the other end, not an answering machine with a ho ho ho message... Doctors made house calls. Rabbis were guys. Kids were raised by their moms instead of in child-care pens like piglets. Software meant haberdashery. There wasn't a different dentist for gums, molars, filling, and extractions – one nerd managed the lot. If a waiter spilled hot soup on your date, the manager offered to pay

> her cleaning bill and sent over drinks, and she didn't sue for a kazillion dollars, claiming "loss of enjoyment of life". (*BV 248)*

The transformation that changes the face of Montreal in fifty yearstime is shocking in terms of sophistication and value system and is a universal phenomenon. Barney represents the people of the mid-twentieth century who find it difficult to accept the old world rotting and being replaced by an age of techno-explosion. In an attempt to make life simpler, easier and luxurious, life had become more complex with increase of intricacies. Richler's inventory of the advanced age signals less human signs and more machine-induced lifestyle, creating voids that can be filled only by the human touch.

Richler maps the transition of Montreal from a most-wanted refugee, immigrant land to non-English, pure Francophone city. Richler considers Quebec's Declaration of Sovereignty as premature. The Separatist Movement creates unrest and displaces a lot of English-Speaking youth. Constant migration from Montreal to Toronto, Vancouver and Saskatoon, places that would favour good environment for bringing up children, left behind a number of homes and stores hosting FOR SALE, *A VENDRE,* TO LET boards during the time on the referendum. This is absorbed into the political contexts of *Joshua Then and Now* and *Barney's Version.* In 1978 when Joshua takes a walk in Lower Westmount, it looked like a thicket of *A VENDRE/* FOR SALE SIGN. Lower Westmount (in 1978) was "a failing city a wasting place, many of the shiny new office towers were crying out for tenants, the construction hammers silenced, the stock exchange mute" (*JTN 55*).

The English-speaking natives were in jitters and inclined to stumble out of bed at 3 a.m. to jot down a list of redeemable assets on the back of an envelope or study French verbs. Many of them were packing their bags, making ready to run. Safety deposits boxes had been emptied and they had their bank accounts cleaned out. While the "The Canadian dollar continued to sink", Richler notes, "In this city, Joshua's Montreal nobody he knew was redecorating. Or planting. Everybody was thinking hard" and even "The Ritz, desecrated" (*JTN 56*). In *Solomon Gursky,* Kugelmass's daughter and her husband joined this exodus of English-speaking people from Montreal fleeing to Toronto. In *Barney's Version,* Saul's trips to Montreal presents a declining city. His old friends had moved out to Toronto, Vancouver or New York. English sign boards in dull colours were shadowed by bright French sign boards. Unilingually labeled *'matzohs'* on display in *'kosher'* grocery were withdrawn and later permitted for sixty days of the year. A disintegration and disappearance of Jewish rituals in a largely assimilated Canadian environment is evident. The cry to get children rooted in Jewish education continues with raving modernization and widespread Canadian assimilation. The struggle remains while the reason wary with time and age as it is a universal phenomenon with tradition that gets dissolved in an ocean of modernization.

The 1980s and 90s the political Separatist Movement in Quebec dispersed Montreal-English families and scattered them in different provinces or abroad. The abandoned down-town streets hosted the CLOSING DOWN SALE or EVERYTHING MUST GO signs. But old people like Barney who had struggled to graduate from the streets of the Montreal-Jewish ghetto to mansions in Westmount, savour to linger longer till the end. Only a group of old, infirm, poor Anglophones was found. The few intrusive ageing parents call their sons in Toronto to hint moving into a neighbourhood nearby. But their calls were either not received or answered as the children were no longer bound by the Jewish communal spirit of staying together. Thus, the 1980s witnessed the once communal large Jewish families in Montreal scattered and dispersed with migration and modernization. Richler's Montreal of the 1950s is buzzing and teaming with Jewish sounds. But the late 80's and 90's sees a dying city, with every effort made to cleanse the city of non-Francophone origins. Richler does not regret the "dissolution of old ways", but sharply satirizes the "diminution" of the old order (Gerson 108).

Be it a novel set in European capitals or St. Urbain Street, Richler's heroes never forget their Montreal roots. For Joshua, Canada, particularly Montreal is what Frank Davey calls, "a world-class site, part of a global commercial network" in which he can market his writing (259). While Noah leaves home in *Smaller Hero,* Duddy in *Duddy Kravitz,* another Boy Wonder roots and spreads himself in Montreal. Jake feeds on aching memories of home-coming through his wakeful nights in London. He yearns nostalgically for days at the shooting pool with his friends or drinking in his favourite bar. He reminiscences, "enjoying being at home. At ease in Canada. The homeland he had shed with such soaring enthusiasm twelve years earlier. Thousands of miles of wheat, indifference, and self-apology, it had seemed. And no more" (*SUH 13).* On the other hand, the novel *Joshua Then and Now* brings home a paparazzied, wearied protagonist to solitary sanctuary and confinement in Montreal after exploring the swinging 60's of London, Paris and Spain. The Gurskys expand their businesses from their Montreal mansions in *Solomon Gursky*. Richler's Montreal in *Barney's Version* is a waning moon. Barney in his declining years chose to linger in Montreal than be with Mike and Caroline in London, Saul in New York or Kate in Toronto. He says, "It suits me to be rooted in a city that, like me, is diminishing day by day" (*BV 81).* Thus, home and exile are a recurrent theme. The streets of "The Main" in Montreal are the home of Richler's characters. It resonates in his texts and contexts and has the power to engage the literary imagination, shape identity and provoke political resistance of the characters.

2.3 The Word and the World

> "There is more to Jewishness than observance".
>
> (Richler. qtd. in Foran xii)

Richler examines the Jewish tradition, culture and relationships between individuals from different socio-economic backgrounds in his novels. He delves into the connotation of Jewish rituals and orthodoxy as perceived by the Jewish-Canadian characters. He analyses how the customs and habits have been reduced to mere observances, clichéd and meaningless to a generation born into Jewish homes in a Canadian space amidst constant conflict between the Orthodox and non-Orthodox.

Richler vehemently criticized the "ghetto-paranoia" of the Jews and openly states "You feel your survival is contingent on the continuing anti-Semitic pressures of the larger community outside, and where they do not exist, you invent them" (qtd. in Foran xi). He possessed an authoritative, public voice which he translated into his novels.

Richler's select novels reveal that the Jewish tradition is an integral part of the Canadian multicultural mosaic memory. They also elaborate on the important Jewish traditions and rituals that are a part of the Jewish-Canadian society. Performing *'Bris'*, celebrating *'Bar mitzvah'*, observing '*Sabbath'*, wearing a '*yarmulke'*, embracing '*Torah'*, keeping '*kosher'* are the uncompromised traditions of Orthodox Jews. Foran records that the Jewish faith is rooted in the '*Torah'*, the literal word of God, handed down to Moses. The Decalogue or the first Ten Commandments, given to Moses on Mount Sinai is the basic foundation for the other '*mitzvoth'*, the codified rules for Jewish living. These numbered 613 in all, as found throughout the '*Torah'*, while a couple of hundreds of them were obsolete and an Orthodox Jew was expected to abide by the rest. Men dressed each morning for prayer with '*tefillin'* on the forehead and a '*kippah'* over the skull, the '*tallith'* around their shoulders. In public they wore black, to show mourning for the destruction of the Second Temple in Jerusalem in 100 A.D. Hasidic men grew long beards and some of the wives shaved their heads, donned wigs so as not to be attractive to other men. "There were rules about these matters, and rules about many of the rules. No compromises were allowed. There was only the covenant and those who honoured their faith, and their fathers, by keeping it" (6-7).

Foran observes, "Orthodox Jews married other Orthodox Jews" (6). They did not prefer to marry Secular or Reform Jews or Conservative Jews to live the faith. Jake's father Issy, vehemently declines the son's wedding to a gentile. He warns him to rethink his decision lest, "The doors of all Hersh family will not welcome you. Not being married according to the Jewish laws your children, if any, will be considered illegitimate" (*SUH* 214). His letter echoes Nnaemeka's father's letter, when the latter informs the father about his plan to marry Nene, a non-Ibo girl in Achebe's *Marriage is a Private Affair*. Crossing religious barriers in marriage is a universal phenomenon. For the Jews the historical divide between the Jew and Gentile aggravates the tension.

Richler's Jewish homes in Montreal are caught between Orthodox grandfathers and non-conformist grandsons. Observant Jewish men kept their heads covered with a skull cap known as a '*yarmulke*', *'kappel'* or '*kippah*'. Abromovitch, the grandparent of Martin complains, "He doesn't wear a hat and he can't speak Yiddish" (*DK 65).* Reuben on the other hand tells young Joshua that observant Jews wear one of those crazy fur hats and side curls and a beard and announces "I'm not very Jewish" (*JTN* 167). Itzik one of Noah's most orthodox uncles rebukes him for not wearing one. When Wolf Adler dies, he asks Noah, "Do you know how to say '*Kaddish*' at least?" *(SH 134). Kaddish* is the prayer for the dead. The ravage of the changing times on tradition is not taken as change but as sacrilege by the older observant population. For the orthodox, "The synagogue was a habit and a meeting place for them The *Goyim,* a mystery" (*SH 110).*

A man of uncompromising strictures, Melech devoured people who never kept the '*Kashrut*' or the *'Sabbath'* holy. *Kashrut* refers to "Rules concerning which foods may or may not be eaten, how they should be prepared" (Sullivan 28). Ephraim and the Jewish doctor the sole survivors of the doomed Franklin expedition attributed their miraculous survival to having brought '*kosher*' food on board rather than eating from the regular crew's tainted tins, "But Ephraim and Izzy, given their secret hoard of Jewish soul food, were not as infected as the rest of the company" (*SG* 432). Foran notes that, "Richler insinuated the diasporic Jewish experience and sensibility into the most unlikely of national narrative myths" with the '*kosher*' salvation and Ephraim found cult. (537).

> The *Sabbath* (*'shabbat'*) is of particular importance in a Jewish home. Jewish law requires Jews to refrain from various acts of "work" on the *Sabbath*, in commemoration of God's cessation of creativity on the seventh day of creation. The prohibited acts of "work" include

> travelling (other than on foot), cooking, writing, carrying, the switching on and off of electricity, using a telephone and any transaction of a commercial nature such as shopping. (*Jewish Family Life and Customs – A practical guide*)

The Orthodox kept '*kosher*' and observed holidays. On '*Sabbath*' it meant abstaining from any labour, including riding in a car or bus, lighting a stove or turning on a light. Melech insisted that buying, trading was prohibited in his scrap yard on '*Sabbath*' days. But his grandchildren hang across Panofskys on '*Sabbath*' days and shopped on credit. Melech reproached them saying, "... buying on credit was only one step away from buying, and if a Jew bought things on the '*Sabbath*' he might as well go without a hat, and if a Jew went without a hat he might as well miss the evening prayer, and if a Jew missed the evening prayer..." (*SH 21).*

In contrast to the Orthodox grandfathers the non-conventional third generations believed Richler's ideology of being more Jewish in spirit than mere ritualistic. For Noah being a Jew was more than wearing a skullcap, reading Jewish Star or observing the 'Sabbath'. It is being Jewish in character and he proves it with his moral choices. It is not only Noah who wants to break away from ritualistic practices, but also the others. We find Ida telling Shloime not to take Melech seriously. She says, "Noah isn't afraid. Tell him if you want to go to Panofsky's on shabus, on the 'Sabbath', that it's your own affair" (SH 21). Similarly, there are Jewish practices in spirit rather than observances by the young generation. Always ten days after the New Year, 'Yom Kippur' or the Day of Atonement was followed. The Boy Wonder abstained from placing bets on 'Yom Kippur' and 'Shonnerer's day'. Reuben tells Joshua that he's got a legal right to repent on that day if he'd hurt anybody or done anything wrong. Henry an observant Jew reconciles with his ambitious cousin Lionel who visited the North as he came during 'Aseret Yemai Tushuvah', the ten days of repentance and it was a 'mitzvah', a commandment to be reconciled with the family members who had wronged as it was written: "a person should be pliant as a reed and not hard like a cedar in granting forgiveness" (*SG* 100).

In Jewish custom, the highest order of Holy work is to be a rabbi. Next are the scribes who wrote 'Torahs' by hand on parchment. Orthodox Melech was happy to be a scribe and yearned for a member of his family to become a rabbi.

> The role of the Rabbi is often more extensive than that of pastoral career, teacher and mediator. They decide questions of Jewish law and may act as an arbitrator. If a Rabbi is asked a question on Jewish law, his answer binds the questioner. Some communities turn to the Rabbi or the Jewish court (the *Beth Din*) for determination of civil issues, including inheritance, in preference to the civil courts. (*Jewish Family Life and Customs – A practical guide*)

While Melech considered being a rabbi as honourable, Jake's father thought it was profitable. Talking about choosing careers Issy tells Jake that one need not have a capital outlay, but a big mouth to become a rabbi. Richler with his red teeth wittily unmasks the hypocrisy in the modern interpretation of rabbinical services.

Weddings and '*Bar mitzvahs*' were times of social gatherings. "*Bar mitzvah,* means "son of the commandment," is the name of a ritual observed when a Jewish boy reaches the age of thirteen years plus one day" (Sullivan 8). It is the celebration of the boy's passage into responsibility for study and the transfer of the *'Torah'* to a new generation. For Duddy, the *'Bar mitzvah'* was a commercial venture and he made offbeat movies on it. For Joshua, his *'Bar mitzvah'* with rituals overlooked, is a lifelong memory of shame because of his mother's strip-tease dance. Richler captures changes from Orthodoxy to Secularization of the Jewish tradition. A lavishly reformed synagogue is called as a Temple. Uncle Benjy calls it a whore house. Mr. Cohen's father said it looked like a church and began to weep when the first chord struck on the organ wailing. ""You hidtome" .... It is a church" (*DK* 147). The '*Bar mitzvah*' scene as Woodcock observes clearly shows, "the division in the Jewish community between the Orthodox who wish to remain enclosed within their tradition and are usually poor people who have never got above the simple occupations of the early immigrants, and the wealthy class of the city in which they live" (*IDK* 38).

Richler gives a detailed account of a transplanted Jewish tradition in a Canadian soil in *Duddy Kravitz*. He objectively highlights the practices of the reformed Jew. The transition is a result to accommodate the changing living conditions of modernization. '*Rabbi*' Goldstone is an example of a modern '*Rabbi*' who kept himself popular with the young married people who otherwise would not follow Jewish tradition. These things were held in contempt by the Orthodox Jews.

While Orthodoxy advocated that the individual existed mainly to uphold the tradition and abide by the customary rules, Richler through the rebellious Noah states "it is in the individual life that gives value to the festival, not vice-versa" (Kramer 25). He projects the continuous conflict between tradition and modernity through Noah. Noah's grandfather Melech is an icon of orthodoxy. While Jenny, Melech's wife tries to understand the changing times, Melech is staunch and adamant. Jenny says of her children to Melech, "We are old. This aint our country. Melech, they grow away from us" (*SH* 23), "we are old. They are even ashamed for us" (*SH* 24). Melech is rigid. For him moving away or growing was moving away from tradition. The news that Noah has moved away is like "things falling apart". Smicha is deadly silent after Duddy acquires the land. His moral standards couldn't accept any short-cut road to success. As Dingleman observed Duddy had frightened the *'zeyda'* with his buy.

The Orthodox Jews stuck to the strictures, while the unorthodox like Panofsky in *Smaller Hero* questioned, "Chosen. You tell me what for we were chosen? Soap? Furnaces?" (81). Richler shows how the old, struggle to bring up the children within their tradition while the young drift away and want to be set free to explore the games of the world. But the young when they grow old enSough to become a father like Jake pepper their bed time tales with stories of Rabbi Akiva[3], the Thirty-six Just Men[4], Maimonides[5], the '*Golem*', Trumpeldor[6] and St. Urbain's Horseman.

> They dwell in my veins, they eavesdrop at my ear,
> They circle, as with *Torah*s, round my skull,

> In exit and in entrance all day pull
> The latches of my heart, descend, and rise-
>
> (A.M.Klein, *A Psalm Touching Genealogy*, qtd. in *TS* 24)

Although set in a transplanted soil, the texts echo the relationship between Diaspora and Zion. The Diaspora like Melech, Lennie and Irv Nausbaum raised funds for and planted oranges in Israel.

Unorthodox families like the Shapiros were seen with surprise and indignation. Joshua is instructed to tell the priests in the synagogue that they ate '*kosher*' food. Societal pressures squeeze out false claim of living. Joshua's home was forbidden by parents of St. Urbain Street. Out of the twenty boys invited for his *'Bar mitzvah'* only twelve turned up while the others were not allowed to attend. Like Noah, Jewish heritage was more of a boulder of stone inveighing Joshua down. "Canadian – born, he sometimes felt as if he were condemned to lope slant-shouldered through this world that confused him. One shoulder sloping downwards, ... a reputation for honest trading, good skiing conditions" (162). Reuben is an example of a father who teaches tradition but finds it difficult to practice it. His attempts to take his son to the synagogue ended in excuses. But his tone is dramatic and reminds Joshua firmly that they were Hebrews and he should not forget it. Kramer summarizes that Richler uses Reuben ironically "to defend the flesh and material concerns against Orthodox notions of purity" and his attempt to map a larger pattern suggests that Richler had not fully reconciled to the absurd (289).

Richler's protagonists are mostly non-observant Jews and in customs of Death and Bereavement they were non-Orthodox. An observant Nialie foresees Henry's death and goes covering all mirrors with towels, and sat on a low stool when Henry failed to return. But Jake Hersh is seen shaven after his father's death as he scorned the ritual of being unshaven for it was only a ritualistic gesture without spirit. The Hersh family mourned the passing of Issy Hersh for a week with the truculent rabbis surging into the night, followed by prayers and more guests. Jenny, Jake's cousin asks, "Sitting *shiva* with the hypocrites, are you?" (*SUH* 394). Being a non-observant family, Barney's father Izzy Panofsky on performing the ritual of the dead "sitting *shiva*" says "My own philosophy, speaking personally, is modern, I don't go in for the religious hocus-pocus" and finally both the father and son drove on to Dink's Bar "to mourn together in Panofsky fashion" (*BV 267).* Jake, Jenny and Izzy belong to a generation which restrained hypocritical observances.

Jewish rituals take a different expression in *Solomon Gursky.* Taken by his energetic grandfather Ephraim to the Polar Sea, young Solomon learns and practices survival and strange mystical rituals of the North based on Jewish customs. His son Henry, an observant Jew, insisted '*kosher*', observed '*shabbus*' and followed a southern schedule for his morning prayers in a diminishing sun-land of the Arctic.

Richler's barbs never spare the mere ritual routines ripped off the spirit of Jewishness in observances. He captures the non-Orthodox spirit of the Orthodox, "Outside the synagogue many of the faithful were gathered together in the sun. Smoking, gossiping" (*JTN 75*). Barney a non-observant Jew secretly fasts on *Yom Kippur* and donated big to charities to bribe Jehovah to waiver off his transgressions and to assist him to continue his blissful married life with Miriam. Rituals become means to please God and seek favour.

With wide-spread unorthodoxy, mixed marriages, vast migration from Jewish centres and decline in Jewish observances, Richler sets his novels in the flux of transition and tension of merged identities. Richler like Ted Allen, Adele Wiseman and his American counterparts Saul Bellow, Meyer Levin and Leon Uris weave in the exotic or arcane details of Jewish life into their stories. Golden quotes Singh who observed that, Richler did lament the modern state of Judaism in Canada, "emasculated, shorn of its mystery and beauty' (62).

2.4 Horror and Holocaust[7]

> A year after the end of World War II, Prime Minister Mackenzie king said: "For the Jewish people the recent war had an especial significance. The way of life of all free peoples were threatened by Nazi and Fascist aggression. In addition the Jewish people were threatened by had the even sterner realization that for them it was not only a way of life, but life itself that was at stake." (*JTN* 129)

Craniford states that "Richler's response was "to bear witness" through his writing – to the atrocities of the holocaust and often unbearable inequities of everyday life, and thereby "show an affirming flame"" (*108*).

Greenblatt in his theory of subversion and containment notes the open indicators of power involves the ideology of who can define others. He says that people who are able to label another group of people exercise maximum power. Hence the Nazis informed by the prejudiced Hitler, badged the Jewish people with a yellow star as a result of subversion and containment. While Greenblatt stresses that Harriot may not have been acting maliciously but shot 'invisible bullets' as Subversion must be invisible to the subverted, it is to be noted that Hitler's 'bullets' were strikingly visible, politically Machiavellian and dangerously exterminating. While there are many theories on anti-Semitism from Biblical days the cruelest action is the Holocaust. Wikipedia on "Theory of Subversion and Containment" explains:

> For Hitler the Jews were a 'statue badly begun' and not capable of being "true Germans." They were a disease, something that needed to be wiped out. Hitler and the Nazis enforced a doctrine of "purity." They believed that only white people were the ideal, and that these "Aryans" were the 'pure race' of Germans. Hitler lashed out at anyone who did not conform to this image and the Nazi policy was to eliminate the impure races. Subversion for the Nazi's was extermination of Jews.

The 1950s was marked by Calvinist mores which had an effect on the literary expression of the age. W.H. New writes that literary history records it as an age of mimetic representation of ordinary lives, at times idealized and works tended to demonstrate the psychological dilemmas in making political choice rather than confront the political issue.

Richler's novels imbibe the tension of anti-Semitism and Holocaust. Brenner writes that although the Canadian Jews were not the direct victims of the tragic history of European Jewry, it affected the tribe in Canada "whose anti-Semitic past instilled a lasting sense of mistrust in its Jewish citizens" (Foreword). The effect of the Holocaust is a part of the post-war Jewish consciousness. On one hand the Holocaust shattered the liberal humanist Jewish identity and on the other the anxiety of persecution instigated denial of the Jewish roots thus pushing modern Jew into an ambivalent position.

In *Smaller Hero,* an angry Polish Jew speaks to the children of aspiring working class to rekindle the lost sense of brethren and a fading Holocaust memory, cries out, "Because you are Jews, and that's a crime in this world" (*26*). Noah Adler is more a humanitarian. He says that, "The important thing is not that they burnt Jews but that they burned men" (*SH 70)*

Richler projects the bigotry and insensitive prejudice of a few Jews towards non-Jews as a post-World War II reaction. Melech justifies this ruthlessness in trade as a reaction to the *Goy's* stealing of the crap and the gentile's discriminating attitude towards the Jews. This is also reflected in Mr. Cohen's viciousness in living a callous and a selfish life. He curses the *'goyim'* and explicates his motto:

> "The more money I make the better care I take of my own, the more I'm able to contribute to our hospital, the building of Israel, and other worthy causes. So a goy is crippled and you think you're to blame. Given the chance he would have crippled you," he shouted, "or thrown you into furnace like six million others. You think I didn't lose relatives? I lost relatives…". (*DK* 311)

The effect of the Holocaust is in the cultural memory. In Bernie's *'Bar mitzvah'* movie, the narrator highlights that besides all material gifts and possessions that the boy had received it is necessary for him to know that the Nazi tormented history that has created a blood-stained memory. This brutal history is passed on along with the *'Torah'* to the next generation to understand one's root and tradition.

Frank Davey observes that although Richler lacks politically active protagonists, his characters indirectly participate or react to the political climate. Jake, Harry and Joshua idealistically challenge and avenge the wrongs of the Holocaust but ultimately withdraw to the familial space and seek individual salvation in the security of home. Modelled on the Bronfman family, *Solomon Gursky* mordantly places the Gursky Empire in building the Canadian domain. Joshua's nightmare at Ibiza with the provoking Mueller that prompts him to head for Ibiza the second time, leaving behind his wife at a critical point and Jake's maniac, vengeful notions of extracting Mengele's[8] gold fillings are repressed, unconscious, obsessive retribution to the horror of Holocaust. He also visits sites of racial trauma in Ibiza. The novels also echo historical grievances encountered individually, that which persistently cripples both Jake and Joshua.

The Holocaust not only exterminated six million Jews in the Second World War, but also the tradition, strength and hope that the generations to come needed to bank on. It left behind ashes and gassed skeletons of unidentifiable bodies, remnants of shocked memories and threatened lives and a maimed generation. Jake suffers innumerable holocaust gassed psychotic reveries. He relives the pain and is guilt-ridden that he had not been participative to fight for these people. Scenes of gassed death invaded him.

> *The bodies are not lying scattered here and there throughout the room, but piled in a mass to the ceiling. This is explained by the fact that the gas first inundates the lower layers of air and rises but slowly to the ceiling. That forces them to trample and clamber over one another. At the bottom of the pile are babies, children, women and aged; at the top, the strongest. Their bodies, which bear numerous scratches occasioned by the struggle which set them against one another, are often intertwined. The noses and mouths are bleeding, the faces bloated and blue.* (*SUH* 262)

Richler voices out the pained experiences of the holocaust from the victim's purview and re-historizes the Nazi's barbaric history of success and extermination. He prompts how Jake and his people were nestled in safety in Canada, while the likes of his tribe such as Harry were endangered during the Nazi prowl. Little Harry was shoveled and cargoed "into a train crammed with squealing mums and babes, other slum kids (some covered with septic sores, still more lice-infested), and frantic teachers; a train without food and insufficient toilets. Each one at floodtide. The floor slithery; to be finally disgorged on a station platform in the outer wilds of Buckinghamshire" (*SUH 28*).

Jake Hersh is Richler's first main character who is self-tortured with thoughts of Jewish sufferings in the Nazi Concentration camps. "His attic study walls are plastered with photographs of wartime Nazi leaders and their survivors" (*SUH* 14), and kept a saddle and a riding crop and an absurd painting of Field Marshal Montgomery. He also has a larder of tins with peeled out labels of stew like substance with a decidedly nasty smell. His traumatic, holocaust-prompted reveries forced him on a search of Joey, help his many begotten families, repay debts and become his spokesperson. He felt obliged to do this for Joey for he believed that Joey had fought wars and championed the cause for Jews. The Horseman fantasy functions as a release of Jake's aggression using violence to avenge the horrors of the Holocaust.

In comparison to all his novels, it is in *St. Urbain's Horseman* that Richler weaves in elaborate, troubling, brutal details of the Holocaust to lucidly explain the fractured self of the Jew, "unembarrassed hatred of Nazi criminals and the imperative of vengeance". (Ravvin 34). From these realistic clicks of the black moments of the Jewish History rises the Horseman, created by Richler through Jake Hersh to avenge the Nazi Mengele. In a heart-writhing account, Jake learns that Mengele gassed the entire infected women's block to disinfect. The Horseman is "the Jewish equivalent of the mythic hero Hercules" (Craniford 90). Jake fantasizes that his Horseman would extract the gold fillings from Mengele's mouth with extreme tardiness. This fantasy is revenge to the vile acts of extracting gold fillings from murdered Jews during the Holocaust.

Joshua's rage against the Holocaust permeates the novel with entry of the German man Dr. Dr. Muller. Mueller treats Joshua cheap not because he was Nazi but because Joshua was a Jew. Ramraj notes that "His preoccupation with heroism and manhood makes him inflate himself into an avenger of the Jews and Mueller into a monstrous Nazi villain" (121). Actually, Muller worked in a government office in Berlin and never saw the front, during the war. He was sent out of France not for Nazi killing but for assaulting a girl in Nice in 1954. Joshua thinks that Dr. Muller is a spy. But Dr. Muller is an eccentric writer of western novels under the pseudonym of Gurs McCabe. Joshua's obsessed idea of Muller does not change even after he breaks into his house and finds no lampshades or bars of soaps made of human skin. Joshua loses his temper when his three children giggle while watching a documentary on World War II, "as Hitler did his notorious victory jig in the Compiegne Forest after accepting the French surrender" (*JTN 97)*. Through his idealization of the Spanish war, he seeks emotional growth and potency and worships the International Brigades for their volunteer to sacrifice.

Irv Nausbaum in *Barney's Version* is an ardent supporter who stands up for Jewish people. He raises his flag against anti-Semitism, raises fund for Israel and restrains from non - '*kosher*' activities. As a principle he advises Jews not to spend dollars visiting Europe especially France, where the French police in 1943 were instrumental in rounding up to thirteen thousand Jews in Paris which included invalids, pregnant women and three thousand children for the gas chambers. While Noah and Duddy are too young to respond to the Holocaust, Jake and Joshua are troubled by the memory of it. While the Gurskys resort to charitable ways of reaching out to the affected bretheren, for Barney it was not fame, but fortune that eventually found him. His search for a life beyond the ghetto was sponsored by a survivor, of Auschwitz, Yossel Pinsky.

Noah, Duddy, Jake, Joshua, Moses and Barney all belong to the frivolous generation. As Jake reviews it:

> Conceived in the depression, but never to taste its bitterness firsthand, they had actually contrived to sail through the Spanish Civil War, World War II, the holocaust, Hiroshima, the Israeli War of Independence, McCarthyism, Korea, and, latterly, Vietnam and the drug culture, with impunity. Always the wrong age. Ever observers, never participants. The whirlwind elsewhere. (*SUH* 92)

When millions were gassed in the holocaust, this generation observed that their parents prospered on the black market. These men were too young to have marched into the wars and later when old they carry guilt and are embarrassed. This guilt-led life guided their ways of helping their community and is the reason behind their ruthless ways that is inherent in all characters in varying degrees. Born into a chaotic political undercurrent in a wrong age, huddled in a safe new world, Richler's select men suffer traumatic holocaust reveries and bear the onus of anti-Semitic rage. This leads them to confront the great ghetto wall which barricaded their freedom and obstructed their visibility of others and hid them as non-existent. It is this wall of separation that they have to transgress or transcend.

2.5 The Jew-Gentile Divide

> In Richler's work, Montreal is the meeting place between the two cultures. The writer's experience of growing up in Montreal in the 1930's and the 1940's in a predominantly Jewish neighbourhood, surrounded by a predominantly Gentile world has exposed him to the complexity of the relationships between Jews and Gentiles. (Brenner 145)

The Jew-Gentile divide imposes geographical, cultural, economical and marital limitations on a Jewish-Canadian and thereby restricts their living. Richler's select novels have an intricate pattern of life of the Jewish-Canadians criss-crossed with lines and demarcations of restrictions. Like Richard Wright, who projects the lines of difference between the blacks and whites in an American soil, Richler focuses on the Jew-Gentile divide with an ironic tone. The texts reflect the play of power, resistance and oppression of the marginalized as depicted in the characters of Noah Adler, Duddy Kravitz, Jake Hersh, Joshua Shapiro, Moses Berger and in a way Solomon Gursky and Barney Panofsky. These contours of restrictions prescribe a way of living within boundaries which Noah repeatedly wants to escape or instigates amoral ways to transgress the boundary wall as in Duddy or escalate to the mainstream through petty thefts and marriage as in Joshua, Jake and Barney.

In the 1930s and 1940s the Montreal Jewish community bore the brunt of the anti-Semitic upsurge in Canada. According to demographer Louis Rosenberg, from 1921 to 1931 there was a trend "for the Jewish population of Greater Montreal to move from the so-called Jewish wards of St. Louis and Laurier to the neighbouring satellite cities of Outremount and Westmount" (31). In *Joshua Then and Now,* Richler has chronicled the rise of his generation, and their flight from cold-water flats on St. Urbain to exclusive Montreal neighbourhoods like Outremont and Westmount. Joshua notes that the Outremont children were dressed classy and were well bred. Their St. Urbain brethren received all their old clothes and second-hand books. The flow of left over from Outremont fed the urchins of the St. Urbain Street. Joshua was sent Sheldon's old clothes and books but was not socially fit to attend an Outremont *'Bar mitzvah'* or '*Kiddush'*.

The moving beyond the boundaries was to move up the social order, escalate economic conditions and settle in better homes. Joshua belongs to the segment of Jewish community who wanted to assimilate into a more "Canadian" milieu. As a St. Urbain Street boy, he wanted to grow into a less visible Jew in a non-Jewish environment. Born to an Outremont mother from the Levanthal family, Joshua and his father were socially invisible to his Levanthal relatives. On one of his forced stays with his cousin Sheldon's family, Aunt Fanny had fixed up his bed in the attic, next to the maid's room. Joshua found them as a rich dustbin of money, fruits and everything. When Uncle Harvey asks him what he'd like to be when he grew up, Joshua replies, "Rich and famous and popular with girls" (*JTN 21*). Joshua does it. He has a passionate love affair in Ibiza, gets a social lift with his marriage to the senator's daughter and establishes himself a writer. Noah's departure from the Jewish area is a move away from the self-prescribed ghetto, an area of the city where Jews lived in a sort of self-imposed segregation, separated from the non-Jewish communities to become "something". An ethically-challenged Duddy becomes "Somebody" after purchasing the land around the lake.

Restriction and Rejection

Restriction is the watch-word that governs the Jewish world. An archive photo of the village of Ste. Agathe reproduced by Weintraub pictures a summer 1939 notice on telephone poles, "Jews are not wanted here in Ste. Agathe, so scram while the going is good". This is absorbed in Richler's surrounding space where Ste. Agathe is Ste. Adele in the novel. "THIS BEACH IS RESTRICTED TO GENTILES" (*SH 54*). Right from nature everything is restricted. Noah suggests to Miriam that they can run away from Theo's house to Ste Adele. But she says "Ste Adele is restricted", Noah replies, "I'll tell them you're an Arab" (*SH 104*). As an act of rebellion and power Noah and his friend attempt to steal the sign of restriction and euphorically replaced it with the new sign "THIS BEACH IS RESTRICTED TO LITVAKS" (*SH 56*). Ste Adele is the retreat of Montreal's aspiring middle-class. The Gentile owned hotels restricted the Jews. Reuben tells that "These are the Days of Awe" and how the Jews' world is restricted. "Says, he won't let you check into one of his hotels, it's restricted but he doesn't want you breaking the furniture or slugging him" (*JTN 169).*This place started to flourish after the Outremont Jews bought lands here. Ste Agathe des Monts is a middle-class Jewish community's resort town in *Duddy Kravitz.*

Persecution and rejection follow the cultural memory of Jews like shadows. In *Duddy Kravitz,* Lennie as a Jew gets the rare opportunity of studying at Mc Gill. "The university's admission standards simply and unashamedly made it harder for Jews to get in than gentiles" (Yanofsky 42). The Jewish quota at McGill required a seventy-five percent while the others were eligible with sixty-five,

""In my day" said L.B. to Moses on winning the Rhodes scholarship said, "it would have been considered presumptuous for a Jewish boy to even put himself forward for such an honor"" (*SG 128)*

Rejection was an expression of anti-Semitism. Career options and advancements were restricted to the Jews. Commenting on the flow of rejection slips to her husband's writing, Bessie said "It would break their heart to give it to a Jew," (*SG 129).* This echoes A.M. Klein's not-so-welcome original writings that drowned him in an irretrievable solitude and eternal silence.

Lennie who admitted that he preferred the company of Gentiles is a victim of self-hatred. He believes in Irwin Shubert's remark of the Jews "They inhabit a psychological ghetto… and dare not step outside of it because they're afraid of being rejected" (*DK* 185). To Lennie being worried and scared was Jewish, being just themselves and glad was gentile. "They are just themselves and glad of it. Nothing scares them" (*DK* 186).

Jews were denied promotions. Barney's father Izzy Panofsky was the only Jew on the police force in Montreal. He had to remain a detective sergeant for nine years before becoming an inspector. His promotions were detained with contrived stories against him. He was hated for being a 'straight-shooting' Jew. While other cops fattened on immoral ways, Izzy was triple cautious not even to slip on a hair. Izzy defends himself as a righteous Jew and claimed that they were more alert.

There is a sword of Damocles hanging over the Jew. When a Yiddish boy had robbed in the neighbourhood, Noah's grandma fears how all the Jews would be branded as robbers. Mr. Cohen remarks that Mr. Calder would not appoint a Jew to clear the scrap from his yard. *Duddy Kravitz* constantly mentions hostile relationship between the Jews and French-Canadians and the Anglo-Canadians. Duddy leads a Jewish gang to chase out a gentile vendor off their street. Duddy had to buy land through a gentile intermediary, Yvette Durelle, because the French-Canadian farmers would not sell to a Jew. The tension between the Jews and the

French-Canadian affected the choice of the shops from which school children bought at recess. The FFHS frequented the Felder's tiny tenement store which had the sign DON'T BUY FROM THE GOYISHE MAN FELDER IS YOUR FRIEND FOR LIFE. Duddy had run a French-Canadian chip man off the street, when he ventured into their territory. Greenstein observes that such signboards mark Richler's satiric revenge which exposes hypocrisy and the brief soul of wit and the comic heroes craftily cross borders and trespass to avenge the situation (*Jewish Wry* 198). Although a non-observant Jew, Duddy was Jewish in every sense. He rebelled against Christians and the like. With stinging humour, he invites the non-Hebe to school and took them to the rabbinical college at lunch time. Duddy's prank turned out to be quite serious and created conundrum. The alarmed students drew back when the FFHS boys began to pelt them with pamphlets and snowballs.

Quebec Nationalism combined with anti-Semitism fuelled the already burning tension between the Jew and gentile and keeps simmering throughout the mid-twentieth century. Each one reproached or avoided the other. Street attacks and incidents caused by gangs of truculent French Canadians were on the rise. When Joey, Duddy, Jake and Arty shoo them away the parents are not happy as there was enough trouble already. Resentment was prevalent high up in Westmount too. Bernard reproached Morrie for selling his furniture orders through a goy shop in Ste.-Adele. He tells him how the anti-Semites would wickedly take pleasure in saying, "… hey, you know who made the crappy lopsided little table for me for ten dollars? Mr. Bernard's brother" (*SG 377).*

Jews were rarely hired by '*goys*' and were not given equal opportunities. People like Wolf confined themselves within ghetto walls. In a disheartening account Wolf tells how he couldn't go beyond the ghetto walls of the scrap yard of his father, "I go to a goy for a job. Go ahead and tell me that a goy is gonna hire a Jew" (*SH* 32).

A Jew rarely took into confidence another Jew. They alienated from gentiles and isolated themselves from each other. Wolf explains that if he asks a Jew for a job, he would doubt why a Jew wanted to work for him. He will suspect that in two months time he'd learn the trick of the trade and win over the employer. An air of distrust hovers like an eagle. The cultural memory shows them dispersed across continents and also individually they find themselves disintegrated. Losing his job Bert found himself working for a Jew in Hornstein's Home Furniture on "The Main", a Jew store: "It's the Main, you sell a French Canadian a five-piece set for $350, ship him only four unmatched pieces from cheaper sets he won't complain, he's probably never been into a real store before and he buys from a Jew he expects to be cheated" (*SG 171).* The owner orders them to memorize the prices from the sheets and to quote them double when it came to Italians or Jews.

The Montreal ghetto was the home of scrap yards and junkyards. It's the Canadian waste bin. Life was junk for the ghetto people. They scraped through the scrap yard to find a living. Just like Wolf who toiled in Melech's yard, Reuben slogged in Uncle Oscar's yard. The yard vibrated with sledge hammering of brass bedsteads. The wastes would earn him a sparing twenty-five cents a pound. Joshua remembers his father wading through the muck while his uncle Oscar sat at the Desk. Young Joshua remembers that his father came home dirty as a miner and drove home in the truck. But Uncle Oscar who had graduated from Commercial High owned a car, was on the executive of the synagogue and played golf with gentile customers. Joshua is seen harping on these differences and yearns to move beyond the social line.

Beyond the Ghetto Wall

Richler describes a certain milieu of the streets of St. Urbain in Montreal's Jewish quarter whose inmates are victims of double discrimination from the Quebec French and the WASPs. Discriminated as second-class citizens they wanted to look across the border. There is a constant obsession in all of the young characters to peep over the ghetto walls into the gentile world. Ida in *Smaller Hero* creates a make-believe ballroom of the Gentiles and dances in it. Everything that was Jewish was odd, small, dirty, cheap or bad. Everything that was Gentile was neat, colourful and beautiful. Kaplan in her report on Mary Douglas' *Purity and Danger* states "Dirt is essentially disorder... it exists in the eye of the beholder... In chasing dirt, in papering, decorating, tidying, we are not governed by anxiety to escape disease, but are positively re-ordering our environment, making it conform to an idea. (p. 2). [Kaplan's emphasis]. Noah repeatedly calls Miriam neat. "You're so neat. Did you know that? You're always cleaning or mopping up or sweeping. I noticed that this afternoon" (*SH* 117). For Noah, Miriam is neat in contrast to the narrow ghetto life, cramped with disorder and unsophisticated. Earlier Richler in his description of the Dorchester Street observes that dirt was found everywhere. 'But most of the people don't mind the dirt too much (*SH* 25). These people always planned to move away and a stint with dirt was part of a lifestyle that they soon wished to outgrow. Max complains that MacPherson called Duddy "you dirty Jew" *(DK 37)*. Duddy reacts to Linda who had cheated him, "You think I'm dirt,' he said, 'don't you?" *(DK 95)*. Duddy is hot with fury for being considered as 'dirt' not only by non-Jews but by wealthy Jews like Linda. It is this 'dirty' identity of being isolated he wants to clean in the society.

> Look at me, he thought, take a good look because maybe I'm dirt now. Maybe I've never been to Paris... I can't play tennis like other guys here, ... I don't trick guys into crazy promises when they're drunk. I don't speak dirty like you either. You make fun of your father. You don't like him... But he sends you to Europe and Mexico and who pays for those drinks in the afternoon? ... May be I 'm dirty today. That bastard of a black marketer Cohen can give me twenty bucks and a lecture about gambling and feel good for a whole week. If you want to bet on something then bet on me. I'm going to be a somebody and that's for sure. *(DK 95)*

Duddy rips the veil of hypocritical acts of Linda and Cohen, values family and pledges to rise above his squalid identity. Joshua recalls painfully "Those Leventhals gave me a lot of trouble. They treated me like dirt" *(JTN 223)*. In *St. Urbain's Horseman* through recurrent scatological images, Richler projects a society of discharge, sewage and flush. He also projects that for the Nazis the

Jews were an image of dirt that had to be wiped clean. This act of brutal killing and cruel cleaning is in the background.

A Jew's image enhanced when he was accepted by the non-Jews of Montreal. "Smicha's stature increased immensely when it became known that he was respected even among the gentiles in the district" (*DK 46).* His 'good-Samaritan' act of helping a gentile earned him a lot of acceptance and respect from both sides of the divided line.

Marriages changed social status. Jewish men wished to get married into Outremont. It was the home of well-to-do Jewish girls. Max in *Smaller Hero* married into the Debrofskys and Uncle Oscar in *Joshua Then and Now* took a wife in Outremont and moved out of the ghetto to enjoy a brief postwar affluence. Marrying a gentile was a taboo. Duddy talks to Hersh about marrying a girl from Outremont. He is interested in meeting the right Jewish girl, preferably a very rich one, while living with a Yvette, a French-Canadian gentile. Falling in love with a gentile was secretive. Noah discovers his grandfather's secret of his repressed lifelong love for a gentile woman.

In the select novels the women counterparts, Miriam, Yvette, Nancy and Pauline are Gentiles. Duddy first do not want to be seen with Yvette and for a brief period of time did not mind it when she was of a great business help. "Duddy looked pained and he wondered if she realized that he was ashamed of being seen with her on the lake" (*DK 97).* One of the very first questions Miriam asks Noah was whether their relationship would be fine since he was a Jew. Noah's short lived love affair seems to have taken him into a world that could be forever his. But Miriam functions not as a lover but as a member of the gentile community. Through Miriam, Noah understands that her world is no better than his own. He feels scattered in a foreign land like a dispersed seed. "He had expected that by moving away from home something wonderful would happen whereby he would end up a bigger and freer man" (*SH* 29). After he leaves St. Dominic Street and finds a room of his own in Dorchester Street, he finds himself disillusioned. He felt he did not belong to both the worlds. "All the dictums of the ghetto seemed unworthy of contempt in retrospect. I'll miss them, he thought" (*SH* 29). Noah felt he was conditioned by the mental ghetto. He found it difficult to confine within the ghetto and found it absurd to stay away. Joshua forever thinks about making a home in Outremont. With his marriage to Pauline he socially escalates to Westmount, the gentile homes of the rich with a garden laced cottage on the lake side. Their love story finally connects the worlds of Westmount and St. Urbain Street, amidst ups and downs.

Mixed marriages amidst denial create a new-breed of children. In contrast to Issy Hersh's stinger, "Mixed Marriages stink" one notices that they shrink the Jew-Gentile divide. Fanny Hersh, mother of Jake Hersh, talks about the children:

> They were a new breed, these mixed-marriage kids. With a Christmas tree in December and matzohs in April. Instead of being unwanted, hounded here for being Christ-killers, mocked there for being bland WASPS, they belonged every-where. With a stake in Jehovah and a claim in Christ. A taste for hot cross buns and bagels. (*SUH* 279)

Money –The Hammer

Rich Jews successfully elbowed their way, transgressed, owned properties and hammered down the ghetto wall. Duddy aims to own one, transgresses, amasses many and so do the Gursky brothers which triggered anti-Semitic rage among the goyishe people. O'Hearne on investigating the Boogieman disappearance case reprimands Barney, "We guys may not own big lakeside properties, but we sure do our homework, eh?" (*BV 333).*

Richler's twist in penning the betrayal of the Gursky brothers is to show that same kinds of manipulation occur between Jew and Jew. Larson writes: "But more than explicating Jewish neuroses, Richler captures most virulently the psychological geography of Canada, a country built-like the United States-by the dissatisfied, Jew and Gentile alike". He quotes Richler's view of Canada as not so much a country "as a holding tank filled with the disgruntled progeny of defeated peoples".

Bert Smith, a gentile plays a near check-mate knock out with the greedy Gurskys, the newly found Jewish royalty. Ironically, the Gurskys do not prove to be the 'law-abiding bunch'. Smith is the check-post for the reckless, ruthless drivers of Gurskys. Bernard's threats and Solomon's skillful reasoning cannot win Bert over. Solomon says: "This country has no tap root. Instead, there's Smith. The very essence" (*SG 382).* Nevertheless, the crime-prone Gurskys bribe Bert's superiors and walk out of the trial clean-handed. But the penalized Bert is a powerful representative not only of the gentiles but of that part of the world which still believed in righteous ways of living. Bert tells Bernard, "You and your sort will have to learn once and for all that not everybody has his price" (*SG 369).* His is a saved flame of truth which he keeps burning and believes that judgement came from above and not from men. At Bernard's funeral Bert remarks: "Over? It's not over. It's just begun. Now he will have to face a Judge that he can't subvert" (*SG 254).* Through Bert, Richler's voice of the absolute echoes loud.

Solomon is a rare Jew, who stomped into the gentile world that threatened him and his kind. When he enters a restricted hotel, his presence stirs an air of discomfort among the gentile crowd who hinted physical distancing. They whispered to each other looking at him, a lady reached for her handbag and secured it on her lap and the waiter tells: "I must ask you to leave" (*SG 381*). When Solomon was told, that it was against the hotel's policy to serve his kind, he nonchalantly announces that he had already bought the hotel and grabbed a golfer who spoke condescendingly and slammed him against the wall. Solomon had particularly purchased the most elegant Chalet Antoine resort in Ste.-Adele. He and the rest of the Gursky trade, highlight how power and money could make them more respectable irrespective of the Jewish lineage. Ironically their power erases the Jew-Gentile demarcating line and restriction turns into acceptance. The Gurskys success projects that wealth elevated the Jew in a classed society. It is this material success every ghettoed street boy pursues, no matter how crooked the road they travel to the Promised Land. When restricted they barged, invaded, plundered space ruthlessly.

Solomon, in fact, is a different kind of Jew who could really fight back in order to establish his rightful place in the world. He conquered whatever threatened their very existence. Later as Sir Hyman Kaplansky, he teases and shocks a whole lot of non-Jews inviting them to a *Passover* celebration. Delaying a hungry crowd with his deliberate deliberations of the *Passover* he offers them to begin the feast with the *matzoh* – unleavened bread of affliction. Much relieved the starving guests start to bite into the sacred food, which Sir Hyman had wickedly engineered to ooze red faking blood from the *'matzohs'*, sending the terrified crowd shrieking and howling. The wizard Hyman enjoys a long belly-laughter over a form of revenge accomplished.

Changing Times

Miriam and Noah of *Smaller Hero* fear restriction in Ste-Adele in the 1950s while Miriam and Barney of *Barney's Version* aren't disturbed with such thoughts and are noted to frequent La Sapiniere in Ste-Adele for their romantic dinners in the 1990s. The desires of the Jewish folk of the mid-twentieth century to live a life without dividing lines as absorbed in the early-novels are realized in the 1990s and are entrenched in *Barney's Version.* While Noah's grandma yearns to walk on the streets of Park Avenue, Barney the street boy is invited to A-list dinners on Park Avenue

Hersh's Grandfather was a peddler. Uncle Abe was the first Hersh to be in McGill. He recounts that those days were bad. "We couldn't own property in the town of Mount Royal, we smelled bad. Hotels were restricted, country clubs, and there were quotas for Jews in the universities" (*SUH* 404). "No Jews, No Dogs" ... Now times changed, his son Irwin does not know about anti-Semitism. Uncle Abe spoke on Talmudic Law in McGill. He said that the struggle was worth and as a content Hersh lives in Canada, raising a family in Jewish tradition, wearing his father's '*talith*' marking the changing times of the age. Irv Nussbaum in *Barney's Version* traces the social change of the mid-twentieth century Montreal to the latter half of the Century that erased the Jew-Gentile divide. He speaks with joy that the once restricted hotels in the Laurentians were now accessible. Gone are the days when it was difficult for a Jew to get a cashier job. "These days there are Jews serving on the boards of banks, and on the Supreme Court, and even in the cabinet in Ottawa" (*BV 203).*

Ironically, Diaspora Jews were not accepted in Israel. "Israel itself could soon become just another goyishe country" *(BV 204)* says Irv. People in Israel abhor them and they call them derogatory "Oh, u must be one of those ghetto Jews" *(BV 204)*

Irv Nussbaum pathetically points out that in the process of assimilation the Jews had lost their roots. He points out that instead of moving out of Montreal to Toronto and Vancouver in search of cosmopolitanism the Jews should return to Israel in search of their roots. "Listen here, my old friend, we didn't survive Hitler so that our children could assimilate and the Jewish people disappear" (*BV 203).*

With his acerbic satire, well-constructed caricatures of his Montreal childhood, Richler projects how the wandering Jews and prejudiced gentiles co-create a world, resisting, dividing on one hand and blending and transcending on the other. Thus, Richler's select novels speak for the marginalized and show how the Jew-Gentile divide, mutually redefines each other's perspectives, living and society.

Contexts and Texts are inseparable. The text cannot be an isolated entity. In the process of negotiation and exchange the difference between the text and the context blurs. It is to be noted that Joe King in *From The Ghetto To The Main: The Story Of The Jews Of Montreal* quotes Richler to describe the St. Urbain Ghetto. He records, "Richler immortalized the St. Urbain Street Jewish ghetto with his award-winning novel, *Duddy Kravitz"* (104). The co-texts by themselves are texts of historical value and circulation widens at a point when Richler's literary texts become co-texts for non-literary texts of the time period. Thus, non-literary texts written on the period begin to borrow from the literary texts of that period each validating the ideology of the age.

Posner quotes Richler's thoughts on writing, "Orwell said that writing was revenge on your own childhood and whatever indignities you suffered. That's true, to some extent. It is a way of getting your own back" (1). Richler vividly recreates the surrounding space of the Montreal ghetto, Jewish tradition, effect of Holocaust, anti-Semitism, idealization of Spanish war and political climate during the Separatist Movement in which he grew, its faults, gaps and discriminations that created the ghetto walls. This outraged the Jews and pushed them to the circumference to transgress and blast the imposing barricade of the Jew-Gentile dividing ghetto wall. While chapter II discusses the surrounding spaces of the mid-twentieth century Jewish-Montreal ghetto, chapter III focuses on how the surrounding space of ghetto-living constructs a socially-conditioned self improvises for mobility in varied degrees of transgression.

End Notes

1. *An Inconvenient Truth* (2006) documentary is on the imperative issue of global warming scripted by the Former U.S Vice President and a long-time environmental activist, Al Gore. The movie documents the scientific facts of global warming and explains how it has already begun to affect our environment.
2. *Barney's Version* (2010) is an indulgent comical film based on Richler's award-winning novel of 1997 centering on Barney's fully lived life.
3. Akiva Ben Joseph (c. 50-135 C.E.) was a famous Jewish rabbi of ancient Israel; a major legal scholar and was also a legendary mystic and martyr. He was tortured and killed at the hands of the Romans in 135 CE. (*JGV*)
4. The Jewish legend of the lamed Vovniks describes thirty-six righteous men in every generation upon whose goodness and merit the world is kept from entire destruction. Based in part on the story of Abraham and his conversation with the Lord about the destruction of Sodom in Genesis [1]8, the Lamed Vovniks cause the Lord to answer, "I will spare all the place for their sakes" (Gen 18:26). (For more check *JGV*)
5. Maimonides (1135-1204). Also known as "Rambam"; from the acronym Rabbi Moses Ben Maimon; rabbinic authority, codifier, philosopher and royal physician. He was the first person to write a systematic code of all

Jewish law, the *Mishneh Torah*; he produced one of the great philosophic statements of Judaism, The *Guide to the Perplexed*; served as physician to the sultan of Egypt; wrote numerous books on medicine; and, in his "spare time," served as leader of Cairo's Jewish community. In earlier centuries it was almost impossible for an educated Jew to pass a single day without remembering Maimonides in whatever field of study the Jew might be engaged. For more on his life and works refer (*JGV*).

6. Joseph Trumpeldor (1880-1920) Early Zionist activist and national hero who believed "It does not matter; it is good to die for our country." (*JGV*)

   Immigrant Jewish parents fed their children with inspiring Jewish stories on Akiva Ben Joseph, the thirty-six just men, Maimonides and Joseph Trunpeldor.

7. Holocaust refers to the genocide of European Jews and others by the Nazis during World War II. *The Holocaust Encyclopedia* defines, "The Holocaust was the systematic, bureaucratic, state-sponsored persecution and murder of approximately six million Jews by the Nazi regime and its collaborators". It explains that "Holocaust" is a word of Greek origin meaning "sacrifice by fire." The Nazis, who came to power in Germany in January 1933, believed that Germans were "racially superior" and that the Jews, deemed "inferior," were an alien threat to the so-called German racial.

8. Josef Mengele (1911-1979?) – Physician at Auschwitz. *The Holocaust Encyclopedia* notes that he made selections at the ramp and was known for his arbitrary and brutal decisions and actions against Jews in concentration camps. (*JGV*)

   After the war, he was hunted as a Nazi war criminal but escaped all attempts. In *St. Urbain's Horseman* Jake dreams that the Horseman, his alter-ego Joey will chase and find Mengele and extract his gold-filled teeth as he had done it to the Jews.

3

'Self-Fashioning' – Confronting Conflicting Conflicts and Moral Policing

> Social actions are themselves always embedded in systems of public signification, always grasped, even by their-makers, in acts of interpretation, while the words that constitute the works of literature that we discuss here are by their very nature the manifest assurance of a similar embeddedness. (Greenblatt, *RSF* 5)

Robson notes that Greenblatt claims "a historically specific sense of self" and attributes its formation to be culture specific and socially constructed (53). Although the term 'self-fashioning' in a sense hints on how human autonomy creates the self, Greenblatt considers this an illusion. By 'self-fashioning' he means how an individual is shaped by religious, political, societal views and living conditions of a period, giving no room for Satre and Burckhardt theories of existentialism and individualism.

> I perceived that fashioning oneself and being fashioned by cultural institutions – family, religion, state – were inseparably intertwined. In all my texts and documents, there were, so far as I could tell, no moments of pure, unfettered subjectivity: indeed, the human subject itself began to seem remarkably unfree, the ideological product of the relations of power in a particular society. Whenever I focused sharply upon a moment of apparently autonomous self-fashioning, I found not an epiphany of identity freely chosen but a cultural artifact. (Greenblatt, *RSF* 256)

Culture-sculpted selves may confront constraints and restrictions and the limitations may be limited to materialistic and social values. But the discernment of a moral choice is based on human autonomy and is guided by a universal value system. Thus redefining 'Self-Fashioning' seeks a mid-way between a culturally-constructed ideology and an existentialist choice of freedom which decides the different paths of individuals with similar conflicts and constraints.

Chapter III studies the various forms of 'improvisations' that Richler's protagonists resort to, in response to the 'constraints' imposed by the 'circumambient space'. It also states that although confronted with societal pressures, the characters' discernment of moral choice defines their 'improvisation'. As a result, they transgress, transform or transcend the barring ghetto wall. Thereby in a sense this 'mobility' negotiates, affects and moral polices the society and hypocritical families that erected the ghetto wall. This is discussed focusing on the conflicts between individual versus power structures of religion, tradition and a Jew-Gentile society. It studies the protagonists' response to moral issues and the choices they make. It elaborates on the importance and influence of families on individuals, deliberates gender-roles and explains how it leads to the "Third Solitude" of the Jewish-Canadian.

3.1. Individual versus some Power Structures

Tamara Myers records in *Negotiating Identities in 19th and 20th Century Montreal* that in 1917 young Jewish men in Montreal were called to root out "an insidious problem that had beset the community's youth" identified as juvenile delinquency which included children and adolescents along "three broad religious categories – Catholics, Protestant, and Jewish" (175). The conditions attributed to the rise of Jewish juvenile delinquency are "as a by-product of the immigrant experience, resulting from dislocation, impoverishment, and a growing gulf between foreign-born parents and Canadian-born adolescents" (197).

Richler's works imbibe the transgressions of the Jewish-Canadian youth of the period who trespass for material success. While the mid-twentieth century ghetto was not totally impoverished like the early years of the century, it was not completely nourished like the Uptown Jews. The widening gap between the immigrant parents and Canadian-born children triggered amoral ways to gain material success. The friction between the inner spaces of the characters versus the outer space of social conditions gave rise to emotional, social, psychological and moral conflicts. The crisis to assimilate with the mainstream, assert their Jewish roots and redefine the hybrid identity is perennial to Richler's protagonists. Conflicts amid the rich and the working-class Jew, Orthodox, Secular and a self-rejecting Jew, Jew and Gentile, self against self, crisis in family and professional life, from being socially non-existent to becoming socially-relevant individuals, cause tension in Richler's protagonists. They are driven by a need to socially escalate and publically be visible like the mainstream Canadians.

This subdivision throws light on the protagonists' relations to power structures and studies how power operates either explicitly or secretly as suggested in the select novels. Power structures refer to the Orthodox Jewish religious strictures, families and a Jew-Gentile divided society dominated by the WASPS (White Anglo-Saxon Protestants). It also traces what model of human personality the novels imply or construct and the type of a historically specific model of truth they reveal.

Applying the Greenblatt approach to literature in three interlocking ways, the analysis throws light on the dialectical sense of production of Richler's select novels. They are a powerful satire of the hypocritical behaviour and ideology of his age with the writer's vehement acerbic tone which is a reflection upon the codes that shaped the age. The disturbance, turbulence and hypocrisy of the Montreal ghetto and a sense of rage boiling under the surface of each character are present in Richler's novels. It presents a glimpse of the morality of the age which opens up a world of undeserving rich, corruption and amoral choices.

Richler's fiction reflects the literary mood of the period between 1960 and 1973 which New observes as, "academic, sometimes arcane, usually middle class in its affirmation and rejection of values, and it was concerned with the psychic isolation that recurs so frequently as a motif in modern literature" (233). Borrowing Max Weber's idea of man as an animal suspended in webs, Geertz attributes these webs to culture in his book *The Interpretation of Culture*. It can be observed that Richler's men try to cut off unwanted strands from the web to weave in new silk threads of their choice. In doing so, men realign themselves by exercising their existential freedom to choose which is in constant constraint with the constructed culture. This improvisation varies from Greenblatt's explication of the socially constructed self.

At the end of the novels a traditionally grown Noah, leaves home. A scrawny, pimply Duddy moves on to own the land around the lake, a St. Urbain Street boy Jake becomes a TV writer and has a home in London, a poor-ghettoed Joshua owns an idyllic home in Westmount, the sons of a truthful working-class Jew Aaron own the Gursky empire and dictate politics and economy, yet another ghettoed Barney has lived a rich life with his first, second and final wife. The question, how do these Street-boys move beyond the dividing lines of the ghetto wall have been critically analyzed.

From a "Know-nothing adolescent" to a grown-up man, the individuals are in a constant state of struggle against the dominant ideas of religion, society, family and a hyphenated identity. As Robson quotes Focault: "Power is everywhere; not because it embraces everything, but because it comes from everywhere" (20). Systems of thought are part of this process of control, and so ideas are implicated by power. Greenblatt echoes Foucault's idea that at a specific point in time, within a particular culture, the relationship between the individual and the society will be governed by certain techniques that can be analyzed to be given a sense of the state. Hence an analysis is made of how the hyphenated identities of Richler's characters confront some of the power structures of the society at a specific point of time, space and culture. It also works on Greenblatt's question – "What kinds of behaviour, what models of practice, does this work seem to enforce?" (Robson 21).

Flyways to Flyaway

Charles Foran calls Richler, "A devotee of shaded characters" who preferred in his novels the lively scoundrel over the boring nice guy who could be strong and powerful with an intimidating presence. The religious strictures ill-suited for a non-Zion environment, with family and its values becoming more of a heavy baggage on a long journey, Richler's men confront society and find ways to reinvent themselves. At many levels, the confrontation being unequal, they transgress the codes of the society. Their criminal transgressions of varied degrees include civil and sexual offences, shoplifting, cheating and forging documents. Their routes many with diverse flyways but the purpose singular, ill-advised by a push to make money, escalate their status and become more "visible", opts short-cuts, short-routes, short-roads called transgressions.

In explicating transgressions, core themes of survival, ambivalent pursuit, guilt, revenge, and revelation abound in the novels. In *Smaller Hero,* Noah is torn between guilt and survival. Craniford observes, "The cost of saving oneself alone involves remorse at the thought of those who are not saved. And this taints the excitement of moving on" (3). It is this dilemma that makes up the undecided Noah shunt between home and his world of moral appraisal. Noah is in contrast to Duddy who is obsessed with personal success and survival, at the expense of hurting others and nearly killing them. It is guilt that knocks an unbent Melech to hire Moore, the man he cheated in his scrap yard. Although he overtly does not accept the crime, he felt sorry and pensive and decided to make the aging man a night watchman rather than scorch him with day work.

The Canadian pride of multiculturalism and ethnic mosaic of cultural diversity proves to be a myth for the early protagonists of Richler. It's conflicting for Noah and Duddy to retain their ethnic roots and be a Canadian too. This turns out to be an ambivalent pursuit and a challenging route for Duddy which he decides to trespass. Noah Adler stands out as a righteous man averse to telling lies. He stands out as a round portrait who loathed the hypocritical

Jewish men who were ritualistic with religious practice but cheated in the scarp yards. Noah is against such men while Duddy moves closely with the "Cohen" men. Yanofsky allows that, "Noah is a sincere model for a young man of promise" (64). Noah's only moment of transgression in his attempt to streamline with the gentile world is breaking into his Professor Theo's home metaphorically and eloping with the man's wife. After a brief period of deviation: "He remembered old Moore, who had been cheated by his grandfather. The way I'm cheating Theo, he thought" (*SH* 96). Realizing that his search is on a higher plane he abandons a neurotic Miriam thus committing another mistake to correct the previous one. Noah's innate quest for the moral self-strays far from his sin and takes him back home. Noah is in constant conflict with the dividing-lines of the society, Orthodox Judaism, hostile nature of the gentiles and deceitful practices of their own tribe, the onus of a tortured cultural memory, man and woman relationship which finally brings him into tough conflict with himself.

Duddy's confronting style is inventive and voluptuous. He dreamed of making "big" and was a shark that devoured any intrusion between him and his money-making endeavors. His fictitious nature of Bradley's exploits was unquestioned and gave a safe distance between his lies and the real self and the space to grow his desired self. He never wanted to be cast out because of his Jewish or Street roots. He was indignant about people judging his taste or strength. "You think I have to be a moron just because my old man is a taxi driver? My brother's studying to be a doctor. I read lots of books" (*DK 22).* It is this prejudice or limitation set by the society he raved to outgrow and he lied, cheated and forged to do it.

From a small, narrow-chested boy of fifteen from St. Urbain Street to a well-built robust millionaire flying countries, Duddy had stomped his way breaking rules, breaking bricks of the ghetto wall and has a serious moral handicap. Smicha's seeds of wisdom, "A man without land is nobody" (*DK 48),* is manipulated by a mean, crafty Duddy. He takes it as the guiding line with infringement as a ladder to success. As an ace prankster, Duddy taught his schoolmates to steal, shoplift, flick, split streetcar tickets and smoke.

"A *pusherke*, a little Jew-boy on the make" (*DK 242)* as Uncle Benjy rebuked him, his commercial adventures were a breach of morality and the flyways he chose were crooked and advised by his innate perverse nature. Duddy always preferred the shortcuts. He knew the art of bribery. He could easily get his orders when he could gift a bottle of rum to his cook as waiter in a Laurentian hotel. All that was dirty and amoral attracted Duddy. Contaminated, he seeped through every system of discipline, flouting rules, initiating trouble and tormenting people who did not agree with him. He even captained a street fire on St. Urbain. In doing this he felt powerful, wanted and noticed who would have been an otherwise invisible scrawny boy, naturally overlooked. Duddy continues to get this attention in his re-appearances too.

Rising up on the social graph there is no looking back for Duddy. His once desolate apartment becomes a place for gatherings and partying activities. William New observes that Richler offers a lively paradigm of adventures where sexual and intellectual discoveries provided the chief activity as in *Duddy Kravitz* and in which rebellion took the form of the standard Bildungsroman (239). This can also be traced in the coming-of-age of the rest of the protagonists. Craniford calls Duddy "A parody of success" (50). Richler through the novel's ambiguous ending relates social success to human and moral failure. The Jews believed that the only way to bridge the poverty gap and move beyond the ghetto walls is to be materially rich like the gentiles. A few like Mr. Cohen pursued money amorally while the others lived off the success of others like Max Kravitz who lived off the Boy Wonder. While Noah continues his search beyond the dividing-walls by leaving home, Duddy discovers himself worthy on a piece of land that he buys.

William H. New notes that the recurrent theme, "'Power' (industrial, political, sexual) was a captivating subject" of the 1970s (235). Power in Richler's select novels apart from the Orthodox Jewry included the political and sexual particularly in Jake in *St. Urbain's Horseman* and Joshua in *Joshua Then and Now.* It manifests itself in its political, historical and social agenda as a response to the

Holocaust memory that maimed the psyche of several Jewish people, a trauma certainly Jewish alone.

Thirty-seven-year-old Jake Hersh, a Canadian expatriate in London is an artist and an individual conscious of his ethnic roots. A far more experienced man than his literary precursors Noah and Duddy, he is rooted in his family with a gorgeous wife Pauline and three kids and managed to remain "an alienated Jew, Modishly ugly" (*SUH* 25). Greenstein notices, "Spatially, instead of Duddy's limitations within Montreal parochial ghetto, Jake Hersh widens his horizon throughout the Diaspora" (*TS* 149). A war-guilt laden Jake chases his fantasized alter-ego Joey avenging the Nazi *Doktor* Mengele in his dreams and reveries. Jake's crisis is triggered by a sense of professional unfulfilment, moral charges and cumulative dissatisfaction of being born in the wrong age. With constant conflicts and a baggage of guilt, Jake is a serious and brooding character, relentlessly reviewing himself with a pained psyche that swells with longings and doubts of being a successful Jew: "What is with me, he demanded. "Wherever I put my foot down, it's quicksand" (*SUH* 343). Vanderhaeghe explains the undercurrent of the self-appraisal: "More than anything else, Jake Hersh wants to be judged worthy" (*SUH* 464).

The conflict between the idealized self and the real one traps Jake. William H. New views, "In *St. Urbain's Horseman* (1971), where guilt (real and imagined) and love (corrupted and refined) are woven into a more densely textured social fabric and the various tensions insist on the profound meaning that attaches to an individual life". He explains that Jake's doubts and nervousness stems from the struggle of being, "Poised between Establishments, he strives to be his own man, but constantly he is compromised by his private self. Horrified by his limitations, he seeks the Muse, art, success; horrified by success, he courts nonentities" (241). Jake is caught between a corrupted threatening world and his indignant self. He lets the Horseman ride in between this chaotic road. "Exploring his guilt and his innocence takes Richler into an analysis of complex moral dilemmas. They become, in the process, a guide to the burdens contemporary people carry and to the potential for happiness which their innate and unassailable weakness still allows them" (New 242).

While Jake is caught in a web of moral dilemmas, the impish Harry Stein lashed the powers of the state with his ruthlessness. He teased people with his vicious, sadistic ways. Being tried for sexual transgressions, undaunted by anti-Semitism, he proclaimed in a London court, ""For purposes of census, taxation, and pogroms," Harry proclaimed in a swelling voice, his St. Crispin's Day voice, to the somnolent court room, "I am a Jew" *It's the rope,* Jake thought. *It's the rope for sure.* (*SUH* 83)

Joshua of all protagonists is in constant battle with various structures of the society. It begins with his childhood struggle to deal with his mother's wanton ways and father's dirty deals, the Herculean effort to impress his WASP Senator father-in-law's respect and consent for marriage with Pauline and blend with the established Westmount elite. His conflicts continue with his friends like Yossel who defame his literary reputation abroad. "Seven years later they return to Montreal where Joshua establishes himself as an outstanding Journalist, a television personality and the author of *The Volunteers* a book on the Spanish civil war" (Ramraj 110). Yossel digs into Joshua's St. Urbain Street childhood and remarks, "Your spurious articles may have won you some kind of reputation outside the country, but we know who you are. I remember your father's picture on the front page of the *Herald* wearing hand cuffs. I was at your bar mitzvah and I still remember what happened there" (*JTN 63).* Joshua had to constantly protect his beautiful wife from the licentious advances of his former friends. He had to deploy sensitive methods to slacken his wife's part-incest affection for her brother. Finally he battles his haunting memories of Ibiza, Dr. Dr. Mueller and the guilt of fleeing without helping the old couple and the tormenting shadow of Mc Master. Craniford calls Joshua a failed soldier because he leaves his home unguarded to fight a contrived battle of revenge with Mueller, while at home Pauline was disintegrating mentally.

Battles continue. On their return to Montreal, Joshua and Pauline with Alex, eighteen, Susy Fourteen and Teddy Ten are busy with their footing problems in Westmount. Craniford traces a pattern of "sin, punishment and redemption" in the novel (106). Joshua's protection and loyalty for his friends Murdoch and Seymour causes disaster which pave way for the pseudo-salacious literary correspondence blackmail and masculinity ridicule. His obsession with the Ibiza past prompts Pauline's disappearance. The novel begins with Joshua's physical collapse and Pauline's emotional collapse.

Joshua's attempts to vandalize Westmount homes and denigrate Sheldon's family are forms of revenge. When an anxious Sheldon pleads literary introduction for his writings, Joshua responds, "Sheldon, you once made a big mistake in your life. You should have let me play with your Lionel train set. We could have taken turns operating it" (*JTN 340).* Joshua carries his St. Urbain Street hurt and avenges them in Westmount. "Richler's Joshua suffers for his immoderate acts of revenge" (*Craniford 7).* As Ramraj traces, in his attempt to confront conflicts, Joshua is hopeful and nihilistic, moral and malicious, accommodating and sardonic (124).

Richler surveys the dynamics of ethnic triumph once again in *Solomon Gursky*. He employs the comic device of parody to highlight ambivalence and displacement fashioned by the Jewish immigrant's dream of discovering a home permanent in the new world Canada. The Gurskys en route to material success are camouflaged gang tricksters who exploit the mosaic culture and expand their empire.

Solomon Gursky is a novel of many men and their varied ways and paths, constructing or creating or moving beyond the psychological ghetto. Each ghettoed beyond Montreal, in a wider world: Henry and Isaac in Tulugaqtitut, Ephraim in London and Arctic, Solomon escaping every ghetto experience while Bernard, Morrie and Lionel in the Gursky establishment.

The novel deals with the Jewish community's search for origins and attempts to create legitimate Canadian credentials through a new Arctic tribe made up of some members of a Jewish family and native woman who consort them. The Gurskys are scoundrels, alternating between a seedy underworld and a normal world in which they war for acceptance, recognition and status. From the underworld of nineteenth-century London, through the Franklin expedition to the Arctic, to the prohibition years of the prairies and eastern township of Quebec, Richler's men and women seem real and come alive against the background of his own peculiar Canadian reality.

Larson comments that the novel is an apocryphal revelation on Jewish family in a Jew-marginalized Canada, linking the frontier to the modern. Spanning across four generations, it records that in every age band, the struggle for survival, the violent psychological battles of the dispersed Jew repeats from Ephraim to Aaron to Solomon and his brothers to Henry and Lionel each inventing, devising different models of existence. Ephraim begets the non-Inuit House of Gurskys. He and his "chosen" grandson Solomon, stand apart in their unique path, resurrecting with reincarnated lives. Craniford notes: "While everyone else, for better or worse, lives only one life, Ephraim and Solomon shed their skins and emerge renewed to live again and again – in Solomon's case, each time with a different name" (110). The phoenix reappearances of Ephraim and Solomon suggest extra-ordinary, supernatural living patterns, are evolved to combat the marginalized living of the Jews. While Ephraim's return had a more personal agenda, Solomon's is political and social.

Richler maps an extensive troubled global identity of the Jews beyond Canada. Pushed to the rim of life to survive as an expatriate Russian Jew, Ephraim Gursky the grandfather of the Gursky dynasty of sinned wealth is kicked out of Victorian England for philandering. He volunteers to go on Sir John Franklin's expedition to find a Northwest Passage in 1845. Ruthless as a risk bearer and capable of contriving mystical power, Richler creates Ephraim through what Kramer remarks as "Judaized narrative" (13). He somehow escapes when the ship is frozen in the waters of Upper Canada, becomes a deity to an Eskimo tribe and eventually teaches the visiting Solomon tricks of the raconteur. Solomon uses the wicked magic wand blessed with criminality to create the Gursky "Booze-Baron" empire, along with Bernard and Morrie (the three sons of the legitimate Aaron). They become millionaires, bootlegging imported Scotch whiskey to American rumrunners during Prohibition. The Gursky family is an example of how a negligently dispersed Jewish seed of Ephraim grows into a mammoth tree feeding on crime and offense to survive and finally pockets the most prestigious visiting card of Westmount in Canada.

The fourth generation of Gurskys is caught in the mire of family feuds fuelled by greed and Lionel, a real vampire of their age. Morrie mourns it: "Poor Lucy. Poor Henry. Poor Barney. It's a shame that their generation had to be caught up in family fights over what? Money. Position. Power" (*SG 211*). Ironically the Gursky Empire survives a series of trials through heavy bribing but confronts a slow decline due to severe greed, revenge and betrayal of the brothers.

While *Solomon Gursky* teams with grave revenge and rivalry, *Barney's Version* is Barney's anticipated settling of scores to the much-expected Terry McIver's autobiography in which he is all set to scandalize Barney, his relationship with his three wives and friendship with Boogie. Barney's plan to write his memoir is "to come clean" with the truth of what he considers to be his "wasted life" (*BV* 1). Jake also considers reviewing his wasted life (*SUH* 96). The novel is a network of familial conflicts which Barney confronts and messes with his moral dilemmas and infidelity.

Richler also echoes the groans of an aging flesh and the "Hagar syndrome" with insight into the wrinkled age. In constant conflict with himself, Barney is consumed of guilt, compulsive regret and is constantly conscious of his death-prone age. He repeatedly scripts his death scene and asks the anxiety prone "what if" questions: "What if this was to be our last conversation?", "And what if Miriam and I were never to be reconciled?" (*BV 21)* and plans to be found with books on his bedside if he died in his sleep. He calls himself "reeking of decay and dashed hopes – an impenitent rotter – a malevolent man" (*BV* 232). He never wants to age beyond thirty and ridicules his aging years, "My breath sour. My limbs in dire need of a lube job. And now that I've been blessed with a plastic hip-socket replacement, I 'm no longer even biodegradable. Environmentalists will protest my burial" (*BV 17).* It is to be noted that Richler does not speak much about women's aging and inadvertently focuses on the elderly like Barney and Hymie. An age-challenged Hymie also writes – "I don't want to die yet". Maggie Humm observes in her definition of aging that "older women are less visible" (5).

Acts of Revenge is a recurrent theme in the novels. Provocation is a form of revenge for Duddy. He annoyed MacPherson and Uncle Benjy with his intolerable vicious ways for he found their "polite behaviour" and what Daniel Coleman calls "white civility" provocative (Deer 43). Duddy is revengeful, he figured that Uncle Benjy, had humiliated him, and he would remember that. Vengeance harboured, Duddy never misses a chance to payback. He unrolls a rumble of infuriating questions of Uncle Benjy's respect for Smicha "How come you care so much? You never even go to visit him anymore" (*DK 62).* Greenstein states that revenge is also at a physical level like Jake's revenge of spraying a murdering lime solution on his neighbour's rhododendrons, Duddy's destruction of Westmount tulips, Harry's slashing a Silver Rolls Royce with his knife and Joshua's vandalizing spree (*TS* 151).

Retribution spurred by memories of Holocaust throbs in Jake's blood. It was entrenched in his daily routine; his "attic aerie" had artifacts of Jewry and holocaust survivors. He had a wall clock adjusted to show the *Doktor's* time in Paraguay. He shelved a Horseman cupboard with a journal entry on The Horseman referring to Joseph Hersh from Yellowknife in Yukon Territories and believes his cousin Joey to be the Horseman, a champion of Jews: "In his mind's eye, Jake saw him cantering on a magnificent Pleven stallion. Galloping, thundering. Planning fresh campaigns, more daring maneuvers" (*SUH* 41). For both Jake and Joshua, *Doktor* Mengele and Dr. Dr. Mueller are targets of revenge to avenge the "six-million" extermination of Jews.

While revenge is meted out in varied forms, guilt is overcome by ruthlessness in the protagonists. Noah quickly gets over his guilt of deserting Miriam with a pinch of insensitivity. Duddy's callous nature forges an epileptic Virgil. Jake's heartlessness comfort his guilty nature. Joshua's insensitivity to Pauline's repeated requests for attention and Barney's juggle with thoughtlessness and thoughtfulness make them tough men at times cruelly indifferent to people.

"Each man creates God in his own image" (*SH 40).* Richler's prototypes negotiate identity traded between the individual's choice of freedom and the cultural construction of identity, thus differing from Greenblatt's 'Self-fashioning' concept:

> Noah's twice-old dilemma to return and quit home;
>
> Duddy's moral transgressions to achieve material success;
>
> Jake's choice to strictly maintain the moral requirements of the character;
>
> Joshua's initial yielding to the cultural pressures of identity but latter makes a conscious individual effort to recoup the family's idyllic peace;
>
> Solomon's exposure to the wild demi-god acts of Ephraim and the conscious effort to use it to rise above the suppressed identity; by choice his benevolence to Moses – a stark, striking contrast characteristic to his inherent bootlegging character; and finally
>
> Barney's conscious efforts (tragic in nature) to succeed in love and life.

All the above choices of the protagonists, despite 'constraints' and 'mobility' of social construction, focus on the existence of the existential freedom to choice. This freedom to choose is influenced both by the value system of the self and restrictions of culture. Though societal influence is large and looming, finally it is the innate choice of the self, like salt to food, which makes the difference. Since all St. Urbain Street boys in Richler's world are bred under similar conditions, face challenges alike, allured by similar moments of transgressions, but it is the strength or weakness of the individual that leads them to their desired not destined destinations. Uncle Benjy at twenty-six had the golden touch, who owned a factory strictly without contravention. Lennie chooses to assimilate denying his St. Urbain's roots while Duddy is a fighter who takes pride in being a Jew boy from St. Urbain Street strives to breakdown the ills of racial and class segregation, transgresses to torment the society. But incidentally Uncle Benjy and Lennie become failures in the idealist world. If these selves had been only culturally constructed then they would have reached the destined destinations of success. Greenblatt's 'Self-fashioning' constructs the Self only from the outside. It fails to recognize that it is the Will that drives the character into a making the final choice. The cultural construction or surrounding space may spread a menu card of options available or indicate unavailability at a particular space or time, while the Will of the self makes or rejects the choices. The dilemmas and choices of all the characters validate this argument.

While power in the form of marginalization of Jewish immigrants operates explicitly through anti-Semitism, the pressure to rise up on the social scale is an implicit social-construction. The protagonists respond to these structures of power by the acts of will to lie, cheat, forge or at times resist with a moral stand. Through transgressions Duddy and Gurskys threaten the operative powers of the dominant gentile world both in Canada and abroad and with the material successes 'contain' the 'subversion' of authority, while the rest like Noah, Jake, Joshua and Barney confront moral dilemma. In the quest to be "somebody" Duddy forges and buys the restricted site for the Jews, Noah leaves the ghetto, returns and leaves in search of a home of his own. Jake, Joshua turns to a European tradition to forge a new identity while Solomon, Moses and Barney struggle in a relatively Canadian homeland of ghetto. Their discernment of choices to choose between moral and amoral solutions is discussed in detail in the following subdivision.

3.2. Moral Issues and Amoral Solutions

He admits "I did it because I detested them for being rich" (*BV 276)*

Amidst varied responses to Richler in "print and flesh", his admirers attribute praises for his moral consistency and integrity. "Richler's bad guys come in two varieties-those capable of greed, hypocrisy, vulgarity, pomposity, lust and betrayal on a large scale and those capable of the same qualities on a small scale" (Yanofsky 207). Simmering rage, frenzied frustration and a mild rebellious tremor are inherent in the characters of Noah, Duddy, Jake, Joshua, Moses, Solomon and Barney. Transgression as an expression of pent-up rage, turns them into silent avengers causing destruction. They are ruthless but not murderous. They are unlike Bigger Thomas in *Native Son* who kills to exert his identity. As Woodcock observes, "(Richler's) His revelation of the ruthlessness of the man who seeks the truth is as deliberate as his exposure of the brutal world where men accept big lies and live by small evasions" (*Introduction SH xii*). The protagonists' amoral choices not only earn them their desired prizes but are tools of moral policing the hypocritical society that had double standards and pushed them to edges of marginalization. Richler in a CBC interview with Robert Fulford admits, "I've really been an old-fashioned moralist," indicating that no one is free from satiric treatment. It's not the values, he says, but rather the corruption of values that he explores in his novels. Yanofsky observes that even "if he was no longer orthodox in observance, he remained orthodox in temperament" (156). Richler is contemptuous as much as he is creative and the select works authenticate it.

Richler reveals how the protagonists find tradition in league with self-delusion and attempt to blow apart the ghetto's illusory walls through amoral ways. Self-driven by a passion to fight against double marginality, the protagonists possess the seed of resistance to the dominant ideology of restriction and marginalization. Greenblatt's says, "...culture is a space of conflict and competition" (Robson 71). He explicates the collision or emptiness of communication when two cultural backgrounds encounter each other. This to a greater degree is ascertained by the decoding and 'interpretative strategies' used by the participants. Hence he throws a link of questions and asks, "...how is it possible for one system of representation to establish contact with a different system? (*MP* 91). 'Improvisation' is his answer to initiate a kind of exchange between the two cultures. He describes improvisation as the capability to include the self in the system. In Richler's protagonists flexible moral standards, amoral choices and hypocritical signs and gestures and moral-policing them become forms of improvisation.

Richler works on the questions of how a Jewish-Canadian copes or negotiates a Jewish birth in a Canadian context and combats the secular and traditional forms of Judaism. It can be traced that the immigrant Jews on encountering the Canadian world decoded by isolating themselves into ghettoed spaces in Montreal. This hostile distancing preserves their tradition and communicates non-verbally the need to resist assimilation. For most of the older Jews in Canada like grandfathers Melech and Smicha, the collision of cultures was a mute wonder. They stick to their rooted Jewish rituals, alienate themselves and never want to communicate or establish relationship with non-Jews. But the third-generation Jewish boys born into a Canadian home had a frequent need to translate the signs, at times break them with an urge to converse with the mainstream. While Melech renounces his love for a gentile woman, Noah breaks into the gentile home of Theo and usurps Miriam.

Greenblatt suggests that mimesis or imitation is a form of improvisation to acculturate into the mainstream. The protagonists in their urge to mimic the gentile world are defiant of Orthodox-Jewish ways. No one prefers wearing the '*kapalah*' which is distinctive of a Jew, except on forced occasions and overlook '*kosher*' food and '*shabbus*'. This is to impose a sufficient likeliness to the mainstream and be more acceptable in a non-Jewish environment. Their dreams of more space, materialistic expansion and escalation of social status are actions to mime mainstream living. To achieve it, transgression and deviant ways are the shortest en route. Noah begins to seek transnational solution and plans to leave his home,

Jake migrates to London but is obsessed by the past and Joshua returns tired and beaten after the journey. Duddy's truant trespasses expand his social space. Solomon's magical re-appearances are avatars of varied survival. Barney escalates socially and moves on to Atwood's "Victim Position Four" (38) where the Jew and non-Jew dividing-lines blur.

Dilemma and Deviance

Deviance means choosing the perverse way that could hurt somebody or something or the conscience. It also refers to ways against the religious moral standards that might have brought them up and may not be a part of the repressive society. In the present study deviant behaviour is triggered by conflicts from the surrounding spaces. In *Invisible Bullets* Greenblatt establishes that fraudulence adds to the authority of the fraudulent. Hence deviance becomes a way to assert ones identity.

John Antony observes, "antisocial behaviour may be part of a protective survival strategy" especially in urban settings and may appear to be associated with low socioeconomic status (70). Richler's characters have traces of what Pritchard calls as "moral insanity" for their repeated immoral behaviours as indicated by Antony's diagnostic criteria for Antisocial Personality Disorder. It points to a pervasive pattern of disregard for and violation of the rights of others with either, "failure to conform to social norms…deceitfulness, as indicated by repeated lying, use of aliases, or conning others for personal profit or pleasure… reckless disregard for safety of self or others…lack of remorse, as indicated by being indifferent to or rationalizing having hurt, mistreated, or stolen from another" (69). They frequently lack empathy and tend to be callous or cynical. They may have an arrogant self-appraisal and may be excessively opinionated or cocky. He also adds that they may be irresponsible and exploitative in their sexual relationships. Noah's non-conformism, Duddy's callousness and ruthlessness, Jake's cynical and pervert ideas of sex and women, Joshua's pilfering, vandalizing and fake homosexual claims, Solomon's inflated self-appraisal, self-assured ways which display a glib, superficial charm and Barney's sexual infidelity and ruthlessness are forms of social deviance to exert identity and moral police hypocritical society, with a slant in the moral compass.

In and Out of the Ghetto

The ghetto of Montreal with Orthodox tradition conditions the protagonists to transgress the social conditioning of their lives. While Noah is rebellious, Duddy is ruthless. Noah breaks with his family's rituals and transcends the ghetto walls and Duddy in order to become "somebody" contrives success through amoral ways. The element of transgression in many ways is depicted as an attack on greed, hypocrisy and culture of the society. Noah's deep sense of justice and a brief passion of usurping his professor's wife and Duddy's forging of Virgil's signature become apparently tools of moral policing families and societies that live in deceit and pretension.

Noah's enthusiasms to move beyond the "illusory walls" frightened the Adlers. "The Adlers lived in a cage and that cage, with all its faults, had justice and safety and a kind of felicity." (*SH* 36). It is this cage that Noah wants to flee as early as seven years of age, intolerant to the hypocrisy of the ritualistic Jews, war profiteering and cheating in the scrap yards.

Noah is doubly displaced. "Noah had renounced a world with which he had at least been familiar and no new world had as yet replaced it. He was hungering for an anger or a community or a tradition to which he could relate his experience" (*SH* 64). His non-conformism leads him away from home. Noah's short lived love affair seems to have taken him into a world that could be forever his. But Miriam functions not as a lover but as a member of the gentile community. Through her, Noah understands that her community is no better than his own. He feels scattered in a foreign land like a dispersed seed. "He had expected that by moving away from home something wonderful would happen whereby he would end up a bigger and freer man" (*SH* 29). He is disillusioned after he leaves St. Dominic Street and lives in a room of his own in

Dorchester Street. He felt he did not belong to both the worlds. "All the dictums of the ghetto seemed unworthy of contempt in retrospect. I'll miss them, he thought" (*SH* 29). Noah was conditioned by the mental ghetto. He found it difficult to confine to the ghetto and found it absurd to stay away. Noah briefly returns and when he no longer could put up with the falsity and pretences of his community, he plans to quit home for Europe to "be something".

Noah of all Richler's heroes, has an inbuilt system of morality; however, his usurping of Theo's wife is a questionable act. It can be noted that Richler as Craniford states, at no point claims Noah to be a perfect man. He skillfully moderates Noah's transgression and attributes it to his age and alleviates the charge by criminally projecting a flawed Miriam. This makes the deviance as a slight deter in Noah and not a grave imperfection. Woodcock in the introduction to the novel observes that Noah in an attempt to rebel against the willful blindness of his tribe and in an attempt to preserve their ghetto isolation becomes deeply involved with the *Goyim* world which leads to the love-affair. As an outcome of guilt, Noah asks Miriam if he could marry her, but her angry "no" snaps all cords from his short-lived love affair with sin.

Noah is ever in conflict with the hypocrisy of his family. He abhors his disciplinarian grandfather's defrauding of Mr. Moore, a gentile peddler. Melech like Cohen stands as a prototype of all hypocritical Jews who were traditional in word than in practice and spirit. Noah threatens to report his uncles and cousins for war profiteering. Noah also understands that "truth was adroitly side-stepped" by the liberated Jews of his mother's family. He comes to know of the deceitful acts of the Goldenbergs. Just as Duddy's brother Lennie is dissuaded by assimilation, Noah realizes that "terror" lurked behind their happiness and they indulged in deviance in their own way. This includes Marsha's love affairs, Aunt Rachel's secret reading of pornographic literature and Mrs. Feldman's repressive beating of the French poodle. "He finally realized that the secret of their humanity was that each one had a tiny deviation all of his and/or her own. None conformed completely" (*SH 180).* As Woodcock observes, Noah realizes that crimes are committed and deviance is common and one supports the system by default. "At last Noah understood about the concentration camps. About the Goldenbergs and Harvey. The Germans had told the truth when they said that they hadn't known. They couldn't cope with knowing. Neither the Goldenbergs. Their crimes varied in dimension, but not in quality" (*Introduction SH xi).*

Noah's leaving home is a statement of quest for truth and non-conformism to live by temptation and evasion. His criticism voices the traditional prejudice against the Jews on inherent deception which he disdains to inherit. In his attempt to turn into a real person, devoid of deception, he leaves home. As he had envisaged earlier, "He was beginning to develop a morality of his own, Still embryonic..." (*SH 106*).

Duddy's lust for money is Shylockian in nature. A third-class graduate with failures in History and Algebra II, Duddy is obsessed to become "Somebody". He is driven by indefinite passion to earn big money, but was not sure of the smartest way to go about it and dreamed, planned and smoked about it all night. He wrenched his brain, had his "eyes peeled" to be that somebody which nobody had made. This quest is induced by the surrounding spaces of the ghetto and a passion to graduate from Street dwelling to a Westmount living.

Duddy is ruthless. He enjoys Lennie's absence for he began to get all of the family member's attention, "Just when everything is beginning to move. That's what you call luck" (*DK* 162). His penchant for a piece of Canaan in the Laurentians around Lac St Pierre was a driving force. He toiled day in and day out for it. As an enterprising kid turned adult, he searched every nook and corner to fill his pocket for the land. Being too sure of his purchase he tells Yvette "... I'll raise the rest of the money even if I have to kill somebody for it" (*DK 121).* But in his wild chase to acquire this verdant land-strip of his dream, he let go of his entire loved ones' trust including Yvette, Virgil and Smicha. Smicha, the grandfather pierces Duddy's conscience, "I can see what you have planned for me Duddel. You'll be good to me. You'd give me everything I wanted. And that would settle your conscience when you went out to swindle others" (*DK 312).* Yvette tells Duddy, "I think you're rotten. I wish you were dead" (*DK 315).*

Duddy magnetized mannerisms of the Boy Wonder. He liked to think that his anger was made of the same hot stuff as that of the Boy Wonder. This fire of anger is sparked off from squalid living conditions of the 'circumambient space', a space that many people wanted to move away from. Its inhabitants never existed to the outside world. Caught between a powerful tradition and drawn towards a lurid style of sophisticated living, boys like Duddy quickly wanted to make it big. They answered the *How to make it big* question as *Somehow* in many cases.

Bribery, forgery and cheating are the tools that Duddy uses to acquire his land. D.J. Dooley accuses Duddy of pollution of environment, "since the Laurentian Lake which he ultimately succeeds in buying is to be turned into a sleazier version of Ste. Agathe" and questions," Is *his* the authentic human response to the conditions of our time?" (93). Scheming, he makes Bernie's father buy the Bar Mitzvah movie, removes the MacPherson and Dingleman obstacles, forges and swindles money from the epileptic Virgil, fleeces and uses Yvette for help by faking love to become an instant *'mensch'.*

Richler's *St. Urbain's Horseman* and *Joshua Then and Now* reflect the social attitude; sexual conventions and moral choices of the period. Both Jake and Joshua are entangled in petty encumbrances and are found battling with both internal and external conflicts at the beginning of the novel. Jake is in the middle of a sexual scandal, a trial on moral charges aiding and abetting sodomy and indecent assault. As for Jake, sex has never been a part of his lifestyle. He refrained from seductive moments of orgy on Ibiza and night clubs and returned to Nancy. Moss in "Richler's Horseman" comments, "Jake wavers between seeing his reticence as a moral advantage and a character flaw" (157). Although he dreamt of being a pervert experimenting women, he was not able to overcome his self-consciousness. Joshua also fights a fake homosexual scandal. Nevertheless, Joshua unlike Jake has passionate love with Monique in Ibiza and played Ed Ryan to a London writer whose wife was his mistress for a short spell. Jake and Joshua have allowed themselves into a mess and are found struggling with doubt, guilt and the excruciating pain of feeling unworthy.

Richler in the epigraph to *St. Urbain's Horseman* quotes W.H. Auden's *September 1939* to throw light on how the just people rise as defenders in an unjust, defenseless world. This is the crux of the characters and mission of Jake Hersh, his alter ego Joey and his dirty accountant Harry Stein, avenging injustice. Jake is against the vile Nazis in his mental space. He sends his Horseman Joey riding the stallion hunting down and whipping his enemies. Harry, the blackmailer misappropriates the tax returns of the rich, threatens the wealthy with pornographic photographs, sirens bomb hoax and burps on ransom notes. Jake is a victim of mental turmoil of the disturbing accounts of Nazi camp victims. For him, revenge is to salve the Jewish blood and he believes that Joey does it. Harry is impish, foul and goes out himself to avenge his contrived injustice. While Jake is immoral in some ways, Harry is amoral in many ways.

Guilt is what drives Jake into the treacherous trap of Harry. As a response to Holocaust, there is a sense of guilt that overcomes the non-victim. Jake tries to compensate Harry's miserable childhood in London during the Second World War, where he lived a rat-life in air-raid shelters, while he safely grew in Canada.

Jake in his premarital days has been lascivious, loaded with urges and would have remained so if not for his ideal wife Nancy. In his thirties, he has a complete life with a thriving career and blessed family. But this thought of completeness only troubles him. He feels restrained as this sense of entirety does not allow him to complain or crave for more. Nancy puts an end to this search for women by being devoted, trustworthy with unconditional love. Craniford states, "Jake is restless and dissatisfied with himself, envying his divorced friends who are once more on the prowl" (94).

Jake sometimes thought, "if only his union with Nancy was oppressive, stale… he could then, like most of his film acquaintances, seek solace with vacuous girls, indulging in sex without love..." (*SUH* 292). It is this secret urge and an undefined resentment of his "singularly happy marriage" (*SUH* 297) that leads him to help Harry, in a way his feigned self that gets him into trouble. Abetting an amoral Harry, Jake is in troubled waters. It is his pervert ideas of sex, women and marriage that get him into a contemptuous maze of the sex scandal. These ideas are St. Urbain Street nurtured and London groomed. They arise from his 'id' craving for drinks and flesh. He is a moral-mess. He can neither sin nor abstain from it. Ironically, he shoves the au pair girl found with Harry in his home as he finds it morally repulsive.

For Jake the ghetto wall exists in his mental space. The Hershes imposed their identity as premier Montreal Jewish families. Hailing from an affluent family that battled against anti-Semitism and cushioned against the harsh realities of the Second World War he realizes his creative dreams as a director. For Jake, apart from Harry, trouble is within him. The mental ghetto barricades the self, bewitched by the fantasy of the Horseman and pained by Holocaust. He has to break down this deceptive wall of fancy and step down onto the grounds of reality of his fairy-tale life of a soaring career, a bold and beautiful wife and three angelic children.

Ramraj opines that, "… *Joshua Then and Now* examines the effects of the past on an individual rather than the doubts and vacillations of an ambivalent mind with which *St. Urbain's Horseman* is concerned" (125). Joshua overcomes his inauspicious beginnings in the ghetto to become a celebrated television writer and a successful journalist in Montreal. En route to this success abounds his deviant directions. Joshua's unfortunate upbringing of poverty and constant struggle, dirt and dust, negligence and indifference instill in him the desire to be renowned. When Uncle Harvey asks him what he'd like to be when he grew up, Joshua replies, "Rich and famous and popular with girls" (*JTN 22*). Joshua does it. He has a passionate love affair with Monique in Ibiza and comfortably married, the married-Pauline, the daughter of the senator. He establishes himself as a household name in Canada with his TV appearances and screen writing and as an author with *The Volunteers*, based on interviews of survivors of the International Brigades.

Joshua's transgressions include the faking of a homosexual claim highlighting his notorious communication with Murdoch to gain media attention and to sell writing to an American University archive. His acts of vandalism, vindictiveness, cunning revenge and usurping the communist wife are amoral solutions to his moral conflicts.

Joshua's early life in Montreal was one of poverty and constant struggle. It is this struggle that Duddy wants to win and Noah although not truly materialistic, shuns the ghetto cage for the gentile world of freedom. In his forty seventh year, Joshua considers himself blessed with good fortune and recalls how he had grown out of the delinquent living in slums and is rich with a home in Westmount.

Joshua in his youth primarily treads on his father's flyway of crookedness. He cheats, steals cars, shoplifts and spends a brief time in the reform school. He also pinches a card from the student locker to access Mc Gill Library. He strips off a letter head from the old boozer-editor of *Sudburry Nugget* and uses it as a letter of reference, type written as "I majored in Spanish history at Mc Gill. I speak the language fluently (*JTN* 102). As a journalist he plagiarized and exaggerated, for instance if a dumpy Canadian actress had a walk-on part in a play on Shaftesbury Avenue, he would write "Toronto Beauty Dazzles West End". He plagiarized Collier's writing with a twist and sent it to *Toronto Weekly* pleading he was a struggling Canadian artist, "who simply refused to sell his proud heritage for a fistful of yanky dollars" (*JTN* 103). To his list of amoral ways added the contrived stories to his friend of a key to a box in Royal Bank of Canada (*JTN* 104).

Joshua's vindictiveness on his return to Montreal as a successful writer is a result of his childhood grudges. When Sheldon invites the Shapiro couple for dinner, Joshua sees it as an opportunity to humiliate him and to establish himself, "They were, Joshua insisted to Pauline, obliged to go. "We are most certainly not obliged to go," she said..." But Joshua persists, "Dress classy. I want your breeding to show" (*JTN* 23). Rejected and humiliated for being a poor Street Jew and son of a crook father and saussy mother, Joshua runs, flees, breaks into boundaries that ostracized him and grows from a promising thief to a renowned television personality.

Richler through Moses Berger traces Solomon's footprints ingrained with crime in *Solomon Gursky.* Moses is on a forensic trail to read the fingerprints of the vanishing Solomon and the ever-looming large empire of Gurskys built on gambling, lies and other forgery. The novel globe-trots and is a gallery of striking characters, themes and motifs, based on the Bronfman's liquor dynasty whose history is inseparable from the rise of the Canadian nation. The novel is an exhibition of innumerable crimes that engineered the rags-to-riches Gursky dynasty.

The novel is a gallery of crooks from the forger-explorer-preacher-grandfather Ephraim to the king-size swindler Solomon and his brothers the scheming Bernard, blundering Morrie to the workers of the Booze-Baron empire, an avarice Harvey Schwartz and ruthless Betty Schwartz. Larsen claims: "However, the more journals, letters and anecdotes about the Gurskys he finds, the more he sinks into their moral squalor. Truth usually triggers despair; only later, freedom".

Ephraim, an outcast Jew is a trickster who swindles a Canadian town with news of Christ's second coming and incarnates himself as God and has a long record of transgressions that builds the foundation of the Gursky Empire. He is the son of a Liverpool cantor who runs away from home at thirteen to work in the mines. Stealing his teacher's candlesticks after a seductive experience with the wife, Ephraim runs off to London ending up in jail for forging papers and pimping off two Irish girls. He uses a forged letter of recommendation and joins the Franklin's expedition in search of the Northwest Passage, and becomes the lone-survivor of the doomed voyage. Apart from being a "ravisher, panderer and gentleman pickpocket" he converted Eskimos to his own trademark of Judaism, founded a cult and defrauded farmers in Quebec, travelled to Minsk (where his family had come from), ran arms in the American Civil War, sold firewater to Indians and swindled miners during the Alaskan Gold Rush. This directory of transgressions is the basic foundation stone upon which his chosen grandson Solomon raises an overnight skeleton of the Gursky Empire with his notorious money-making skills and which the greedy business-tycoon brother Bernard bricks and cements and the weak-willed Morrie takes shelter. The Gurskys were grown in the prairies and later when business expanded found office in Sherbrooke, Montreal and home in the Laurentians. They bought and built hotels, distilleries and liquor factories in Ottawa, Regina, Saskatoon and almost in all provinces. Like the raven, they flew all over Canada, making business, money and exercising power.

Mr. Bernard Gursky becomes a Jewish icon in Canada. A photograph with him is considered to be a status symbol and adds value to one's identity. Irv Nussbaum in *Barney Version* treasures one in his office (188). Bernard proves to be the-most-ruthless crook in coat and suit, betrays Solomon, hoping to save his hide from prosecution. When young Bernard is set to marry the daughter of a Winnipeg Jewry, his future father-in-law demands assurance of Bernard's majority stockholding in McTavish. Knowing that Solomon will not cede his own stock, he takes out a contract on him in which McGraw, his underling, gets hit. Bernard tries to frame Solomon for the murder. Bernard's sins are veiled behind Solomon's overt crimes. Bernard is a selfish, greedy money minter but Solomon is a generous crook.

Travelling across continents and chronicling generations, the novel is preoccupied with greed for money, power and flesh. Solomon, the invisible black sheep is the most notorious and mysterious of all Ephraim's grandsons. He is an ambitious gambler; self-dictator, undaunted risk taker and daring lover who changed overnight the Gursky family from bootlegging to a multifaceted commercial empire. Solomon's disappearance by itself is an unsolved mystery furthering crime and murder. A self-dictated King

Solomon could have possibly killed himself not admitting to failure or could have moved to the solitude of the Arctic if not for the cunning brother Bernard who could have killed him for the thriving empire.

The Gurskys are a powerful and threatening tribe who rise to power through transgressions. In facing trials on evasion of customs and excise duties they are acquitted due to clever bribing. Bert Smith, the rightful moral police is doomed for taking them into task. When Moses investigates the crimes of the Gursky dynasty, he finds all newspaper accounts of the murder of Mc Graw and Bernard's trial are found missing. Lionel exceeds his father Bernard in his baseness of character to hold on to the reigns of Gursky dynasty. As Larson observes, he wages a stock battle against his Uncle Morrie and his cousin Barney, an equally sleazy would-be producer, until the mysterious Corvus Trust of Zurich joins the fight. Barney Gursky, the son of the feeble Morrie had a checklist of his crimes that included fraud and alimony payments. Gitel calls them: "the Gurskys were mobsters as far as our group were concerned. Capitalism's ugly face, as we used to say" (*SG 74).* "Continuing to slide downward, the Gurskys display the ultimate symbol of their moral decay when the repulsive Isaac Gursky cannibalizes his father on Passover in the Arctic wilds" (*Craniford 118).* The Gursky action thus begins and ends in the iced Arctic, every part of the story iced and frozen and Moses had too many to defrost.

As endless are the crimes of the Gurskys, endless are the cob-web of lies that copiously cover the façade of their empire. Trekking myriad routes, unraveling mystery after mystery, globe-trotting, Moses' maniacal inquisitiveness neither finds Solomon nor finishes the biography. Getting to the root of the four-generation family saga of crime could not be completed by the feeble Rhode's scholar single-handedly. The doctor tells Moses "is filled with bottled-up rage. Shake the bottle hard enough and the cork pops" *(SG 99).* Gurevich observes that Moses in engrossing more deeply in Solomon's buccaneering life, he seems to be seeking an underworld King of the Jews, a hero, to whom no trick is too dirty in order to rise in the *goyim*'s world. Solomon in one of his messages to the adopted non-Gursky Moses writes, "I once told you that you were no more than a figment of my imagination. Therefore, if you continued to exist, so must I" (*SG 556).* Moses' journey into mining minerals for the book by itself had done the job more than the writing of it. Moses is both angled and appointed by Solomon. If Moses is the protagonist, then Solomon is the hero. The novel's shimmering web of disappearance and deception weaves in wicked tales of larger-than-life image of crooks and treacherous transgressions of not only Ephraim, Bernard, Solomon but also of the hypocritical and morally feeble Schwartz couple.

The Jeanne Mance Street boy Barney in *Barney's Version* promotes his dwelling to the Montreal suburb of Hampstead where he buys a house. From a cold-water flat, a seedy, sordid, grubby space co-inhabited by sewer rats his business prowess earns him the bourgeois style home. As a wily lover of women, he has three marriages. His baseness and a night of sexual infidelity, pours cold-water on a long-lived love marriage with Miriam, which disperses the family, imprisons him in guilt and reduces him to an Alzheimer patient.

Barney throbs with enterprising ideas like Duddy and ventures into all sorts of business to soar high above the Jeanne Mance Street walls. Initially he deals with ancient Egyptian artifacts, stolen from minnow tombs in the Valley of the Kings. Barney claims, "But I have my principles. I have never handled arms, drugs, or health foods" (*BV* 5). He churned crap for the Totally Unnecessary Productions television and added to the pollution of programmes aired in his pursuit of money-making skills and became a successful Westmount man. He admits, "I became a sinner not by stealing but by filming" (*BV* 5*).* Barney felt that being righteous never helped. His father Izzy, a truthful cop was denied his rightful promotion. May be this instigates Barney to be more prudent and resorts to trespass than impress God. He recalls how he suffered mediocrity in his profession. He calls it "A sewer". He discloses, "But until I cheated, I was blessed with a sanctuary. Miriam. Our children. Our home...Where I was never required to be deceitful" (*BV 357).*

Barney's sundry acts of a revengeful avenger led him to fake letters and send trouble in sealed envelopes to Blair and The Second Mrs. Panofsky's mother to humiliate them. He is helplessly revengeful when he forges letters of nuisance and takes child-like delight after redirecting supplicants to disturb Blair after Miriam deserts Barney. He feigns concerns for Blair of whom he is noxiously jealous and takes effort to wipe him out of his life. All his efforts would have been worthy but for his one moment of sin which he suffered primarily because of a wonky-system of values. The memoir itself is a sweet revenge he takes on all whom he could not win over in life. The list includes Blair, Caroline, Terry and to an extent Miriam.

Harvey Schwartz, the Gursky's former employee, is the senator in *Barney's Version*. As a crime-accessory to the Gursky Empire he graduates from his squalid living street conditions to a penthouse in Westmount. As an inside trader, currency speculator, property-flipper, hostile-takeover-bidder-cum-asset-stripper, tax evader Harvey is another Boy Wonder who travels on the flyway of transgression.

Celebration of physical pleasure began to be recorded in extravagant detail in *Beautiful Losers* (1969) by Leonard Cohen. It gave a break through psychic and social censorship and is a guide to the mid-1960s sentiments. Richler's works abound with the protagonists' sexual activities. Duddy's indulges in amateur experiments of the body. Noah trespasses and usurps his Professor's wife Miriam. Jake's youthful experiments with girls culminate with the perfect wife, giving him an ache that Nancy has punctuated his sexual adventures. But his Id traps him into a much-publicized scandal in which he played a negligent part. Joshua's rapturous primal youth sexual activities including the one in Ibiza, his fake homosexual scandal and his wife's list of lovers along with Barney's trio marriages record the growing fantasy of sexual activities in all forms that constituted the social life of the mid and late twentieth century.

Hypocrisy – Signs, Gestures and Language

> "Every act of unmasking, critiquing, and opposition uses the tools it condemns and risks falling prey to the practice it exposes"; (Vesser xi)

Richler rips open with caustic teeth the contrived niceties that glossed the Westmount living. Spiritless deep-sighs at fund-raising dinners, empty head-nods in an effort to empathize victims, plastic smiles of recognition and machinated heart(y) laughs add to the pseudo-socialistic trends. Pauline is never able to adapt herself to the synthetic-society of Westmount where people effortlessly feigned concerns to pry into her life. Her friends especially Jane manufactured the ills of the masked society. It made Pauline sick to the point of insanity. She declines all invitations to glitzy dinners and is happy only to be with her family. The hypocritical claws of the Westmount crowd nearly kill her. After being acquitted of murder, Barney is more accepted by the Westmount snooty wives. They were delighted when he accepted the heinous deed rather than deny it. The Westmount society accredited superficial grandeur, money, white-collar crime and extravagant exhibitionism.

Richler satirizes Mackenzie King's hypocrisy in his two extended accounts of the William Mackenzie King Memorial Society. King is ridiculed as a hypocrite and anti-Semite. The members of the society are ambitious and solipsists and as Ramraj observes "try to outdo one another in subtly announcing their various achievements and who snub those with lesser intellectual and cultural attainments" (111). Richler's cynical description of King's wealth, his association with mediums and ethereal appearances of his dead mother are passages of hilarity unveiling the political mask (*JTN* 138). Richler points out that King was recklessly amassing wealth. In 1920 King had purchased a lot of land "to prevent a sale to Jews, who have a desire to get in at Kingsmere and would ruin the whole place, possibly by opening a *kosher* delicatessen" (*JTN* 137). Ironically, a year after the end of World War II, King in his address to Jews empathizes their plight: "For the Jewish people the recent war had an especial significance.

The way of life of all free peoples was threatened by Nazi and Fascist aggression. In addition, the Jewish people had the even sterner realization that for them it was not only a way of life, but life itself that was at stake" (*JTN* 129). Richler further exposes that King in 1934 met Adolf Hitler and glorified his kindred spirit and noted that the world would rank Hitler someday with Joan of Arc and deliverer of Europe. Richler continues the irony by noting that, "Just as he died thunder and lightning and torrents of rain came without any warning. The rain fell only at Kingsmere, not in Ottawa" (*JTN* 138). Richler with his crafty skill uses history and avenges the hypocritical King through his storyline where an annual day in honour of the scheming old fraud King was organized at Kingsmere by the FFHS team ruining the whole place with champagne to tease hiss efforts to buy a lot of land to avoid a Jewish enterprise. The meeting is also an act of angry defiance against King and his politics. Joshua echoes Richler in his conversation with the senator who was on King's war-time cabinet, "I was never an admirer of Mr. King" (*JTN* 134).

Richler vehemently laughed at all forms of pretention. Jake prefers a WASP to a Jewish lawyer because he wanted, "no twisting, eloquent point scorer who would outwit judge and prosecutor, eat witnesses, alienate the jury, shine so foxily in court in fact as to ultimately lose him the case" (*SUH* 179). The Jewish boys feigned, lied and contrived situations to claim attention from an otherwise inattentive society. In one of Joshua's attempts to impress a girl in his youth, he took on a pseudo identity claiming out to be Robert Jordan, a Mc Gill student to allure and dine out with Bessie who later becomes Yossel's wife. Barney says, "… I must say I was not the real me in those days but an impersonator" (*BV 190).* It was masking that Barney had adopted to regain himself after the Clara disaster and get footing in the Jewish community of Montreal which finally gets him entangled with The Second Mrs. Panofsky. Saul derides Mike's deception especially pretending to be a vegetarian to please his wife but digs into a huge steak when in New York and goes out of his way to bait Aviva.

Richler's microscopic eyes dig into every facet of masking of the rich Jewry. Becky Schwartz gestures her husband to order caviar at Ritz since the Moffats were watching them inspite of Harvey's distaste to it. Becky lived a life of exhibitionism, throwing extravagant parties in their Westmount mansion. Richler unmasks the phony The Second Mrs. Panofsky who read not for pleasure but to keep up her talks at dinner parties. She flaunts her rich lineage, littered her conversations with starry names and classy places of visit. She suffered from verbosity and spoke with endless effusions, insensitive to dumb listeners who muted her voice and waited to snap the conversation. The most laugh-aloud account is her shopping spree where she squeezes a fortnight schedule into a tight three-day extravaganza, fanatically induced by book-marked advertisements. She went window shopping at elite shops to borrow brand names for party conversations and bought at discounted shops, collecting fabricated heavy bills and sewing labels of renowned names.

Richler's depiction of Hymie in *Barney's Version* is tragically comic. His life is a portrait of a rollicking star who endlessly entertained people at parties. But he wept over innumerable former wives, broken relationships, unsettled children and endless financial drain. Norman Charnofsky in a remorseful retrospection of his self blames that he had unconsciously been subjected to hypocritical ways in order to be seen as a more benevolent, pro-feminine person as criticized by Jessy and Shirley.

Duddy is pimply with hypocritical gestures. His pseudo signs are a resource for business contracts and to exhibit his materialistic acumen. In his encounter with Hersh in the music shop, an FFHS mate he pretends a happy reunion. But Hersh says, "Why pretend we're friends, Duddy? We hated each other at school" (*DK 223).* Davidson notes, "Through that authorial dispassion Richler also examines the hypocrisies of many (Gentiles and Jews) most honest and honorable than Duddy" (81). Noah protests against people who raise his father's death to martyrdom.

Bernard's hypocritical statements of fidelity are broken when Kathleen O'Brian reveals her intimacy with the old man. The revolting Isaac smirks at his father's religious pontifications as hypocritical because he knew that Henry, whom everybody counted as a holy man, hid a lot of filthy photographs in his desk. Children question Jewish practices and double standards. When Moses smokes on the Sabbath day, Isaac questions how come Uncle Moses was allowed to do so while he was not allowed to play hockey or even watch TV. Noah also questions in the same way.

Richler opines to Gibson that we "live in chaos without any agreed-upon system of values which we can refer to, and so the more we disentangle from the hypocrisies of our background, the more chaotic our life becomes" (289). The act of masking and unmasking is indicative of a superficial system of society in existence.

Tools of Moral Policing

The protagonists use their deviance and transgressions also as a tool for moral policing the hypocritical families and societies. In an attempt to moral police the pseudo nature of his tribe, Noah transgresses, returns, questions, endures, breaks and sails away. What may be considered as a transgression for the ghetto people is a flight into freedom. This bon voyage towards finding one's voice and identity is repeated in Jake Hersh of *St. Urbain's Horseman* who appears as Hersh in *Duddy Kravitz.* He is an extension of Noah who sails for Europe and further returns to Montreal as Joshua, the prodigal Son in *Joshua Then and Now* and settles as an aged Barney in Westmount in *Barney's Version.*

Moments of moral-policing are seen in other characters too. Duddy liberally forges Virgil's signature and brutally involves in acts of fraudulency, severing his lone, selfless well-wishers to spiral up socially. Favouring a scrap deal for Mr. Cohen, a Jew, from the white Mr. Calder, Duddy moral polices an anti-Semite society, fitting as the ring master of the game and earning a commission for it. He informs an unhappy Calder that the business was to make him look less hostile, less anti-Semite and to enlarge a white man's reputation in the public opinion. From a pimply Duddy in *Duddy Kravitz* to a million-dollar business man in *Barney's Version,* Duddy acquires more than one land and sets up his empire. He flies a first class on a 747 instead of a Concorde so that he could walk through the economy class to show a society that condemned his Street roots.

While Jake is a brooding avenger, loaded with guilt, his alter-ego Joey whips and lashes on his horse championing for his men. Although Joey is a gambler, liar and bigamist, he like Solomon stands apart from the rest of the crowd. He rides above the victim position and is a master of his own destiny. Both Joey and Solomon disappear and reappear without clues. Compelled to cross-over the towering ghetto-wall, they literally and metaphorically fly planes to take wings and overcome the barrier. Joey returns home with a commercial pilot's license and Solomon flies his Gypsy Moth. They never wanted to be mute observers of a victimized society. As Jake frequently questioned, 'What are we going to do about it?', Joey had his own ruthless means to avenge the situation. He burst into the cigar stores, barber shops, urging and mocking at men, questioning what they intended to do about such insults. Solomon the large-scale crook, answers the question by championing Jews through negotiating talks with people in power, financial help, raising funds and hilariously avenging and scaring a group of invited elite non-Jews for a *Passover* with bleeding *'matzohs'.*

When in trouble or in near discovery of truth, Joey and Solomon flee or destroy themselves, not out of fear, but change their station of operation, leaving behind traces of colossal wreck. After Joey's disappearance, his car was discovered upended and gutted, burned out alongside the road to New York. Solomon's Gypsy Moth bursts and strewn parts are seen in the barrens. Unlike Kevin, Pauline's brother he does not kill himself but fabricates a scene of self-destruction. Later in his avatar as Sir Hyman Kaplansky drowns himself vouching his story with the left behind glasses, slippers and stick on the beach. These men will not allow themselves to be trapped, tried, punished, charged or even questioned by a society that is hypocritical and unjust to them and their men. Elusive, they fly on horseback or plane, to continue their mission.

Joey is also believed to be the '*Golem*'. Joey and Solomon are avengers of a society that dehumanize and marginalize their tribe. They are brave, mythical and magical in their ways. They are the alter-egos, incarnation of courage, respect and dignity, the supermen of the troubled conscience of helpless ordinary men like Jake and Moses. Jake is shocked when he hears of Joey's death: "He wept because the Horseman, his conscience, his mentor, was no more" (*SUH* 460). Robin Noel calls Duddy, Jake and Moses as protagonists and Jerry, Joey and Solomon as their heroes. Duddy surpasses his local hero, the Boy-Wonder whom he adores initially. He does not chase but outshines him in the economic rat race. Noel notes, while the protagonists are "self-aware, conscious of themselves as world citizens, ethically paralyzed and class bound" Joey and Solomon are "compensatory heroes…not bound by class, geography, or history…communicate through action than speech…traverse the globe…represent the epitome of male honour" (92).

Moses fights for justice as a moral editor of the Gursky Empire. His obsession is not merely with Solomon but with truth. "As far as Callaghan was concerned, what redeemed the young Moses so quick to anger, was that he had not yet grasped that the world was imperfect. He actually expected justice to be done" (*SG 163).*

Joshua apart from his "developmental defects" of borderline Kleptomania, breaks into the homes of Westmount colleagues to commit such malicious acts of vandalism such as peeling labels off vintage wines, cunning defacing of valuable paintings and planting stolen money. As Frank Davey observes, Joshua at times dons as a lone-artist burglar to avenge as an outcast, "self-styled hero" and in his own term as a "heroic" defender (256). He vandalized to punish the pompous and threatening Westmount '*kosher*' people and friends like Pinsky who eye his wife. He brings along with him nabbing and jabbing from St. Urbain's Street to Westmount, to rob not wealth but vanity and as Eric Wright observes "the victims' egos" (373). "The general figure of criminality operates throughout the novel as the renegade individual's answer to a culture of greed and hypocrisy" (Davey 136). Greenstein notes that Joshua with Maimonides' *Guide for the Perplexed* struggles through the labyrinths of history against his own confusions and unmasks those characters hiding behind the superficial facade of a present concealing their roots. "An interloper and a vandal, Josh rewrites history for those who seek to forget" (*TS* 157).

The Second Mrs. Panofsky and her bunch of people were Barney's undesirables. He found them snobbish and yanking at safe distance in opulence being severed from their miserable brethren. Barney avoided the dining table talks with the Panofskys because it was the golf versus hockey talks. Golf is a game of the rich and hockey was the favorite of the rest. Barney was more anxious about the Stanley cup results than his own wedding which was on the same day. On their travel junket Barney follows her as on a porter's appointment. His intolerance towards an ostentatious living style of his second wife and the necessity to get married to Miriam manipulates the Jewess-Boogie scandal and heads for a divorce. Thus, Barney puts an end as a pretentious couple of being an ideal man with a deserving wife.

Barney hated his production job but still pursued it to ensure a free flow of money. Miriam questions Barney, "You hate those TV shows you produce, and you're filled with contempt for just about everybody who works on them. Why don't you give it up before it gives you cancer?" (*BV 166).* This act of self-immolation in pursuing a career which he hated is to provide a good life to his family. It is an act of an insincere indulgence to moral police a hypocritical society that marginalized him.

Guy Vanderhaeghe in the Afterword to the novel writes, "... I naturally assumed myself untainted by the hypocrisy, pretense, and stupidity. Mordecai Richler so savagely pilloried, and I reveled in this exuberant novel without too many anxious second thoughts"

(*SUH* 463). Richler took fierce delight in laughing wickedly at people who could never speak their mind. He guffawed at the pretensions of his society, human venality and vanity in all forms in a postmodern civilized era.

Prestigious moments

Veeser notes Greenblatt: "Society's dominant currencies, money and prestige, are invariably involved" (*Introduction* xii). Circulation for new historicists involves not just money and knowledge but also "prestige-the 'possession' of social assets as evanescent as taste in home furnishings or as enduring as masculinity" (*Introduction* xi). This is found in Gurskys' owning and furnishing mansions in Outremont and Westmont as assets of prestige symbol. The novel also deals with how the Schwartz trade richness for uprightness. The main reason for the protagonists' treason and transgression is to cross boundaries to mimic gentile richness and 'circulate' prestige. The idyllic setting of Joshua's house with a garden and Duddy's possession of land are evidences of this circulation. Yvette tells Duddy when he gets everything inside the Mount Royal house sold to save the last forty-five hundred dollars needed to buy the last strip of the land, "There's not a decent sentiment in your body" (*DK 296).* Duddy pines, "All I needed was to be born rich" (*DK 298).* Noah trades with infidelity to buy the freedom and comfort of gentiles, which he discovers is a failure. Joshua fakes a homosexual affair to trade fame and popularity and Barney trades with crap production for a home and living.

> Symbolic capital accrues in the ruses used to enhance one's social standing in the marriage mart, or in the symbolic meal given in the mason's honour when a house is built – a bonus disguised as gift. All such practices have cash equivalents and aim, even if unconsciously, at material advantages. (Vesser *Introduction* xi)

Richler's men are prone to be materialistic because of being born into poor homes. The primary circulation of the protagonists includes trading morality for status and prestige. There are instances of Jews' marriage with Gentiles to trade tradition for social advantages as in Jake and Joshua. Ephraim trades religion for power. In studying the dilemmas of the protagonists all transgress to trade morality for physical or materialistic pleasures except Noah. Noah's search involves the soul-satisfying quest for truth and human values. Even when rewarded materially he is not happy, he breaks with Miriam and gets back home. His search is one at the moral and spiritual level which cannot be liquidated to materialistic values. Although most of Richler's characters exchange goods and morality for cash equivalents in terms of money, business, mansions, tasteful houses, prized wives to escalate social status, people like Noah and also Henry search for non-material values. Ideals and virtues when withheld for moral claims cannot be calculated in terms of materialistic value as suggested by New Historicists. Smicha and Henry hint a non-cash equivalent exchange system. But they do not sustain till the end. This could be a symbolic profit. The tell-tales of Smicha are limited and expresses only one aspect and that too symbolic of the material profit in hinting to Duddy the need for a man to own land. Henry's saint-like life covers the tabooed pictures which he enjoyed secretly. Hence it is discussed that there are no real spiritual nomads in Richler's world, who trade for truth and freedom like Jesus and Gandhi whose negotiations cannot be reduced to cash equivalents. But all of Richler's men are governed with the principal motive of materialistic profit, except an undecided, ambivalent Noah.

Transgressions in Richler's novel begin with childhood kleptomania, then the primal experimentation of bodies and relationships, criminal as in Duddy and Solomon and sexual at times including fake sexual and asexual claims as in Jake, Joshua and Barney. These transgressions trade morality, integrity for social advantage and escalation of economic status, a compulsion induced by the surrounding spaces of the protagonists to bridge the Jew-Gentile gap and acts as tools for moral policing the hypocritical families and societies that compelled these transgressions in varied ways. Thus, as Woodcock observes, "The great collective crimes are committed with the consent of men and women who cling to such private caves of withdrawal, who cannot recognize the brutalities of a world they support by default" (*Introduction SH* xi). Doug Fraser in his script on *Accident* outlines the reasons for accident-prone drivers as: "*An inability to adjust to the codes of society* and a common trait of "*An underlying aggressiveness directed against authority*" (*SUH* 154-155). This may be true of the moral accidents that occur in the select novels.

This section of the chapter presents how Jewish individuals responded to the strictures of the Jew-Gentile divided society, the choices they made and the flyways they opted. It discusses how the Self is obviously influenced and fashioned by social-constructs but to accept or reject such patterns of fashioning falls into an existential trope. This gave rise to resistance, aggression, rebellion, transgression or transformation. These men out of their restricted identity emerged socially, geographically and economically through the most opted route of transgression. The following subdivisions focus on how people at any level of society exercise control over others within the same society such as families on individuals and man or woman and vice-versa.

3.3 Knots and Ties

The Jewish community has a celebrated communal life where familial and marital relationships are part of their great tradition. The *Jewish Family Life and Customs* states that, "Families are the building block of society and Jewish law and tradition highlights the centrality of the Jewish family". It can be traced that family is a strong influence on Richler's protagonists, where they imbibed or shunned their traditional and hypocritical value systems.

Family and belongingness are strong and ambivalently dealt in the novels. Richler throws light on the Post-Modern effect of breaking up of extended families, with sons leaving the ghetto on moral delusion as in Noah or for career prospects like Jake and Joshua. In both cases the ghetto a part of the Canadian experience is cast off. Jake contrives visits for family occasions to Montreal; but his gentile wife was unwelcomed. Duddy stays in Montreal, frequenting business tours abroad and Barney refuses to leave his Montreal home. Joshua returns to Montreal and sets up a home around Lake Memphremagog. While Noah fears that familial ties would clog and strangle him with its vicious tentacles and retreats into narrow individualism, the magical Solomon sets up an empire and aviates across the globe. When in conflict, Duddy, Jake, Joshua and Barney end up finding an answer in home. For them home is the final recreation of the self and this is liberally dealt in the novels.

Noah Adler's story reflects the pressures applied on an individual by polity. Exasperated he remarks, "I should have had the right to begin with my birth" (*SH* 62). His conflicts arise from his love-hate relationship with his family and community. Although Noah leaves home in search of his moral compass, there are family moments and belongingness to which he was attached. His innate goodness and loyalty save his grandfather's reputation veiling the life-long affection for a gentile woman. He "blankets" his father's foolishness, a misconceived act of heroism of saving the *'Torah'* while Wolf risked his life for Melech's cash box. He also refrains from telling the truth that the grandfather's youngest son had set ablaze the scrap yard. His selfless kindness from time to time is the "Noah's ark" that saves the family from drowning in dishonour. He hated the hypocrisy of the family and not his family.

Inspite of his rugged ways and wicked pranks, Duddy is protective of his family. "What a family, Duddy thought, what a bunch we are" (*DK 229).* He tells Lennie that he'll take up a job as a waiter to help him pay his fees. Duddy avenges a soft MacPherson, the teacher for accusing his father of irresponsibility: "Nobody gets away with insulting my old man" (*DK 10).* This sense of protection is seen in Joshua too. He is intolerant to Uncle Oscar's humiliation of his father Reuben and abuses him. Togetherness and coming together is a part of the Jewish family tradition as Mrs. Hersh puts it, "we stick together you know. In a crisis we always stick together" (*SUH* 44). A similar spirit is echoed in Joshua, "Pauline called out. "Ding a ling". And Joshua, filled with delight, thought, they, were some family. We really are some family" (*JTN 40).*

Jake Hersh is contemptuous of the imposing identity of the Hershes in Montreal. He despises their "self-contained world" that failed to focus on reality of their brethren. His anxiety of imbibing a callous attitude is echoed, "We're all becoming our fathers" (*SUH* 288). Greenstein remarks that Jake in order to moral police the hypocritical families with his "allsorts bag of anarchy" cause "border troubles and destroy, self-contained worlds" (*TS* 154). Jake's non-conformism to the ritualistic practices is similar to Noah and in his quest to create a real world, grooms a Diaspora family raised from his mixed-marriage.

Joshua Then and Now is more of a domestic drama on marriage and family. It revolves around the lives of Joshua and his wife Pauline along with Reuben and the senator as guardian angels: "Two old men, Reuben and the senator, guarded against intruders" (*JTN 4)*. Family is a solace for Joshua after a breathtaking rat race of fame, fortune and scandal. He feels accepted when he is with his family and they cheer his presence. Josh prided: "me, Joshua Shapiro, My family" (77). After all the battles in Joshua's life the novel ends with the "family tableau" on togetherness. "Joshua wasn't leaning on his cane; Pauline was supporting him" (*JTN 370)*. Eric Wright in his Afterword to the novel observes that it ends with winning the battle for honour, decency and love. Like Joshua, Jake Hersh retreats to the peace and love of his family with Nancy and his three children.

While the earlier novels are based on individual lives, *Solomon Gursky* widens its focus on four generations of a family. *Barney's Version* is a tale of Barney's trio marriages and his family. An analysis of the bond between the grandfathers and grandsons, fathers and sons, mothers and sons and mothers and daughters is done to understand the intricacies of relationship.

The 'zeyda'

Montreal lapped stranded Jewish immigrants whose preferred destinations were either New York or Toronto. Grandfathers in Richler's novels have been instrumental in rooting their Jewish stems in Montreal, many a time accidently or for want of money to travel further. Duddy's grandfather Smicha's CPR ticket took him only till Montreal although he headed for Toronto. He settles as a shoe-maker in Dominique Street in Montreal. Barney's grandfather; a ritual slaughterer immigrated to Canada from Budapest because he had only twenty-five dollars and could never reach New York. For Jake's great grandfather Montreal was the chosen destination where he begets an enormous family of fourteen children and his brother limited to twelve, while their disowned brother Baruch, Joey's grandfather had three children.

The grandfathers toiled hard to root their grafted families. They were honest and hardworking and stood by the value system of their Jewish tradition. Although a shoe-maker, Smicha commanded respect for himself and family. Boogie's grandfather Moishe Moscovitch rose by dint of hard work and parsimony from a pushcart chicken peddler to sole proprietor of a '*kosher*' butcher shop and then into Peerless Gourmet Packers. Melech, the grandfather of Noah is a prototype of the deceitful Jew in trade but hails as the King of his family. He was a coal merchant who dealt in scrap and old tires as a side-business. Joshua's grandfather started a scrapyard after prohibition and had ended his services as a wheelman on the back roads leading into Vermont, no longer needed and had finally begun to make what the Shapiros considered big money with office on King Street. Ephraim is the *'zeyda'* of the Gursky crime Empire.

The moral compass plays an important role in the rapport between the grandfathers and grandsons. Grandfathers of Noah and Duddy are the pivotal point in their grandsons' lives. Melech's deceitful dealing sends Noah running away from tradition and Smicha's inflexible morality and misconceived advice sends Duddy running after money. Melech tells Noah, "I wanted you to be a somebody. Something. Something not like them" (*SH 39).* Smicha echoes Melech, "A man without a land is nobody" (*DK 48).* Melech, who wanted to make Noah "a something" feels punished by an upright Noah's decision to sail away. "*Goyim. Goyim.* Now go. Go. Go. Join, become my enemy" (*SH* 55). Arnoldson writes, "Melech has to have the *goyim* and the ghetto as his excuse for being Melech" (55). Smicha punishes Duddy with his deadly silence as a sign of reprisal, who becomes "a somebody" by cheating. *Smaller Hero* begins with the estrangement between Melech and Noah while *Duddy Kravitz* ends with a rift between Smicha and Duddy.

Joshua learns from his father that his great-grandfather in Russia used to mutilate the Jews who wished to avoid the Czar's decree of Jewish conscription to the Russian army. Joshua's preoccupation with his manhood begins with this story of physical castration that proceeds to the haunting lines of Dr. Dr. Mueller's "Are you a man or mouse?" His father Reuben chaperoned the grand-children as a caring *'zeyda'* when both Joshua and Pauline collapse.

The *'zeyda'*-Ephraim and Solomon combo is the most unique of all Richler's grand-relations. It echoes the Baruch-Joey combination in *St. Urbain's Horseman*, although the two had not met but Joey gallivanted and rebelled truly like his grandfather. Solomon-Ephraim's trip to the North, their love-hate relationship and the cruel lessons of survival and mystical tactics of living are the basis on which Solomon raises the Gursky dynasty. Ephraim is the hyperbolized imagination of adventure and success that all other Richler's fictional *'zeydas'* never even dreamt of. While the others passed over to their grandsons nuggets of pain-filled advices of a spent life such as "Be somebody" and "Be something", Ephraim outwits them by whisking off the school-going Solomon to the far-far of North Canada and exposing him to his maniacal adventures and engineering of the Gursky tribe. Although a "quirky-companion" and a cranky grandfather Ephraim fed Solomon with doses of wisdom, sometimes even in the middle of a sleep. He taught Solomon the hard way, a heap of skills – Latin verbs, map-reading, hunting, sledging, navigating and aviating skills.

> Since the name "Ephraim" means "fruitful", Richler riffs on the meaning of the name by having Ephraim Gursky scatter his seed far and wide in Europe and Canada. He becomes patriarch to the Gursky family after first impregnating various Inuit tribes in the far

> North. These northern tribes imprinted with his name are ever after known as Gor-ski, Girskee, Gur-ski, and Goorsky. (Craniford 112)

In their own ways the families' fulcrum and the points of reference in the protagonists' lives are the grandfathers. They are either a mine of traditions and values like Smicha or at times the directory of hypocritical values like Melech or diction of criminality like Ephraim. The Jewish cultural memory that the grandfathers and grandsons shared can be best worded through a nineteenth century Franco-Jewish proverb – "The grandfather believes, the father doubts, the son denies". The *'zeyda'* thus becomes the seed of the families, making, marking or breaking rules.

Fictioned parents and children

Richler in *Barney's Version* records the everyday life of Jeanne Mance Street mothers who force-fed their sons with stories of inspiration to pursue medicine, cheated on the grocery money or bargained tough with French Canadian farmers to save money for books. These show the mothers' urge to groom their sons to outgrow the ghetto life. Brenner observes, "To "do very well" away from the Montreal "ghetto" has become the parents' most cherished ambition for their children" (87). Richler in *The Street* records that the mothers on St. Urbain read stories from *Life* of Harvard graduates and M.I.T nerds. The children were forbidden to memorize baseball batting averages or dirty limericks but improve Word Power with *Digest* and gain inspiration from Paul De Kruif's medical biographies.

> No sooner had (our grandparents and parents) unpacked their bundles and cardboard suit-cases than they were planning a better, brighter life for us, the Canadian born children. The Main, good enough for them, was not to be for us, and that they told us again and again what was the struggle for. The Main was for "bummers," drinkers, and (heaven forbid) failure. (70)

The focal point of parenting anchored on financial provision for children. Brenner explains that the parents set financial, material success and fame as goalposts. Preoccupied with wealth and social recognition the parents failed to insist traditional, cultural and moral value system for younger generation.

Richler talks about his father as an, "Insufficient straw, *NO SUCCESS* story of his life" (*HSH* 57). Repeated failures and criticism marked the life of Moses Richler. This poignant story of an unsuccessful man is ingrained in the fictional fathers, Wolf Adler and Issy Hersh. Wolf's failure as a "smaller hero" is an effect of Melech's patriarchal tyranny. As a defeated man he is of little source of inspiration to Noah unlike the pampering fathers of Joshua and Barney. Noah like Moses had a mixed feeling towards his father. For Noah it was one of pity and fear and he did not want to become another "smaller hero". Moses despises his father's decision to become a speech writer and scribe for the Gurskys. It is this anger and tryst with truth that sets off his quizzical venture to solve the Solomon-mystery. He reflexively reaches out to Solomon for a surrogate father. The doctor points it out: "that your obsession with Solomon Gursky can be explained by your self-evident search for a father, having dismissed your own as unacceptable" (*SG 223).* Moses wanted Sir Hyman to look upon him as a son. The Henry-Isaac umbilical cord is disjointed and as Foran says "lethal" of all (545).

Duddy shares a comrade relationship with his father. Max Kravitz tries in small ways to cheer him. He applauds the third-class holder on the graduation day, while Lennie, Uncle Benjy and Smicha were reserved. He does not approve Duddy's deviant ways and constantly reminded him not to embarrass him. But he delightfully repeated Duddy's success story to onlookers like the Boy Wonder's tale. Issy Hersh constantly insists on Jewish roots to the expatriate Jake and disapproves his marriage to the gentile Nancy. He sends him a parcel containing a Jewish calendar, listing holidays to be observed, a skullcap and a prayer book to remind Jewish observances.

Reuben Shapiro is the savior of a mortally wounded Joshua. He is one man who does not suffer wifely disrespect of Richler's fictitious fathers. He is armoured with a doting wife and an equally tender, affectionate son. Joshua learnt a lot to be "big" from his father's prizefighter's album. He is the most resourceful of the fictional fathers who could save Joshua. With years of unlawful experience, he skillfully bribes and dupes the scavenger journalist greedy for morsels of Joshua's story and devices the master plan to free Joshua from the crooked cop's blackmail.

Izzy Panofsky the Jew-cop strictly observes professional ethics. Barney inherits his sense of humour and non-observant Jewish ways. The two drink at the Dink's to mourn the death of the mother instead of sitting *Shiva.* The father-son rapport echoes the Max-Duddy buddy-bond. Barney of all select protagonists dons the role of an aged-father. He largely plays the role of a provider in the family. "My parental role had largely been confined to providing a good life, teasing the kids at the table, leaving Miriam to settle disputes..." (*BV 133).* Barney has a hard relationship with his first son Mike, a better one with Saul and a close one with his daughter Kate.

Fathers persist with clichéd advices and models of success just as Max repeats the Boy Wonder formula to Duddy until Duddy becomes his success story as a boy born "with a rusty spoon in his mouth" (*DK 315).* Joshua's father insists on morality through idiosyncratic Biblical lectures, Issy Hersh with practical nuggets: "*You have to be discovered"* (*SUH* 102) and "Making money isn't everything" (*SUH* 103) and his airmailed parcels with letters of Jewish wisdom. Izzy's airmail letters with built-in satirical stings are similar in notion. Richler's fictioned fathers bear the onus of a failed Moses Richler, whom the sons love but do not want to relive their lives. Their failed lives indirectly inspire material success.

Richler's literary men relate with reserved affection with their mothers which reverberates the author's strained relationship with his own mother Leah Rosenberg. Leah's leaving Moses Richler is repeated in the characterization of Joshua's mother and Miriam leaving Barney. Foran in the E-mail communication notes:

> The soul-defining moment involved discovering the remarkable letter that Richler wrote to his mother in 1976. On reading it, I realized it

> was a key to understanding his character, and many of the decisions he had made in his life, and once I thought it through, I realized that the 'narrative' of his terrible relationship with Lily Rosenberg was perhaps one of two key underpinnings to the biography. (The other was his marriage to Florence.)

Richler treats the fictional mothers with less dignity and sympathy. They are not the clichéd legendary Jewish mothers who doted over their sons, feeding food, stories and ambitions of pursuing medicine. They were discontent beings, unsatisfied with their marriage to failure-prone husbands. Apart from being a stinging wife Leah, Noah's mother is an ace homemaker, prissy with details of home-keeping. Davidson observes, "Leah is, in some respects, the standard caricature of the Jewish mother and a master at manipulating through applied guilt" (50). Leah plays an emotional blackmail when Noah plans to leave home. She is the unsung queen of the "smaller hero" Wolf and yearns to graduate from St Lawrence Boulevard to Park Avenue Street. Duddy's mother Minnie died when he was a child and hence Duddy lacked maternal rearing that makes him a puzzle. Greenstein observes that the absence of the mother points out to "an absent origin for his homelessness" in Duddy. He further associates that Duddy in order to compensate the missing mother in his life, turns to the land, "an illusory Mother Earth, for a sense of security and rootedness" (*TS* 147). Jake Hersh has a guilt-inducing mother. The fussy Mrs. Hersh cherished Jake's atrocious, "ice cruelty" towards her as "acts of filial kindness" (*SUH* 32).

Mothers of Joshua and Barney grudgingly tend their Jewish homes. Joshua's mother Esther born into Outremont affluence, defied a cultivated family and married into a family of thugs on the grubby street. Joshua could never draw her attention as she was a self-absorbed woman smitten by her husband. "My mother has never given a damn what I do and so far as my father's concerned, anything that makes me happy if fine with him" (*JTN 132*). However Esther has a protective son and consistently bestows affection even after she becomes increasingly promiscuous and a porno star. Even as an embarrassed son of a cockamamie mother who performed a strip tease dance at his *'Bar mitzvah'*, he never outgrows his warmth for her. Later Esther Shapiro turned Esty Blossom supports Joshua in his period of disgrace by marching with placards to establish his innocence. She was an active member of the women's cause and was on the executive board of parents of gay in Canada. Although an indifferent mother she had an attachment to the son. Of all the mother-son relationship in the select novels, Joshua and Esther are the closest. An aging Esther Shapiro and Mrs. Hersh simmer with envy against their ravishing beautiful daughters-in-law. Barney's mother like Esther is negligent, indifferent to report cards, TV glued and self-obsessed person, who finds time for him between commercial breaks. One of her gestational wish for Barney was that he should grow up to be a radio personality. Barney partly realized his mother's dream by becoming a TV producer.

The only visible father-daughter relationship is between the Senator and Pauline. His paternal protective nature is revealed in his conversion with Joshua, "I am afraid Pauline's not much disposed to happiness. Neither was her mother" (*JTN* 133), "Take care of Pauline, I love her" (*JTN* 135). Similarly, there are no significant mother-daughter relationships but for Miriam and Kate in *Barney's Version.* It was one of tension and argument and Kate was naturally more loving towards Barney. Kate could never accept Miriam leaving her father nor could be better associated with Blair. She tells her father, "We used to be some family. I can't forgive Mom for leaving you" (*BV 133).* She is constantly concerned about her father, the lonely Barney.

Communication gap exists between the children and the elders of the family because of the different ideals they held. It was Barney and Joshua with their uncaring mothers, Solomon with Ephraim and Moses with his father. Barney recalls that the closest he ever came with his mother was when he had performed her favourite tap dance when she was ill. Solomon as a young kid struggles to understand the enigmatic Ephraim and longs to touch him with affection. Joshua recalling his mother notes that he "could do nothing to please her" (*JTN 9).* "Moses clung to his father, constantly searching for new ways to earn his love" *(SG 15).* The ideological gap that existed between the third-generation immigrants, their parents and grandparents also contribute to conflicts in identity in the select novels. Thus, families with their traditional and hypocritical value system signposted directions for the protagonists, who by their choice 'self-fashioned' their lives in an (un)Greenblatt way.

While Richler has a galaxy of male characters, he suffers from a deficit of women characters. Nonetheless, limited in number and expression, these women attract, influence, support, distract the men and co-create the spirit of their age.

3.4 Gender Roles

> A bungled Joshua tells Pauline, "I don't understand women and their relationships, I really don't" *(JTN 116).*

William New marks that the literary point of view of the 1960s was male (234). Hutcheon writes that with Cohen's *Beautiful Losers* began the so-called sexual revolution and questioning of sex and gender roles has been a major force behind the continued development of the novel on women written by both men and women.

Richler's novels are male-dominated. A typical Richler's man is a Jew and woman a gentile. The gentile women are seen as passages to the world of freedom for the ghettoed Jews. Noah seeks liberation with his short-lived unmarried bliss with Miriam Theo. His Orthodox grandfather had sought it a few years ago and Uncle Max with Miss Holmes, the blonde secretary. Woodcock in his introduction writes, "These men of the ghetto yearn towards the feminine personifications of what seems a freer world beyond the invisible walls" (*SH* x).

Women in Richler's early novels are subjected to Essentialism, like the ones in his grandfather's Shmarya's home as Foran notes were "largely silent figures, moving from room to room like discreet servants" (22). His novels are based on male experiences and lack feminine sensitivity. Unlike Ian McLachlan's *Helen in Exile* (1980)

David Helwig's *Jennifer* (1979) and Jack Ludwig's *A Woman of Her Age* (1973) that is concerned with sexual wars or power relations between men and women, Richler's women exist only in flesh and body. He talks on this to Gibson saying, "... my feminine characters tend to be one-dimensional... the women in my novels tend to be rather idealized creatures" (287-288).

Richler's parade of male characters, both major and minor leaves less room for visible women characters. A woman in Richler's story is reduced to a gross mother, an obsessed wife, a lost lover, a call-girl, a sleep-mate or just a female role that has to exist. They are workers at home, unheard and slogging without much presence like Noah's grandma Jenny or suppressed, manipulative and immoral like Miriam Theo or Pauline (before her second marriage to Joshua) or used for business ends like Yvette, or a whore or striptease dancer. Women on St. Urbain are restricted and are the givens of the society. The rich women flirt as part of socialization. The scents of women are noticed but their senses are ignored. It is not that Richler chauvinistically overlooks them, but he didn't feel the need for them. Richler fails to evolve complete or rounded portraits of women. They are either shadowed or objectified in the galaxy of over-powering male counterparts. This reflects the attitude of the Jewish society towards women.

Voice of a Jewess

Jewish women find less voice and importance right from the historical past. Their roles are stereotyped and limited to domesticity. Rosenberg cites a story of an adventurous Jewish girl who disguised as a boy, arrived in Quebec in 1738 on the ship "St. Michel" commanded by Sallaberie, and was consequently deported (58). This appears as the only story of an independent Jewess immigration into Montreal. In explaining Jewish Feminism, Humm quotes Adrienne Rich who points out how "Jewish women suffer a double disadvantage of being both a target of biological determinism and also invisible in Jewish history" (107).

Women are mostly gentile in Richler's fictional world and the few Jewess did not hail from "The Main". Jenny Hersh the sister of Joey Hersh, is the only Jewess from St. Urbain, with the strength of character and spirit of the "adventurous Jewish girl". Unlike Ida in *Smaller Hero* who dreams and complains, Jenny rises up to shoulder responsibility in a male-absent family. She quits day school, takes up a job and mothers her younger brother Arty. She has a taste for art, literature and plays. She like other St. Urbain youth works to leave the cluttered living and leads the family out of the ghetto, to Toronto. While Richler's Jews flaunt their gentile wives, Jenny exhibits her gentile husband Doug Fraser. As a ghetto-emancipated woman she hosts parties with non-Jewish food. Ironically, she turns showy with the increasing big names at her parties to win a class-race-society that she abhorred.

A mimetic analysis of the select texts uncovers stereotypes of invisible girls and women that characterize the role of the female society of 1950's and forty years later. Mothers were extremely unkind. Clichéd nagging wives of fathers like the sarcastic Mrs. Wolf or the shrew Mrs. Smicha with warts on her face and a sharp tongue, or doting or negligent mothers are some of the typecasts. The characters also included cheaply available lovers like "somebody's gift package" (*BV 30)* or reduced to a *Girl Friday* as Yvette or a hypocritical, infidel Aunt Ida who accused Benjy of castration complex or an unsatisfied Miriam Theo who entertained lovers one after another or a nymphomaniac like Clara, a virago like The Second Mrs. Panofsky or passive supporting beautiful wives, victims of drudgery like Pauline or Nancy. A troubled neurotic Royal Lucy with changing lovers, the daughter of a mad-mother and an absent father also adds to list of blurred women characters. Girls are found strewn all over the novels as paraphernalia to be possessed by men. Girls are commoditized as "female flesh" and are objects whom boys like Duddy gain access. Women were bimbos and silhouettes of them walk in and out of Saul's dark flat in St. Urbain Street.

Richler does not fail to spray his acidic laughter on "overdressed, bejeweled women" benefitted by a series of cosmetic surgery. He is criminally witty on women's infidelity. Hymie's daughter is a woman prone to divorce and remarriage, "Shop, Get pregnant. Marry, divorce. You've heard of serial killers? She is a serial bride" (*BV* 34). The depiction of women as bimbos projects the ideology of the need to be beautiful or only the beautiful are seen as women. The physique is optional for men. An aging, hairy Leo, an established artist has a twenty-two-year-old mistress, a veritable Barbie doll in *Barney's Version*. A beautiful, polio-affected Diana Morgan fears and refuses to runaway with Solomon because she knew that he would resent her imperfection later and his passion and appetite would turn into pity. In her letter to Moses she confides, "Cripples are not the stuff of romance... but such a failing in men is regarded as interesting, even provocative, rather than disfiguring. Women must submit to a more exacting measure" (*SG* 406). The ideology of a beautiful body and ravishing beauty qualifies a girl or a woman to a human status. The others are invisible, doubly displaced as the "Second Sex" and are unwomanly because of a lack of physical features. Bimbos are traded as products in bars and mansions. The position of the bimbos is ambivalent. It is both a socially-constructed and self-imposed, exhibited ideology. But Miriam in *Barney's Version* breaks the stereotyped class.

A reader moves to a point to attribute Richler with Yvette's accusation of Duddy, "You don't know how to treat a woman" (*DK 233).* Nonetheless, Richler narrowly escapes this indictment with his characterization of Miriam in *Barney's Version.* In a 1997 interview with Yanofsky he admits "I think I'm finally pleased with the female characters in this novel... I'm sure being married to the same woman for almost forty years helped" (179). Richler's obvious failure to write on women is salved with his portrayal of Miriam, a Jewess of substance in the whole of Richler's fictional world. Barney says, "ill at ease among so many strangers at the rich, my mood unspeakable until everything changed. Then and forever... there stood the most enchanting women I had ever seen" (*BV 206-207*). Miriam is a subtle tapestry of the bold and beautiful, intelligent and engaging, principled and modern with astonishing grace and endearing of all fictional mothers.

Only through the realizations of feminist aspirations of Miriam, Richler breaks the stereotype of a homemaker which Nancy and Pauline complain but could never overcome. A pragmatic reading of the novels unveils a double discourse especially in the characterization of Nancy, Pauline and Miriam. Nancy begins to complain the loss of self in the monotony of endless chores in mothering three children. Pauline's hectic day makes her feel as a drudge. "I'm a drudge. Well, you've all made me into drudge" (*JTN 115).* While Pauline complains, endures, breaks and returns, Miriam explains and walks out when Barney fails to understand the woman's world and commits an act of infidelity.

Through Miriam, Richler graduates from delineation of passive or hysteric female stereotypes to a prototype of women with self-value and dignity. He touches on the micro politics of the "Third wave" of Feminism with issues on social equality and a space of one's own. Miriam proves that Virginia Woolf's "A room of one's own" is not only the physical space required for the modern woman but also the mental legroom needed to pursue one's interest in a married life. Miriam's walking out of the marriage has two definite reasons. The obvious being her life-governing principle of fidelity in marriage and the shadowy reason of feminist desire to get back to work. Her walk-out is an attack on the sexist ideology of domesticity and breaking of what Humm calls as the "conservative image of women's social condition" (102).

Man-Woman relationship

Barney says to Hymie "I'm committed to a woman in Toronto" (*BV 33).* Commitment in a man-woman relationship is the language of only a few of Richler's men. Jake tries to keep it, Joshua lives by it and Barney pledges his life by it. Duddy does not believe in committing oneself in love to Yvette. He remarks, "Imagine guys getting married and trying themselves down to one single broad for a whole life-time when there's just so much stuff around" (*DK 192).*

Richler justifies Barney as the most responsible husband. He does not desert the sick Clara post-delivery of a still born child that was not his own, until physically fit. Barney was committed to Clara and reassures the reader that he wasn't a wife abuser, but a considerate man who supported Clara's writing posthumously. Barney accepts that he married Clara out of pity, stumbled into a marriage with The Second Mrs. Panofsky out of spite and anger at Clara's judgement of him and swore that he had never been in love before, until he had met Miriam. Miriam is nourished with Barney's profuse expressions of love but starts to suffer from lack of attention when the children leave and she decides that she can no longer be only a homemaker and wants to go for work. It is at the flux of this tension Barney commits his playboy-mistake which eventually makes Miriam walk out of his life.

The thirty-year Barney-Miriam love tale is poetic with selfless, mutual devotion for each other with re-romanticizing instances, love-language of gifts, faithful exchange of expressions of love and moments of standing by each other. After Miriam leaves Barney he says, "I am not only alone but also incomplete" (*BV 274).* Craniford observes that, "It is not the death of Boogie but the death of his marriage that leaves him alone, unhappy and afraid" (131).

Nancy is a woman with "transcendental thoughts" and "high-flown sentiments". She is a solid support to the messed Jake Hersh and a conscious mother who hid the stories and photographs of Jake's trial, keeping the children in the dark of it. Jake's prediction of a rock marriage survives all shaky circumstances. "Marriage is a rotten bourgeois institution. It stinks. I keep up with the times, you know. But Nancy, ours would be something special. A rock" (*SUH* 20). Nancy silently juggles myriad roles during Jake's trying trials. She mutely minced her husband's state of disgrace without creating a tantrum, "Oh, Jake, Jake, my darling, why did you have to go and make such a fool of yourself? And me" (*SUH* 62).

On reading *Solomon Gursky* one is made to guess and awe at Richler's ability to create a woman-less world with abundance of men. The novel is a story of the rich Jews money-making factories but poor family relationships. It succeeds and precedes two family dramas of Joshua and Barney. The novel is void of family get-togethers save the passive, clichéd homes of Henry and Nialie, a scheduled Bernard and Mintzberg couple, a meek Morrie and troubled, hot Ida, a sleep walking, grief-stricken Clara along with the man of many mistresses-Solomon, alive and dead at the same time, a superficial Barney and Darlene affair and a many-husbanded Charna. Moses' maniacal obsession of the Solomon-mystery makes him incapable of a family and let go of a "could-have-been-good-wife" Beatrice or his childhood friend turned lover, Lucy of the Gursky lineage and his other limited moments of fortuitous companionship with others. But Richler does not fail the reader of a fiery love-affair between Solomon and Diana Morgan. Diana is sensible like Miriam in *Barney's Version* and faithful like Yvette in *Duddy Kravitz.* While other novels suffer from promiscuous women like Miriam Theo, Clara and women with a freaky past, Diana is true to life, a sincere lover to Solomon. But their relationship failed because she was terrified with Solomon, his eye of the hurricane spirit, audacity and marked with callousness which she knew would not make their love last long. Diana refuses to runaway with Solomon, unlike Miriam with Noah, for she had an insight that the "fly away to a new and dangerous life" would never be secure, for she felt that he had something dark, deep and "Gursky" about him. Although Diana regretted her decision, she for sure broods over it at a safe distance from a risk-prone relationship: "It seems to me that our lives are consumed by countless wasting years, but only a few shining moments. I missed mine. Yes is what I should have said" (*SG* 407).

Married to the much better, better-halves, Richler's men, time and again fear losing their wives. This fear begins with Jake, continues with Joshua and culminates with Barney. While Nancy stands by the tormenting moments of Jake's scandal, Pauline heads for a nervous breakdown because of Joshua's insensitivity towards her troubles. Miriam walks out of a beautiful marriage because Barney could not stretch more to survive the test of fidelity for over three decades and interestingly, he would have married endlessly had he not met Miriam.

There is an evolution in Richler's characterization of women from a stereotyped woman subjected to cultural and social inequalities as in the case of grandmothers and mothers in a Jewish home to becoming what Oprah Winfrey calls as, "I am my own woman" like Miriam in *Barney's Version,* while Nancy and Pauline's domestic struggle and cry for change transits individualism. This reflects that the Canadian society was in a transitional stage between with patriarchal authority gradually being eroded and the family structures were undergoing changes. The post effect is absorbed into the select novels where there is a constant binding and unwinding of relationships between the man and woman which in turn affected the lives and choices of Richler's protagonists. A Richler's man is inevitably cleaved to his family, society, and milieu and at the same time is in constant conflict with the above entities and self. From this complex, multiple displacements arise the "Third Solitude" which is discussed in the final subdivision.

3.5 Multiple Displacements and Mental Fractures

M.F. Salat notes that post-colonial, nations inevitably suffer "from an inadequate and / or fractured sense of self in their hesitant 'new beginnings'" (1). The same is true of Richler's third generation Jewish-Canadians who suffer multiple displacements and mental fractures in an implanted culture.

Mordecai Richler is among the ace-writers who echoed "Klein's melancholy" and the prime voice of the third-solitude (Greenstein, *TS* 4). The tension of transcending, transgressing or transforming the ghetto walls constitutes Montreal's "third solitude". Ironically, in a land of multiculturalism, Richler's characters with their Jewish ethnic origins are not visible to the English-Canadian or French-Canadian and are caught in the slush of "third-solitude" combating marginality and exile in their quest for identity. The hunt for the self-amidst the tension of "raising and razing" ghetto walls leads to multiple displacements and a fractured personality which in turn evoke fear and surprise in the protagonists. They deter from their roots and divert to deviate. Subjected to "third solitude" they become more than one-self, ambiguous with moral dilemmas, searching for the real values in them and are charged with contradictions. Noah becomes a puzzle to a frightened Miriam. "I am living with you yet I don't know you. You seem to go only so far and then… There is a part of you that I can't reach or understand" (*SH* 118).

Duddy fails to kill the "others" in him to become a man according to Uncle Benjy's letter: "You're two people, that's why. The scheming little bastard. I saw so easily and the fine, intelligent boy underneath that your grandfather, bless him, saw. But you're coming of age soon and you'll have to choose. A boy can be two, three, four potential people, but a man is only one. He murders the others" (*DK 279).* Greenstein remarks that Duddy is very busy doing many things and in his chase for the land he is "Scattered in time, place and personality" (*TS* 146). His mad rush and race blind his relation to others. He explains that Duddy, "… instead of murdering conflicting drives within himself, he destroys other characters, his alter egos" (149). To a reformed Lennie, Duddy subtly summarizes the thesis of the Jewish conflict, "It's hard to be a gentleman – a Jew, I mean – it's hard to be, Period" (*DK 292*).

While Duddy continuously runs, Jake constantly indulges in introspection of the self and matters of his obsession. Nancy Croft comes to notice that Jake was full of contradictions. He was not all of a single piece as a person. She notes:

> Ostensibly consumed by overweening ambition, he was, on black days, filled with self-hatred and debilitating doubts, largely because he took himself to be an imposter and his work, given its fragile nature, a con. She began to wonder why he had chosen to become a director in the first place and feared, in agonizingly lucid moments, that if he did not rise as far as he hoped, he might yet diminish into bitterness. (*SUH* 229)

A *Rabbi* tells Jake that he was a troubled spirit. Jake had a fractured self, troubled by various issues. He was inquisitive about the Mengele family. He could never be calm over the many injustices done to his tribe. At the same time, he had an immoral past, seduced woman, unpaid debts and cheated people.

Obsession is a recurrent pattern in the characterization of Duddy, Jake, Joshua Moses and Barney to combat their fractured selves. Fascination for the land around Lac St Pierre and acquiring acre by acre, dreaming, planning and purchasing of Duddy's "God's own acre" and routes he takes form the narrative lines of the novel. Jake is obsessed with his cousin Joey. He refuses to believe that Joey is dead and gets a notion that Joey is in Paraguay, seeking out Dr. Mengele. Greenstein detects that Jake's obsession with sleepless nights of nightmare and shifting to the *Doktor's* time in Paraguay is to focus that he belonged everywhere (*TS* 150). Joshua is obsessed with his Ibiza past and revenge of Dr. Dr. Muller. Running away is running after, hunting down and being hunted by the Solomon-obsession for Moses Berger. Gurevich claims Moses Berger to be Jake and Joshua updated. Kramer states that through the hero images of Joey and Solomon, Richler clearly wished for "Jews-with-an-attitude" (289). Barney obsession with Boogie entangles him in the murder scandal.

Joshua is also charged with contradictions. "He sent his children to private schools and complained in other people's houses about being the father of children who attended private schools. Anybody good on camera was an abomination to him, yet he owed his reputation to television" (*JTN 96).* Greenstein considers him as a paradoxical character born into a frivolous generation who finds it difficult adjusting to the norms of his society because of a seething aggressiveness directed against power structure and its authority. "The *pusherke* in him wants to conquer the rest of the world while the comic *schlemiel* is thwarted by society" (*TS* 150).

Although a minor character, Jake Trimble in a nutshell is all of what Duddy, Jake, Joshua, Solomon and Barney feared and yearned. He rejects his past ghettoed Canadian family of poverty. He dons a pseudo-British identity to be accepted into the mainstream and becomes Captain Trimble. Through impersonation and deviance Richler's men break the looming ghetto-wall and make themselves visible.

To convey multiple displacements Richler uses recurrent motifs of escaping, running and pursuing. Greenstein remarks that, "Richler's Jewish-Canadian anti-heroic sons of immigrants emerge from a double ghetto to avenge lost time and a lost place by trespassing on foreign landscapes and histories" (*TS* 142). He explains that the men "run a frenzied race away from origins towards elusive goals". He further elucidates that the running motif is a parody of the Wandering Jew "who must "make it" in a hurry in a newly found land of opportunity, who yearns a speedy transition from immigrant margins to mainstream status" (142).

Actions of running, fleeing and sailing abound in Noah's life. "He ran away from home at seven years and again at ten, the last time getting as far as Toronto" (*SH 36).* Melech slaps Noah when the boy tried to explain the fraudulency in the scrap yard to his grandfather. When he realized it, "Noah turned away from him swiftly and ran off across the yard, stumbling on a rock and falling down" (*SH 19*). After this, he never stops running. "He ran and ran and ran" (*SH* 55) after they yanked at the signboard and raced with it. He ran away from his grandfather, his pseudo-morality, from an untruthful system of ritualistic practice, at times away from his own value system when he befriends Miriam and finally away from home.

Duddy's wild chase of his bourgeoisie dream to own a land keeps him running both in the literal and symbolic sense. Uncle Benjy observes, "Run, run, always running, he thought, he can't ever walk to his car" (*DK 243).* Duddy runs when he cheats also from guilt in his dreams of McPhearson. Yvette tells, "You almost killed yourself running after that land, Duddy" (*DK 282*) and "Duddy ran, he ran, he ran" (*DK 306)* after he was discovered cheating Virgil.

Joshua also "ran-stumbling-rising-running again. He ran and ran" (*JTN 306).* Joshua while fleeing from the haunting police, his car crashes because of the failed brakes. In Noah and Duddy, fleeing is an escape but for Joshua it brings his whole life to a grinding halt after years of continuous fleeing for varied reasons. At Teddy's prize distribution, Joshua recollects, "*I ran once*, Joshua thought. *Me, your father. Leaving a couple of mice behind*" (*JTN 97)* remembering with shame and guilt how he had left behind the Friebergs, an old Jewish couple on Ibiza, helpless. Joshua flees a Mc Gill university dance floor when Sheldon with malicious pursuit says, "You're not supposed to be here unless you're a student" (*JTN 99).* Fleeing, flying and running are recurrent actions in a Jew's life from Biblical ages. Greenstein comments, "All of Richler's perplexed runners seek guidance to endure a race which has no end in sight: even if they overcome paralysis of the will, they are condemned to run in circular repetition within and without the ghetto walls" (*TS* 154). Ceaselessly running, Richler's men parody the Wandering Jew who flees and is ever on move to survive and establish himself.

Solomon is a man of myriad lives. He reincarnates himself to combat multiple identities, fractured self and "third solitude" to become more powerful and visible. "Whereas Solomon exemplifies the tough Jewish attitude, Joey is the embodiment of the tough Jewish physique" (Nobel 97). Joey and Solomon like Ephraim reincarnate their selves. "I am Ephraim, the Lord thy God, and thou shalt have no other gods before me" (*SG* 439). Ephraim is reborn. He is in the form of Solomon and then Isaac. The pace of running is accelerated in Joey and Solomon than other characters and these men go galloping horses and flying planes, not only to flee but also to chase, inversing history. There is a recurrent eluding chase of Joey, Boogie, Solomon all mysterious men on move, gallivanting and disappearing. Like Solomon, Joey lived many lives. Joey Hersh is Jessy Hope, Yosef Ben Baruch and also Joseph de la Hirsch. Moses traces that Solomon, juggling many identities had secretly participated in political schemes of the plot to kill Adolf Hitler in 1944, the Watergate burglary, Mao's Long March, the birth of Israel, Israeli raid on Entebbe rescue and at the site of Marilyn Monroe's suicide. He is also the Swiss banker Otto Raven, California naturalist Mr. Corbeau and Africana expert Mr. Cuervo.

He is a phoenix who rises from his ashes to set fire to the entourage of anti-Semitics who teased every Jew and planned to wipe them off from the face of the world. These acts of disappearance and reincarnation are tools of moral policing the deceitful and unjust world.

The once widowed, twice divorced Barney slows towards the end as an aged-man and is in a state of flux. Combating a list of accusations by Mc Iver of his past and the vacuum left by his Miriam the old Barney is struck with Alzheimer's, after a life of struggle to wriggle out of "The Main". Kramer traces him as "an insecure, unassimilated Jew, pathetically grateful to hobnob among artists" (352). His fractured and fading memories vividly bring to life his extraordinary story of his attempts to find success and happiness in both his professional and romantic life. An ambiguous Barney has early ruthless roots of deviance and a mixture of redeeming qualities of a fine family man. Strangely enough the reader unaware comes to care for the deeply, flawed "King Lear" who literally has a fractured and decaying memory.

Richler summarizes in *Barney's Version* that the political climate of the mid-twentieth Canada suffered the aftermath disillusionment of World War II and was surviving a Great Economic depression when Canada as a Dominion was in its gestational phase. Cold War, drugs, pollution, pornographic magazines and movies affected the social weather of an already troubled nation. This was accompanied by a drastic decline in church and other religious attendance. These distressed state of affairs had an adverse effect on the young (75). Further the Jewish immigrants were doubly displaced as a Canadian and Jew and were prone to transgression. In an unsettled milieu they search to settle their "third solitude". Thus multiple displacements resulted in ambivalence, contradictions and duality of character.

Richler's ambivalence not only renders his tone ambiguous, but makes it difficult to discover his moral position. His characters abound with exceptional ambiguity. As Vanderhaeghe notes, dilemmas of moral choice play a vital role in his novels. This makes the characters more human than being mere caricatures, although it is society induced. A tortured history, hyphenated identity, hypocritical set of people, family and society all team up to make ambivalence and dilemma a part of the protagonists' existence. They either conform or break away based on the choices they make.

It can be concluded that conflicts of Richler's surrounding spaces refashion the individuals who improvise for mobility in varied forms of transgression, exercising existential freedom in the context of the mid-twentieth century Montreal ghetto. The contests between the individual and some power structures are dealt to bring to light quests of immigrant adolescence, parents, families and homeland. The familial patterns of influence and gender roles have an effect on the individual choices to combat their "third solitude". It also explains how characters celebrate material and social success over human and moral failure.

Richler's men are prototypes of protagonists with ambivalence and moral dilemma and with transgression as the most opted choice. They mostly trade integrity and morality for money, prestige and social status. With multiple displacements the Jews in Canada impose their identity, accept or resist assimilation or recreate identity. They flout rules to moral police the hypocrisy and greed of the family, culture and society. As Woodcock explains Richler lights up a universal theme of the dilemma of men who set out (a few honestly like Noah, others through their own devices of deceit), to find and to be themselves in a world where men fear their own fabricated natures and try to live by "comfortable falsehoods" (Introduction *SH* vii). Through deceit they try to moral police a society that preaches but breaches practice of its teachings. They struggle to contain the very authority that subverted their existence. Thus from a new historicist perspective, Richler's texts absorb and display the "creation and replication of systems of power" (Hall 301), that has affected both the reading and non-reading population.

The prototypes many times unable to transcend or transform, initially and primarily transgress the ghetto wall. As ambivalence is inherent in the hyphenated identity, these transgressions lead them to the flyway which seeks transcendence as in Noah who chooses to look out for a greater value system and transformation in Jake and Joshua whose transformed selves reunites the family. As for Duddy, a flat character transgression is a way of life and Barney shuttles between transformation after his break with the Second Mrs. Panofsky and seeks transcendence during his thirty odd years of love and marriage with Miriam and an untimely transgression that crumbles all his love and hope. In all of these although the ghetto wall is socially-constructed it moves on to a psychological and private level with choices purely personal.

Greenblatt states, "Texts do not allow you to see *through* them to the world, they are part of the fashioning of that world" (qtd. in Robson 58). Richler's texts are fashioned by the surrounding spaces of his period and have absorbed the cultural fabric and social presence of a conflicting age. While chapter III makes a study on thematic concerns, chapter IV will explore Richler's 'cultural poetics' focusing on the formal aspects of his literary skill that make his works stand the test of time.

4

Textual Relics

> "'Textual Relics' enable us to glimpse the social process through which objects, gestures, rituals, and phrases are fashioned and moved from one zone of display to another" (Greenblatt, *LC* 162).

Richler's select texts are literary artifacts and relics that resonate with the Greenblatt's 'wonder' of the 1940's and 50's Jewish Montreal ghetto. This chapter analyzes the formal aspects of narratives that intersect with the historical understanding which Greenblatt calls as 'cultural poetics'. It explores how Richler recreates the conflicts from the surrounding spaces of mid-twentieth century Montreal ghetto and Jewish life in a Canadian space through narratives, language, imagery, allusions, parody and satire.

The sardonic eye of Richler inundates with wit and humour. This chapter evaluates Richler's dynamic narratives and the vitriolic diatribe against the mediocrities of his society. It traces the capacity of Richler's works to absorb a lot of energy from 'cultural mobility' drawn from his literary readings. It elaborates how the writer, narrator and characters employ, irony and satire to laugh aloud and unveil the pretensions and hypocrisy of society, interrogate and critically evaluate the Self-caught in the conflicts of the surrounding spaces. Although it can be argued that Richler's barbs have caustic energy, his concern for values and the sense of Jewishness preoccupies his purpose.

Critics opine that Richler recycled heavily. But Richler applies what could be called as a phoenix effect, resurrecting universally or regionally relevant motifs, images, themes and localizes the fabric by rooting it in his Jewish-Montreal ghetto.

> What we think of as 'great' writers are those most effectively engage in a process of cultural 'exchange', taking an existing item such as a familiar myth, symbol or character type and transforming it into something else, usually through an alteration in its content or by combining it with materials from another, often unexpected, source. (Robson 23)

The ideologies behind creating Schulberg's Sammy Glick and Richler's Duddy Kravitz are different. 'Cultural mobility' trades in specific themes, plots, images and gives rise to newer avatars renovated by its 'contact zones' and developed out of new tension and mobility between the individual and cultural constraint. This phoenix effect resurrects the spirit of the text and can be read separate from its sources. Richler's works draw a lot of power from 'cultural mobility' drawn from his literary readings, take pride in his honest voice and artistic 'cultural poetics' and resonate with the 'wonder' of his time and place.

4.1. Narration and Thick Description

According to Gallagher and Greenblatt, Geertz's 'thick description' in a new historicist practice is to cause the "touch of the real" and "a confident conviction of reality" (31) through ethnographic realism in the study of literary texts. Geertz states that thin description explains only the sign and thick description explains the context of the practices and discourses within a society. An explication of the narrative technique used and detailing of 'desired anecdotes' employed shall elevate the text from a mere sign board of "what is said" to an illumination of "what is communicated".

Liu explains that the thesis of Geertz's concept of culture as text is to study culture to interpret the meanings of symbolic systems and to thickly describe the complicated cultural phenomena. Liu in his essay proposes an intertextual reading of text to analyze culture as a text: "To "thickly describe" culture, I therefore call for a dynamic textual perspective, that is, one that examines the depths of metaphor in conjunction with how a text is intertextually read, narrated, and performed". Ryan traces that this pattern of intertextual analysis forms the basis of Greenblatt's 'cultural poetics'. He draws on Foucault's *Annales* School of social history, cultural anthropology of Geertz and deconstruction and argues for a 'cultural poetics' that would study the social and cultural negotiations involved in the creation of a literary work. The collective beliefs, social practices and cultural discourses leave "textual traces" in a work of literature and connect it to the extra-textual representational systems of the culture in which it is implanted.

Richler's novels draw energy from surrounding spaces and enumerate the ethnographic realism of the Jewish-Montreal ghetto and these cultural moments have an effect on the mind of the reader. "For Greenblatt this power comes not from the hand of the artist, but, instead, from a series of negotiations, exchanges and movements" (Robson 69). Although the central issue of social energy is 'exchange' and no sole proprietorship of genius is attributed, Richler's literary techniques along with his "honest voice" mark his writings authentic and native. He freely takes objects and ideas that already exists, blends it with his intricate narratives and weaves in cultural contexts and literary imagination. His intricate narrative technique uses linguistic creativity to establish this.

He indulges in 'appropriation' in which he freely absorbs from the public domain, Yiddish inflected phrases to express the Jewish nature of the characters.

He 'purchases' ideas from books of writers and parodies the sources to suit his thematic conceptions exposing and moral policing pretentions and masks.

He engages in 'symbolic acquisition' of Jewish practices and with his caustic satire laughs at the hypocrisy of the families and societies.

Greenblatt from Herder, draws the "historicist insistence on the differences between artistic forms that derive from their different locations" (Robson 91). For Herder climate and culture are aspects of the "originality" of a nation and its cultural products. He binds literature, language, land and people together. It can be stated that the moment that produced Richler is distinctive and cannot be repeated, imitated or continued. Richler thus belongs to his mid-twentieth century Montreal and to avoid omission, he is a transnational writer of London and Spain of his early years.

Greenstein opines that Richler's dualistic confusions and cultural hyphenations, in response to an unstable inheritance mediates in Jewish-Canadian literature, between the marginal man and his discourse. The marginal Jew fills the absence of identity with a quest to rediscover and reaffirm his existence in a shadowed world. Daniel Golden states that, Richler "has a splendid ear for the rhythms or speech in diverse social groups, from ghetto gutter-trash to shabby English aristocrats" (71). He also commends Richler's capacity to parody literary and popular culture forms from "*Bildungsroman*" to television game shows and exploits humour that is "at once black, grotesque, scatological and pornographic". Richler binds all these techniques with the strand of moral outrage set in in humour that lashes Jews, Canadians and the entire "culture" establishment (72).

The narrative focus takes place through Richler as a writer, narrator or the character's voice. Richler dexterously concedes the author's voice, but his moral stand and honest voice unveil it. There is so much of Richler revealed in Noah's story narrative. *Smaller Hero* is basically melodramatic and has a simple, narrative written in the third person. It is introspective with sprawling sentimental interior monologues, overpowered by the writer's obsession with the story-line and amateur narrative skills. Ramraj observes "It is not unlikely that Richler is conscious of this element in his work and that he – who so often draws on his own experiences for his novels is attempting, like Joshua to locate himself from a possessive past" (126).

Richler as a narrator distances and engages in a non-didactic narrative voice. "Richler neither castigates nor exonerates Duddy... Instead, Duddy is dispassionately assessed!" (Davidson 81). With his dispassionate voice he castigates both the Jew and gentile. *Duddy Kravitz* is marked by a brisk authorial ambivalence with a broad projection of Duddy as a Jew, Canadian and struggling individual. Ambivalence is brought out by rich dramatic scenes and a dominant comic tone which include his ordeal in buying the land. Woodcock analyzes that the narrative is flat-toned, "in an apparently conventional manner, that at times hits the rapids of absurd and incongruous situations, with a dialogue that is highly comic..." (*IDK* 47). Lack of interior monologues leaves the reader fishing for lies and evasions to get close to the heart of the characters.

Richler writes the narrative prose with a telescopic eye for minute details, magnifying the theme and behaviour of the characters in the first few chapters of *Duddy Kravitz*. The narrative gently hooks on to the deeper implications of the real-estate trade that Duddy is greedily involved. The lively narrative pace and quickness of Duddy's obsession with the land repeats itself in Jake's quest of the Horseman, Moses' search for the Solomon's hoof and Barney's pursuit of Miriam. McSweeney detects the influence of his working with screenplay or film script, "Through working in this medium, Richler learned to set a faster narrative pace, to use quick cuts and jump cuts, and to add flavor, zest, and entertaining set pieces to his fiction" (136).

Narration by characters possesses a tone of self-interrogation with a struggle for personal and social definition and space in family and society especially in Jake, Joshua and Barney. William New observes that simple linear narrative was giving way to complex artifice around the 1970s. Richler employs a complex pattern of flashbacks to explore the obsessive nature of the protagonists with their past, the ironical inversions caused by the passage of time, and the sad aspects of uncertainty in *St. Urbain's Horseman* and *Joshua Then and Now*. The narrative is richly structured with Jake's scripts of a movie, cinematic inserts, and newspaper items. His attempt to review his life occasions major flashbacks of his boyhood, youth and early manhood with accounts of Montreal and Ibiza and returns to Jake's present in his London home with family.

The narrative gallops with Jake's chase of the alter-ego Joey across the globe, with multiple symbolic structure of the Horseman, seasoned with parts of the trial in court. Richler puts to use the flashback technique and stream of consciousness with great craft. John Moss in his essay "Richler's Horseman" observes, "Chronology is a convenience for Richler, rather than a major plot device. Flashbacks and forward flow simply allow the author to work in the necessary details" (156-157). For Moss the form does not arise inevitably from within the context and suggests that Richler imposes it to order his materials. A reader has to keep track with the shifting narratives between dream and reality and the weighing details of Jake's stories. Vanderhaeghe praises the novel's epigrammatic prose.

Dvorak notes that *Joshua Then and Now* and *Barney's Version* dazzled readers with a dozen labyrinthine narratives interwoven with virtuosity (162). The "Then" and "Now" narratives of Joshua projects his two worlds of struggles; St. Urbain that he wants to escalate and Westmount in which he wants to remain. The meaning of the double narrative in *Joshua Then and Now* delves into the rash and spineless moments in Ibiza. The novel is intricate and interesting with the mystery form of story-telling. The mysteries of Joshua's scandal, his silk underwear, Pauline's break down, the Ibiza nightmare and the marriage between the St. Urbain Joshua and the Senator's daughter Pauline are a fascinating jig-saw puzzle. A puzzle solved leads to another, which makes the reading entirely amusing.

Richler's narration is not direct when concerned with Joshua's malicious deeds. They are mentioned in forms of "hints and insinuations" (Ramraj 124) or from the reports given by Mc Master like that of the Seligson's episode in whose house Joshua planted the stolen money. Ramraj allows the possibility that Richler chose the "indirect form" to suggest that Joshua's socially noxious behaviour originates from Jung's concept of shadow. The third person narration, "in a manner that often seems merely to disguise a first-person narration by Joshua himself" (Davey 130). McSweeney writes about the advantages of the presentational methods common to the Joshua and Jake story, "It also makes it easy for him to interpolate the incidental vignettes, skits, anecdotes and apercus… the interweaving of various story lines and the canny withholding of information stimulate the reader's interest in seeing how the various pieces of the central characters' lives will fit together" (163). This is true of Solomon's story too.

Richler handles massive narrative lines in mapping the history of a titanic timeline over two hundred years with ace dexterity in *Solomon Gursky*. The king-size narrative, intricately weaves in stories within a story of the rise of the Gurskys, spreading across the globe and shuttling between generations, in a non-linear fashion with threads of magic realism. He baffles the reader in the first hundred pages and continues to introduce elements of surprise and suspense until the points of revelation. Richler with "structural sophistication" (Foran 608) is at his peak narrating a complex sequence, leap frogging with interesting events from history, geography, inscribing with achronological journals, letters and desperate unwinding of the Solomon-mystery with revealing anecdotes and the narrator Moses' struggle with the self.

Larson observes that Richler in *Solomon Gursky* writes like a modern-day Swift, bitterly satirizing our unflattering pasts with the wisdom of hindsight and this culturally gruesome tale has a lot of despair to uncover. Richler combines narrative tedium and quickness without any authorial intrusion and is copious in his skill as a story-teller. Gurevich breathtakingly declares that scenes come down in an avalanche, dialogue follows a page from a script that follows a diary entry, all done in rich, meaty prose, generously peppered with witticisms and cultural allusions. Though the Gurskys form the narrative backbone Richler's cast includes a gallery of secondary characters as Larsen points out to the Shwartz crooks, holy fools like Solomon's son Henry, guilt-ridden media celebs like Moses's childhood friend Sam Burns; and there are simple souls, like the welfare boozers with whom Moses carouses at

The Caboose including the Puritan, gentile Bert Smith. Although there are multiple voices, it's Moses' account and in a Moses-absent scene, Solomon's story, that the reader is led to believe.

Barney's Version is "simpler in design than *Gursky,* brimmed equally with character and incidents" (Foran 628). As the title prompts, Richler abandons the favoured technique of multiple viewpoints and settles down to the "single perspective" of Barney. Barney is a first-person unreliable narrator, poignant when it comes to "Miriam, Miriam, my heart's desire" story, but caustic otherwise. The stream of conscious technique is frequently punctuated with sentences of reminders starting with "…I couldn't remember the name of the thing you use to strain Spaghetti" followed by repetition of the names of the seven dwarfs which indicate that Barney is at the verge of Alzheimer's. The unreliable narrator is corrected for factual details in Mike's Afterword. Richler's fast paced dialogues add interest. The following conversation between Barney and The Second Mrs. Panofsky is one:

> "Couldn't you put that damn guide book away while we sit here?"
>
> "I'm embarrassing you?"
>
> "Yes."
>
> …
>
> "Can you speak Hebrew?"
>
> "No."
>
> "Have you got an M.A. from McGill?"
>
> "No."
>
> "Am I embarrassed?"
>
> "I began to growl" (*BV* 219)

Richler excels as a show-all-but-don't-tell narrator. Barney's accusations on Terry as a pathological liar is confirmed at various places especially when Terry reports that "Forty-five people" were present at his reading (*BV 104),* wherein only nine of the forty chairs were filled according to Barney (*BV 93).* This art of narration leaves the reader to decide the facts. Apart from the main fabric of the story, Craniford observes that the narrative hook of whether or not Barney murdered Boogie "is a theme as tragic, powerful, and human as Shakespeare's *King Lear*" (*BV 137).* Richler's craft narrative introduces water bomber planes gulping tons of water and dropping loads on a distant mountain. He hints that consequently a similar water plane "the big fat water bomber" the last piece of the missing-Boogie puzzle had scooped up the drunken Boogie's drowned body and dumped it on the top of Mont Groulx where it was subsequently ravaged by animals and found thirty years later. Craniford comments that the water plane becomes a *dues ex machina* to exonerate Barney (125). This adds to the dramatic twist to the novel and to the theatrical effect of the movie version produced in 2010 in amassing profuse sympathy for the tragic hero Barney.

Richler's narratives are masculine from a feminist reading perspective. Conversations and discourses fail to incorporate the female experience. They are either mechanical expressions that sequentially follow a male-line or a woman's response to the situation. The "double consciousness" of the woman's world is absent (Humm 55). This is evident in the female responses of Pauline, Nancy and Miriam who complain drudgery. Pauline pleads "I don't want to be left alone", she said. "I hear every creak in the house. I dream I'm in my coffin" (*JTN 329).* This domestic tension in Pauline and Miriam's lives and the inability of their men to understand the female consciousness cause cracks in their marital relationships. The Second Mrs. Panofsky's convoluting discourses ridicule the female impulse prone to verbosity.

Narration through Dreams

Richler narrates the repression and obsession of characters through dreams and reveries. Wolf's dream is a premonition to his death. "He dreamed that his father was dead. A mysterious woman handed him a key. He didn't ask her what it was for. He knew without asking" (*SH 61).* The woman is his father's Lodz girl, whose letters and not money which Wolf thought was within the box and for which he would die for. Leah's reverie of her dead father

Goldenberg gives insight into his character and states that if he was alive, her life would have been different. He would have understood Noah for the old man held the spirit of tradition and people above rituals. He had said to Melech "Your children must come to God out of love. Otherwise, their prayers are dead prayers. And are not heard in heaven" (*SH 93*).

Obsessions are converted into dreams. Duddy wakes up from a recurrent nightmare of his land being bought by Irwin Shubert or someone. Sounds of bulldozers, carpenters, plumbers and someone else's plans and surveyors plundered his land of dreams from his dreams. Guilt and pain are rehearsed in Duddy's dreams of Yvette's absence and of Mrs. MacPherson's death. While Duddy's dream has a cathartic effect, Yvette foreshadows Virgil's fit while driving the truck and warns Duddy, "I'll never forgive you if anything happens to him. I swear it" (*DK 217*)

Jake Hersh is prone to psychotic Jewish nightmare. Joshua shuttles back and forth between his twenties and forties in his nightmares confronting Dr. Dr. Mueller. "If you think you can rob me of my manhood, you're out of your mind. I'm not running, Mueller. Neither will I allow you to screw the Freibergs. Because in the years ahead I'm going to fall in love with Pauline. We're going to have three children. I will not be ashamed. I'm a man, not a mouse" (*JTN 157).*He sets right the sequences of his life which are not straight in his real life. Dreams are also deployed as tools of revenge. Barney's dreams of imagining McIver in pain and death, Jake Hersh's vengeful dream of killing Dr. Mengele and Joshua's dream of confronting Dr. Dr. Mueller avenge the troubled psyche of the restless men. Barney indulges in the pleasures of the flesh with his filthy reveries of Mrs. Oglivy feeding the passions of his id. With it he pampers his lonely life post-Miriam's departure and uses it to elevate suspense before disclosing the missing-Boogie story. It could be argued that Barney's night of sin is perpetrated as an outcome of these reveries.

Recurrence and Repetition

Reappearances of Duddy in *St. Urbain's Horseman*, *Solomon Gursky* and *Barney's Version* and of Jerry Dingleman, The Boy Wonder, the Gurskys and Harvey Schwartz in *Barney's Version* is an effective tool of narration that connects episodes, sequences of life, time and surrounding space of the Jews from "The Main". The reappearances of Duddy establishes the locale of Richler's protagonists from "The Main" and ascertains a sense of locality, thereby bringing alive the Montreal of the 50s. His brief but strong appearances also suggest his growth and graduation from St. Urbain Street to Westmount. Recurrence for Solomon Gursky, Ephraim and Joey as discussed earlier is reincarnation. They die to themselves and reappear in the same novels signaling sheer survival and add to the magic realism of the novel.

Richler employs repetitive lines for rhetorical purposes. The line "A man without land is nobody" in *Duddy Kravitz,* is a life-long contemplated sentence of Smicha who dug the coarse hostile soil without much yield. His grandfather's touch-words, "acts as a catalyst for his quest to possess land and self" (Greenstein, *TS* 146). Duddy repeats the repetitive line to the Boy-Wonder and Jerry breaks into a fit of laughter on a Jew-boy's echo of someone's platitude. Jerry's laughter is Richler's mockery and a reader's subtle smile of the boyish obsession. Melina Singer explains that the phrase is a universal resonance of "a larger cultural view of communities wanting to share in the possibilities that middle-class resources and, alternatively, civility can endow" (17).

Greenstein detects a "triple repetition" and rhythmic pattern in the lines "He ran and ran and ran" (*SH* 55), "Duddy ran, he ran, he ran" (*DK 306),* "ran-stumbling-rising-running again. He ran and ran" (*JTN 306).* This has an ingrained rush and speed in linguistic structure which is indicative of the mad rush of the protagonists to reach the centres from their marginalized positions. Greenstein explains that this rhythm creates the "narrative pace to match much of his rapid dialogue" (*TS* 143).

The repetitive lines, "*Mengele cannot have been there all the time*", adds intensity to Jake's psychotic Jewish nightmare. *"In my opinion, always. Night and Day" (SUH* 79, 178, 270, 271, 374). Joey's repeated question, ""What are you going to do about it?" (*SUH* 137) echoes the universal Jewish alter-ego's question on their plight. The lines "These are the Days of Awe" (*JTN* 65) by Reuben is an ironic commentary of the value system of his times. The line signals the ideology that immorality and transgressions are a way of life. The repetitive line, "Human dignity. The dead. The sanctity of the word" (*SG* 22*)* said by L.B. Berger's friend stresses on the ethics of creativity and creator and is contemptuous of what Foran states as the "literary sins of self-pity and inflated self-regard, and the larger artistic sin of "selling out"" speeches and writing (542).

Richler diligently scatters pieces of jig-saw puzzle all over his novel. A careful reader has to keep collecting the pieces to decode answers later. Richler does not follow a technique of book-back answers preserved upside down for his intriguing brainteasers. As a narrative-trickster he casually litters the pieces of the puzzle and unceremoniously reveals them. He gives a passing description of a missing portrait of a young lady which Henry tells Moses as a child. "When you looked at it closely you saw that one of her eyes was blue and the other brown" (*SG 26*). The line reads as if Richler mischievously makes Henry dismiss it with a child's interpretation that the painter should have been angry that he was not paid and so he had painted the eyes revengefully different. The importance of the painting dawns with repeated references and accidently the reader bumps into a Mrs. McClure, "a one-eye brown, one-eye blue" lady, (*SG* 74, 167, 315, 362, 382), thus inferring her to be the lost-lady love of Solomon, Diana Morgan. This is revealed through Moses' meeting her and later with the letter she writes to him. While the lost-love of Solomon surfaces again and again with a recurrent line on Diana Morgan's physical clue, Barney repeats, "Miriam, Miriam, my heart's desire" as frequent as his heartbeat. This adds a pathetic effect to his "wasted life" and lost-wife and earns the reader's sympathy. This nonchalant skill of teasing the reader with massive motifs and riddles with recurrent lines and reappearance of characters marks the matured style of Richler's later novels.

Greenblatt sees language as an explicitly potent or social self-fashioning force to the temporal aspect of history. Richler fashions his characters with language. His natural inter-usage of language with Yiddish inflections and French al carte of responses add to Quebec nativity. Richler uses crass language to mark the street talks of the people and the class language to differentiate the educated. The ghetto language is inflected with Yiddish inflections and is rustic which characterizes the marginalized. Melech uses "hankink" for longing and "Nuttin", for nothing. People said "brudder", "thinkin" for "brother" and "thinking". Mrs. Hersh's spoke English punctuated with errors, "So I says to the fella, what do you think, I've never flown before, I don't know how *other* airlines do things… With Air Canada I says if you had to wait two hours…" (*SUH* 42). Issy Hersh creates laughter with his grammatical errors and flubbed words.

The WASPS like Terry scoffed at Barney's peculiar syntax and ridiculed the Jewish use of the language where the sentences were inverted as if they were translated from Yiddish like "had I known it would have been different, my behaviour" (*BV 98).* This often constituted the language of Duddy, Soloman and Izzy. Greenstein analyses Duddy's ungrammatical iteration "like they say" serves to introduce clichés such as "anatomy's the big killer" which constitute the ghetto language (*TS* 149). Minor characters like Cuckoo Kaplan and Mr. Cohen speak clichés and pet phrases like "That's show biz" and "We're a small family, but we're loyal" that express the language of the ordinary. D.J. Dooley observes that Duddy through clichés like "You can get killed crossing the road", "I can trust nobody", "tries to cover up his tracks or to disclaim moral responsibility" (107).

Refinement in the use of language marked social status. Richler captures moments of superficial statements of the well-to-do Jewish wives. Their conversations sign post material success with exchanged niceties and flatteries.

> "Jack's going to buy a Cadillac. You try to stop him."
>
> "Me, I don't live for show. Lou doubled his life insurance instead of buying a new car this year. He says you can never tell…" (*SH 17).*

The wives were brand ambassadors of their family and their conversations masked hypocrisy and jealousy. The talks of Solomon, Boogie, Terry, Saul and later Barney have an inbuilt nature of jibes.

Anecdotes

"Anecdotes in compressed form (show) the ways in which elements of lived experience enter into literature" (Gallagher and Greenblatt 30). The anecdotes on the Scot teacher MacPherson reveal the scandalous behaviour of boys like Duddy and Jerry which nearly kills an enthusiastic teacher. Duddy bullies Mac's twenty-year-old reserve against strapping students and breaks it triumphantly. It shows the incorrigible ways of the boys caught in a traditional set up, troubled by strict codes of discipline and how rebellion flowed freely in a hyphenated, adolescent blood.

Max's repeated anecdotes of The Boy Wonder infinitely for the sheer joy to live through the success of a street boy who had the whole police force on his pay roll. The circulation of the story of the 'Boy Wonder' finds ambiguous responses in Duddy. On one hand it trades with the ethos of the upwardly mobile Jewish-Canadian's obsession with material success which Duddy mimes. On the other hand, he finds the Dingleman's story oppressive and aims to surpass it. In both cases the result favours social escalation.

Anecdotes from the past lives of Joey and Solomon enhance the suspense and meaningfully interrupt the historical grand narrative of the novels. Richler handles the massive plotting of the Gurskys with anecdotes from Eskimo folklore highlighting the deceitful nature of the scavenger raven. Ephraim's several anecdotes of his North expedition reveal the king-leader quality of the old man. These anecdotes of struggle, survival and power transfer a super-natural energy to Solomon and a tradition of a Demi-god status, which his great-grandson lives throughout in Tulugaqtitut.

Barney's Version abounds with digressions which have a few 'desired anecdotes' of real value and are mostly digressions. Barney in constant conversation with his reader tells, "I'm digressing. I know, I know. But this is my one and only story, and I'm going to tell exactly how I please" (*BV 47).* Self-instigated conscious digressions on the phony Henry Newbolt, on writers and painters' self-promotion and avarice for fame, the parody on the Biblical Abe and Izzy, explains Barney's story telling skill, wide reading and indicate his isolated living. The anecdote of the TV pirate who unscrambled non-licensed American channels is used to grieve Barney's inability to unscramble authentic pictures of his past. The anecdotes or "little stories" in Fineman's words, refers to the real (Gallagher and Greenblatt 49) in the everyday life of the Jewish-Canadian space. The conflicts are brought out through shifting narratives, multiplicity of perspectives and authentic language to examine the fragmented consciousness of the protagonists to give a "touch of the real".

4.2. Resonance and Wonder

Greenblatt states, "Wonder effects the crucial break with another that can only be described, only witnessed, in the language and images of sameness. It erects an obstacle that is at the same time an agent of arousal" (*MP* 135).

Richler's texts house, places such as St. Urbain Street, cottages and memorials and Hebraic artifacts as places and objects that resonate the spirit and ideology of the age. He also employs verbal images of flood, land, horseman, raven, silver doktor, salmon fly as strong symbols for narrative purposes. These places, objects and images strike one with wonder and encapsulate a sense of surprise that is produced by reading it. From a new historicist reading it furthers to 'resonance' exploring an excavation of "its context and of the life to which it is, or was, connected" leading it to a study of the surrounding spaces. This marks the 'cultural poetics' of the texts which arrests the reader with wonder and progresses into a query to unravel the resonance of the literary artifacts which echo the mid-twentieth century Jewish Montreal ghetto life. Richler's Montreal based novels by themselves leads one on a journey from 'wonder' to 'resonance' connecting the reader to the cultural exchanges of the time. Thus Duddy, Noah, Jake, Joshua, Moses, Solomon, Barney, all become artifacts of literary value caricaturing the hyphenated identity and the conflicts that arise out of their context, time and space.

Signposts of Resonance

> (The Main) was a great place to grow up. For a poet nothing could have been better. Nothing. Raw, vulgar, dynamic and dramatic: their smells and sounds and fights. It was altogether a rich and wonderful life. Sometimes I'm sorry for my children who lived in the suburbs and never had anything like this. (Poet Irving Layton as qtd. in King 104)

The editors of *Text, Theory, Space* write about how landscape helps to "create and naturalize the histories and identities inscribed upon it, and so simultaneously hides and makes evident social and historical formations" (qtd. in Bethlehem 140). The review states, "It is culture, they stress, which transforms the seemingly neutral category of "space" or "geographical territory" into "place" – with its concomitant associations: imagined, seen, historicized, remembered" (140).

Richler writes, "Our street was called St. Urbain. French for Urban. Actually there have been eight popes named Urban, but ours was the first. Urban I. He was the only one to have been canonized" (*TS* 17). Richler's St. Urbain Street material arrests the reader on the track and works on as an agent of stimulation to go back to the past. It excites readers to visit the streets of "The Main" to relive those literary moments of Noah, Duddy, Jake, Joshua, Moses and Barney although the lanes are no more the same.

Today much of St. Urbain's Street has been gentrified. Sian Griffiths in an article "Mordecai Richler's Montreal" written in 2011 observes: "Today the area has lost much of its Jewish character as the earlier immigrants became more affluent and moved to better-heeled anglophone neighbourhoods, such as

Westmount". Also a news item on "St. Urbain Street just not St. Urbain enough" that appeared in 2006 notes that "It's been widened, it's one-way. As a location, it just didn't look like it did back then". But Richler through his writings has immortalized St. Urbain's Street of the 1940's and 50's and the street continues to attract a lot of literary tours even today for its power of 'resonance and wonder'. On a walking tour on the Street led by one Stan Asher who reads the nostalgic piece *St. Urbain Street Then and Now,* Yanofsky says, "What he reads is supposed to connect with where we happen to be on the tour..." (78). Richler's St. Urbain stops one in wonder as it resonates the old world and is a coveted textual artifact of prime Montreal. It moves beyond its formal boundaries and evokes in the reader the complex dynamic forces from which it has emerged. Greenblatt explains that such artifacts are a metaphor or a metonymy for the reader. Foran in an E-mail communication notes:

> St Urbain Street is maybe the most distinctive, realized, and ardently mapped 'urban' neighbourhood in Canadian literature. It was certainly unusual, given how rural many early Canadian novels were, and it remains an actual 'destination' for admirers of Richler's work, the way people go looking for Joyce's Dublin or Dickens' London. That is very rare, and a testament to how vividly Richler created this world.

Ryan observes that Greenblatt's use of "wonder" and "resonance" are representations of power and the way it maintains itself through representation. They describe modes of representation "that efface the social practices, interests, and desires that motivate and mobilize power" (130). The landscape of "The Main" exerts its presence, what William H. New recognizes as formidable both as an ally and an antagonist in characters' various quests for answers, identities, comfort and consolation. This is specific to the select novels where Richler's characters continued to question their own failings and that of the society. Encumbered in a claustrophobic ghetto dwelling, childhood revisited by Richler's gross heroes consistently record acts of stealing and lying as common "developments defects". Even when they grow into a respectable adult, a few momentarily fail to outgrow the St. Urbain-syndrome of thieving. Richler's discourse of wonder, resonates the particularities of St. Urbain's Street's social psychology and its distinct neighbourhoods.

> Also interested in the working life of a city, with an even stronger focus on class and ethnic topography, Mordecai Richler in *Duddy Kravitz* (1959) highlights Montreal's St. Urbain Street Jewish ghetto in the era following World War II, focusing on the difficult temptations facing a poor boy scrambling to succeed in an exploitative world. (Fiamengo 256-257)

St. Urbain Street is representative of the life on the streets of "The Main" which also include Jeanne Mance Street, Dorchester Street and St. Laurence Boulevard. These Streets housed the floating immigrant population especially Jewish in the mid-twentieth century. Richler pays detailed attention to the physical layout of his working-class neighbourhood in *Smaller Hero, Duddy Kravitz, St. Urbain's Horseman, Joshua Then and Now and Barney's Version.* In a series of autobiographical sketches in *The Street* he chronicles ethnic differences and miniscule distinctions in income-level. He recreates Baron Byng of his time as the Fletcher's Field in his novels and writes a definite record of the street's location, sketching the tenement buildings, shops and institutional structures as the Fletcher's Cadets march through it. Richler recreates the delicatessens of the period with the aroma of the hot, spicy smoked meat. He echoes the sound and psychology of the neighbourhood through Yiddish inflected idioms. Max's mythic tale of the Boy Wonder is a perfect example. Thus Richler's St. Urbain's street as a textual relic, resonates the lives of the working-class Jews of the mid-twentieth century Jewish Montreal. Overall, he depicts Montreal's centres and margins, the local Jewish culture and the gentile in opposition, a deep intimacy with St. Urbain Street and an insightful awareness of disempowerment of being a middle-class working Jew.

The characteristic spirit of St. Urbain and the neighbouring streets is to move beyond the cluttered space into a widening area to make one's own self visible. This spirit is a recurrent theme as discussed through the characters of Noah, Duddy, Jake, Joshua, Moses, Solomon and Barney. None remained in the Streets as it was a home of leftovers and every kid of the frivolous generation dreamt leaving it early. It was the mental ghetto they wanted to quit. Jenny Hersh says: "This is nowhere, St. Urbain. We're nothing here. We have to leave" (*SUH* 143). St. Urbain Street was grub. No one lives for long, but leaves. Ironically, nostalgia and a feeling of get-back-home add to the ambivalent attitude of protagonists towards the Street-homes. Noah did not hate the ghetto altogether. He knew that it was the place his journey's beginning. Whenever he found business slack, he drove through the streets. An old Barney longed to walk on the street that grew him.

Richler in his CBC Television interview of 1975 recollects that he tried his very best to run away from St. Urbain Street and also away from Canada. But he realized the far away he ran geographically, the closer he reached St. Urbain in his literary space and writings. He admits that like the people of his generation he suffered from a fragmentary sense of Canada as a nation but still it was home to him especially the very rigidly circumscribed neighbourhood with five streets, the synagogue and his school an eight block away. He emphasized that life on the street was not being poor in a slum or a sense of deprivation but was a kind of a self-contained village with their own appetite, enjoyment and enthusiasm. Richler does not talk about the economic poverty of the street alone. He spoke of the cultural vacuum, the constraints of a hyphenated, restricted, orthodox living with hypocritical values. The ghetto was not economically poor, but it was a mental ghetto, culturally fragmented.

Richler records Jewish Montreal as a chapter in history especially in the 1950s with never-before and not-now moments and his older characters walk in and out of the street with reminiscence. St. Urbain in the mid-twentieth century was largely composed of middle class Jewish kids. The Montreal featured in the film adaptation of *Duddy Kravitz* and *Barney's Version* were not just the hangouts of Richler's literary world alone bur also where the author liked to hang his hat in real life. The Dink's bar and other ghetto places have turned out to be literary landmarks. People like Barney who graduated from the streets of St. Urbain to houses in Westmount, Hampsted or Ville St-Laurent occasionally strolled into their old neighborhood in a quest to locate familiar faces and old landmarks. Richler notes in *Barney's Version* that St. Urbain Street now is no longer Jewish but teams with Italian, Greek and Portuguese kids. Barney's old-neighbourhood's the shoe-shine parlour, lending library, *Kosher* Meat Mart are displaced and replaced by unisex hair stylist, video-rental outlet, New Age Bookstore, a vegetarian restaurant and a Buddhist Temple (67). Flats lived by activists like Saul continue to reek of stale living and were an abode for objectionable activities. Family dwellings continued to house the struggling parents juggling with overdue household bills and were certainly out of breath like the Jewish parents who preceded them. St. Urbain Street retained its characteristic struggle but with a different cast. Though Richler's St. Urbain can no longer be relived but can be resurrected through his works.

If St. Urbain Street is a textual relic that resonates the squalid living conditions of the childhood and youth of the ghettoed boys, then their lake side cottages reverberate their dreams realized of a comfortable living with contended family. The cottage is a concrete, architectural evidence of success in both *Joshua Then and Now* and in *Barney's Version.* Cottages resonate with idyllic peace that the characters yearned to live in their St. Urbain childhood. The cottage around Lake Memphremagog has been earlier the welcoming home of the prodigal Shapiros. Outside his cottage is the idyllic setting with sole serving loon, golden finch swooping between the budding birch trees and in the evening Joshua could see the robins feeding on water spiders. The cottage opened up rooms for nature and natural beauty in contrast to the bricked buildings in the streets. Davey states that the archetypal resonance of the "garden" suggests the loyalty of the family and regeneration of Joshua and Pauline's marriage against the ruined marriages of the rest in the novel (140). The cottage is a mental asylum for the wearied, beaten down Joshua. Post scandal, the cottage is under surveillance of the police and scanned with telephoto lenses of the journalists. Lake Memphremagog could be the ultimate resort for a Jew boy to settle around. Like Richler, Joshua returns to settle and Moses Berger borrows money from Henry to buy a cabin around it. Barney's family looked forward to their weekends at the cottage. The cottage resonates with the city people's recline into an idyllic space. "…I was luxuriating in the remembrance of family good times past…" *(BV 247).* Barney's cottage is an artifact that resonates moments of ecstasy, family times, peace and old age. Joshua recollects the family moments of tilling and gardening when he waits for Pauline. The cottage gardens thrived with vegetation in contrast to Smicha's sickly garden in *Duddy Kravitz.*

Objects of Wonder

The Artifacts of William Mackenzie King, the Prime Minister of Joshua's boyhood resonated the vile memories of Canada's leader for twenty-one years at the memorial programme. Photographs of King, his mother, poster of a Lili St. Cyr, tapes and records of Kay Kayser, Harry James and others and other newspaper cuttings reverberated the mean-spirited, cunning, somewhat demented, hypocrite on a grand scale, leader of Canada. The memorial by itself is an occasion of ridicule which Richler amply satirizes and the inventory of artifacts resound it.

Uncle Oscar's junk retrieved in St. Dominique Street flat included a spiked German army helmet from World War I, shoeboxes overflowing with medals and pocket watches, stacks of paintings, lampshades of multicoloured tinted glass, a player piano, an old captain's sea trunk with intricately uniformed grenadiers and toy soldiers, a wind-up gramophone, grandfather clocks, old typewriters and telephones, an ancient cash register and much more. Richler through these artifacts of baseless value recreates the bygone days of war, art, music and communication. The checklist reverberates with antiquity and remains of an age that lived off these big mechanisms. Joshua found them interesting and Hetty, Uncle Oscar's Outremont wife picked one or two interesting items, remodeled it for antique value and strictly ordered the rest to be discarded.

Jewish symbols, artifacts and memorials have a resonant value. Richler in *Joshua Then and Now* recalls the butchers of the auto de fe that resonates in the places that Joshua visits in Ibiza even five centuries later. The square where Joshua hoped to relax in Ibiza resonates with the incidence of auto de fe which took place on June 30, 1680 at six in the morning and lasted for 14 hour (163). Joshua's Jewry obtruded on him time and again. For Joshua it is in Ibiza he connects with Jewish suffering and his roots rather than on the streets of Montreal. "Making Ibiza his base, he had come to Spain to look at battlefields, talk to survivors, learn what he could about the Spanish Civil War. Instead, he was discovering that he was Jewish" (*JTN 189*). The aerie attic along with Jake's Jewish allsorts bag in *St. Urbain's Horseman* echoes the brutality of the holocaust. Jake "fashions his "aerie" as a place where he can focus his energy – and his anger – on the escaped war criminal Josef Mengele" (Ravvin 36).

While many of the fleeing Jews of the earlier century settled in cities in Canada, Ephraim "the ordained" the skinny Jew, risked being a part of the John Franklin expedition. One of the remnants of the failed expedition was a "black satin skullcap with curious symbols embroidered on it both inside and out" (*SG 47*). Written in Hebrew the inscription read, "Observe the Sabbath, to keep it Holy". The *'yarmulke'* was one among the many Hebraic artifacts found later including a *'siddur'* or a Hebrew prayer book and *talith*, a prayer shawl. These indicate the travel of the Jew in the expedition which Moses tries to decode later. "One or more members of the Franklin expedition has been of Jewish extraction and the artifacts had been among their personal possessions" (*SG* 49). Richler's far-fetched imagination weaves in Jewish connections to the historically acclaimed John Franklin expedition connecting the crookedness of Ephraim and deporting him in a calamity-prone voyage of which he is a lone-survivor. These resound the survival skills of the Jew who resorts to dramatic schemes of existence.

The *'Torah'* scroll echoes the religious nature in the *"Bar mitzvah"* celebration as a Hebraic artifact in *Duddy Kravitz.* It is the armour of protection that shields Melech's secret letters to a gentile woman and interprets Wolf as a religious hero who died to save the *'Torah'* from the raging fire. But ironically it is the *'Torah'* which saves Wolf's idiocy in his uneventful death. Noah although a secular Jew wants to treasure his grandfather's scrolls which as Craniford observes: "an affirmation of the tradition even for those who do not follow it" *(37).* The skull cap a symbol of Jewish observance is an ironic symbol that resonates pretension in *Smaller Hero.* An observant Melech wears it and defrauds the peddler while Noah without a *'yarmulke'* stands for a truthful value system. Melech had inherited a prayer shawl and Phylacteries from his father but his son Wolf is forever obsessed with possessing Melech's cash box which he believes contains the hidden money. While the wonder of St. Urbain Street and cottage arrests the reader with surprise, Hebraic artifacts connect to the Jewish culture and horror of holocaust. These retrieve as far as possible the historical circumstances of their original creation.

Verbal portraits, Imagery and Symbols

Richler constructs 'resonant stories' through effective imagery and trades with 'symbolic economy' in developing images of his Jewish world. Parodying Noah and the Ark, *Smaller Hero* is plentiful with flood and drowning as a metaphor. Ada Craniford analyzes that the flood at the symbolic level drowns the unrighteous metaphorically. It is swallowed by the fire in the scrap yard and with Wolf drowns the tainting family secrets and his foolishness. Leah Adler scornfully replies to Wolf's movie outings, "Go, Go to the movies. There would be another flood as sure as I'm sitting here if you missed a double feature" *(SH 33).* The image of drowning is repeated to signal Theo's faint suspicions of something going wrong in his house and Miriam surrendering herself to the force of water in her bath after betraying Theo and in a sense Noah also. When Miriam realizes that Noah's love for her was waning, she fears that she would drown. Noah finds himself engulfed by troubled waters and closing in on him when external pressures are applied by a caging mother and a tugging Miriam. "The broken oars burst free of their locks. The boat itself broke up underneath him. And Noah, who did not call out for help, felt the waters close over him" (*SH 163).* "Adler" in Yiddish meant "eagle". "Noah Adler – the young eagle- is genetically programmed to leave the nest. And as a righteous man bearing the name of Noah, his biblical destiny is to sail away" (Craniford 32).

The image of the land, cane and telephone are recurrent symbols in *Duddy Kravitz.* Greenstein observes that the cane which Jerry Dingleman uses becomes a metonymic substitute for his antagonistic nature (*TS* 145). The telephone acts not only as an instrument of casual communication but is a tool of provocation and Duddy's guilt in Virgil's fits, "Above him the telephone receiver dangled loosely" (*DK* 306) causes the death of Mrs. MacPherson, "The receiver dangled idiotically from the hook above her" (*DK* 32) . If the telephone reminds Duddy of his guilt of fatal misbehaviours towards others, the land around the lake is the bait that allures, magnetizes and estranges him from his beloved people. The land is a destination to Duddy's dreams and a beginning of his commercial flicks.

> Before him spread a still blue lake and on the other side forest of pine trees. There was not one house on the lake. Some cows grazed on the meadow near the shore and over the next hill there was a cornfield and a silo. There were no other signs of life or ownership or construction. Duddy cracked his knuckles, he beat his fist into the palm of his open hand again and again. (*DK 98)*

The fascination of land by itself is a cultural memory. Duddy's life-obsession traces back to the struggle to return to the Promised Land, the dispersion of the Jews and The Diaspora itself. It is more than a land. It is Duddy re-invented.

Richler's Horseman symbol in *St. Urbain's Horseman* performs the function of Greenblatt's adaptation of Marx's 'reproduction and circulation of mimetic capital' (*MP* 6). The creation of St. Urbain's Horseman by Jake (echoes Richler's voice) to battle and avenge the horrors in Nazi concentration camps is an image of a Jewish superhero from the very streets of their childhood. "Jake's respect for the Horseman is motivated by his own feelings of irrelevancy in the face of Nazi's crime" (Ravvin 41). The Horseman on his white stallion who would rise and ride all over the globe to hunt down Doktor Josef Mengele is a fantastic creation of visual fantasies. It is a symbol of relief when the world in and around Jake was crumbling during the tormenting trial. Craniford says that the Horseman offers, "...an alternative set of pictures for the mind's eye, and thereby offers consolation to the heart" and two, "...represents everything that Jake himself is not, but wishes that he could be" (90). The image is a hope, a defense in an otherwise defenseless world, which guarantees that evil can be punished and the principles of moral rectitude can be restored. The galloping image is the sound of assurance of the '*Golem*' that help is at hand, the good is guarded. "Somehow, miraculously, the Horseman will be able to resolve Jake's discontent and disgust with his own professional inadequacies and with the hypocrisy of his artistic milieu" (Brener 98).

Craniford rightly puts it that the Horseman is a cleanser who would clean the world of Nazi "filth" as the mythical Hercules washed out the Augean stables. Drawing from the Jewish tradition, Richler identifies his Horseman as one of the thirty-six just men, who rise up every generation and fight for the just and God would not destroy the world on their account. This reference elevates the Horseman to the highest level of symbolism as a soldier of God. The Horseman image as a mimetic capital achieves "reproductive power, maintaining and multiplying themselves by transforming cultural contacts into novel" (Greenblatt, *MP* 6) and thereby the representation is not just a product but also a producer of varied meanings at different levels.

The same can be traced in scattered references to the scatological imagery which reeks out with filthy smells and stinking odours in *St. Urbain's Horseman*. "For most part he uses lavatory symbolism to connect characters, plot elements and themes in an intricate subterranean sewage system" (Craniford 87). The recurrent mention of sewers, lavatories and stench-filled citation of excrements and the public toilet are a link to Jake Hersh's problem in "letting go". Secondly, Jake's brother-in-law', Herky's obsession with lavatories and a tour of London lavatories act as a comic relief. His high-flown sentiments on the subject not only evoke laughter but as Craniford insists it is a "fusion of comic and tragic elements" strung together dramatically as in these lines,

> In London, above all, he wished to pay obeisances at the shrine of the incomparable Thomas Crapper, repository of stools immortal, where the Cascade had first been successfully flushed and the Niagara invented. Herky, warming to his subject, told Jake of the sparkling enamel toilets of Copenhagen, each bowl a joy to behold... (233)

Thirdly Richler's concentration is focussed when he draws a realistic picture of the humiliated female bondages in the concentration camps having to defecate in the open under military eyes of the Nazis and the brutal Mengele. This vivid, cruel, verbal photo reports the atrocities of a dehumanized treatment of the Jews, innumerable humiliations and responds to Holocaust with black humour and moral indignation. Finally, "On the level of language he tries to flush the pain out of Jake's mind through the symbolic power of toilet imagery. Since Jake's name evokes a lavatory, when relatives call him to account for his behaviour, his retort is "Flush, flush" (Craniford 94).

The raven is a symbol of dirt. While *St. Urbain's Horseman* stinks with scatological imagery, *Solomon Gursky* abounds with the scavenger symbol, The Raven. From the dust-free cover image of the raven to the end of the book, the scavenger weaves itself into the story. It is representative of all the scavengers including the Gurskys who feed on everything, not to clean the society but to pollute it. They feed to claim the lot as their own, to grow wings and soar higher and higher. The raven symbol works on different levels. It is the representative of all the greedy acts of the hungry scavengers in the novel. Raven the bird that failed Biblical Noah is perched on Ephraim's shoulder and he claims that he could communicate with it. (*SG 37*). One of the stories that Ephraim entertained Solomon was how an Eskimo folklore of Iktoomi, a Noah figure cursed a greedy raven which fed on a dead body when sent on an errand: "'Since you have such a dirty nature, you shall have a dirty colour'. Right then the raven was turned from white to black and that colour he remains to this day" (*SG 43*).

The raven like Richler flies all over the globe mapping lives. Solomon in his Chinese Journal notes "Then a raven appeared out of nowhere, soaring and swooping, and the men followed it to the banks of the Hou River" (*SG 78).* Moses also notes that Chang-feng Chen and Hi Hsin also wrote about the raven. Hsin wrote: "that just before the appearance of the big black bird Solomon had tramped up and down, searching the skies, some sort of sad clacking noise, an inhuman call, coming from the black of his throat" (*SG 78).* Larson translates that *Corvus* is Latin for Raven a name related to Solomon. The raven's presence like Solomon's is global. The supposed reincarnation of Solomon, Sir Hyman Kaplansky hints about the deceitful nature of the raven to Moses, "I see that you've been seduced by the deceitful raven" (*SG 191).* He narrates an Eskimo folklore of how a raven swooped over a cluster of igloos and duped them into building new shelters at the foot of the cliff. Later the deceitful raven flew straight to the top of a cliff and jumped and danced starting an avalanche which buried the trusting inhabitants, who become the raven's food in spring.

Sir Hyman once told Moses the Haidas significance of the raven. "Because the raven had always existed and always would" (*SG 493).* "He was slowed down in his pursuit of food and other fleshy pleasures and in his constant and notorious need to meddle and change things. And so inevitably, he took it upon himself to steal the light of the universe from the old man". Later he points out to a picture "A raven perched on a half-open sea shell, human beings struggling to emerge from it" (*SG 499).* This raven as Solomon indirectly claims is himself not hungry for once. On the news of Hyman's drowning, Moses declares: "Obviously the raven with the unquenchable itch was at it again, playing tricks on the world and its creatures. *Once by air,* he thought, *and now by water"* (*SG 501).*

One constantly hears the fluttering wings of the raven "whose natural habitat is north" all through the novel. Richler allows it to fly right through the novel each time with a different purpose either in the literal or metaphorical sense. "A raven skewered and harpooned to the grave" (*SG 257*) operates at the physical level as a symbol of warning and revenge. "…his Gypsy Moth with the raven painted on the fuselage" (*SG 484*) marks it as an image of power and identity. "The night before Henry was to start on his journey a big menacing black raven pecked at their bedroom window, wakening Nialie with a start" (*SG* 523) indicates a bad omen.

Craniford observes that the impish raven in the mythology of many nations was able to change from bird to man and back again performing supernatural deeds. Likewise, "Ephraim and Solomon lead a magical, God-like existence" (*110).* The raven is the friend of "the shape-changers" like Ephraim and Solomon. The book Mrs. Mc Clure prescribes Moses is *The Quest for Corvo* supplies the raven symbol that Richler adopts and parodies as a leitmotif. He appropriates this symbol and weaves it into Solomon's many disguises and activities. Craniford unravels that Solomon is the shadowy genius behind Corvus Trust of Zurich and a major shareholder of the Raven Mine in Yellowknife. He owns mythological paintings of raven, plants a stuffed raven on his brother Bernard's grave and at the end of the novel flies north in a plane that turns into a raven with flapping wings. If the raven is Richler's image from the natural world, he automates it into a mechanized Gypsy Moth airplane which Solomon flies.

The raven is also used as a metaphor and simile repeatedly indicating the dark hair of Miriam in *Barney's Version* and to indicate the darkness inside the coal mine "It was dark down there, dark as a raven's wing…" (*SG 227*). It denotes the dark working conditions of the coal mines. The raven is not only Solomon's symbol but Richler's too. He rightly employs the image of the scavenger, powerful and scheming, an oxymoron to the Biblical Dove to carry the figurative image of all that dark, black and attractive. Craniford states, "For the good guys Richler's raven show themselves to be friends and familiars, but for the bad guys and those who are about to make a terrible mistake they are signs and portents of doom" (115).

Another image of significance in the novel is the Salmon Fly and Silver doctor. Moses keeps searching for the salmon fly and acknowledges that he didn't need the Silver Doctor which he loses at the beginning of the book and later retrieves it when a friend sits on it. Through the metaphor of the salmon lure, the Silver Doctor, Richler contemplates the rapport between a fisherman and the fish he is trying to angle. Moses applies this relationship to the link between the writer and his subject. Craniford notices: "He wonders whether he had decided to write a biography of Solomon and the Gurskys of his own free will, or whether it was the crafty Solomon who chose him to be the Gursky scribe" (116). There is a point in the novel where one doubts whether Moses is the fisherman or the fish. But towards the end of the novel a baited Moses frees off the Solomon's angle and is convinced that he will never be able to write anything.

Richler in *Barney's Version* uses natural, simple, common and less far-fetching images. The opening lines of the novel suggest the grit in Barney's life through the metaphor of splinter that drives him to write the memoir of his life. "TERRY'S THE SPUR. The splinter under my fingernail" (*BV* 1). This image of the sundry splinter earlier occurs in the previous novel where Mr. Bernard complains about Bert Smith's moral policing, "I'm stuck with a little *goyishe* splinter under my fingernail" (*SG* 472). The prickly character of Jane whose pin pricks pain Pauline is expressed through the image, "Well, Jane is the stone in your shoe and I wish I could get her out. Stop seeing her" (*JTN 116).* Talking about Terry's view of life, Barney notes that for Terry it was "a responsibility". So he unlike Barney will not have pages of regret of "wasted years". In a child-like wonder image Richler through Barney compares Terry's "trust" on life to a "black-and-white drawing in a child's colouring book that was his to crayon, filling it with the utmost autobiographical care, mindful of future criticism" (*BV 91-92).* This imagery brings to light the child-like wonder and love of Terry to live life worthily. For

Barney, Blair was that "unwanted polyp "who entered into his life in 1969.

Richler's select novels do not abound with a deluge of grainy images. They are sole, isolated and strong as a boulder of stone and loom large like mountains in meaning, operating at many levels of symbolism. They do not superficially ornament or glamourize language but are ingrained technically and integrated in the storylines.

Places such as St. Urbain Street and the cottages resonate and revisit places of history with Jewish experience. Historical and Hebraic artifacts echo the ideology of pretension and how they are used as outward religious symbols and men manipulate its religiosity to conceal their small or grave misgivings. Imagery and symbolism are integrated, have an omniscient presence and are prone to recurrence. Thus, when a reader confronts these landmarks, objects and images one is struck with the 'wonder' of the age and pass on to the 'resonance' of Richler's age and space having a "*re*-turning effect to the past" (Lai 12). They are 'textual relics' which have a meaningful desire for cultural resonance with a strong narrative purpose to connect with the reality of the age.

4.3 Parody, Irony and Allusions

Richler employs lavish parody which echoes past works that give a postmodern perspective to his works. Through parody and irony Richler speaks of his culture, from within, but without being totally co-opted by it. Hutcheon recognizes that parody allows a certain distance for the writer for separation at the same time the doubled structure of both (the superimposition of two meanings or texts) demands recognition of *complicity.* Richler's use of biblical and literary sources as 'ironic subtexts' in the select novels evaluates both the world he mimics and the one he fashions. Thus parody both asserts and undercuts that which it contests. Richler extravagantly parodies and alludes Biblical structures, stories, characters and the conventions of the Jewish tradition.

Craniford observes that Richler skillfully creates an ironic distance between the Biblical Noah and the Noah of *Smaller Hero.* "Both Noahs sail away, but Richler shows us in detail what happens to the people left on shore, and the conflicted emotions of the one who leaves them behind" (*3*). Richler through his parody states that each one is responsible for his salvation and failing to do so they drown. Craniford traces a blend of literary sources parodied in the character of Duddy that includes the Biblical story of David and Goliath, and Budd Schulberg's *What makes Sammy Run?* Duddy is a Jewish nickname for "David" as pointed out by Michael Greenstein in one of his essays. David's strength, power and loyalty to his family and Sammy Glick's crass nature make up the dual nature of Duddy. This duality of character frightened Uncle Benjy. "Duddy has a conscience; it's just that it's crammed with loop-holes" (Yanofsky 110). This makes him both hateful and admired because he did not just want to prosper but get even with all who looked down on him unlike Sammy who had an appetite without conscience.

Barney's "Troika" has earlier shadows in the Wonder-Olive story in *Duddy Kravitz* where Olive had gone through three husbands, twice divorced and one committed suicide. This supposed parody is elaborated in Barney's character throwing light on marriage and relationships. Jake is named after the biblical Jacob, son of Isaac who stole his brother Esau's blessing. Jake also tricks his dying father Issy into blessing him. "This parody, rather than denigrating the biblical source, lends dignity to Jacob Hersh's otherwise profoundly foolish behaviour" (Craniford 7).

Hutcheon states that Richler uses and abuses the '*Golem*' myth, making it recount the ironic triumph of living art that helps the oppressed. He lodges an ironical twist with questions on the Horseman's morality who invariably is Jake's moral editor. Richler builds in sequences of gambling, blackmail, family desertion, drink and drugs to the Horseman idol, which leads to questioning Joey's moral compass. He does it objectively and leaves behind an ambivalent reader guessing. The reader has to decide between an angry Joey prompting people to rise, playing the ringleader role in an unprovoked attack on an Arab village, a warrior of the International Brigades and a debtor, pathological liar drugged in hashish and a bigamist.

Richler's *Joshua Then and Now* harbingered his return to Canada. It parodies the famous battles of Biblical Joshua who led the Israelites over the Jordon River into the Promised Land, clearing everything and everyone who stood on the way. The novel pictures a recouping Joshua as a fighter, dauntless hero. Craniford states that, parodying his "coming home", both Richler and Joshua have to reinvent themselves to reestablish in the land of their birth and youth. She also hints that Esther Shapiro's appeal is a parody to the Queen Esther's beauty and strength of purpose in *The Book of Esther.* Richler is quick to parody the Biblical stories. In a comical rendition of Abraham's test of faith, Barney writes at the end of the story, "But I doubt that things were ever the same again between Abe and Izzy" (*BV 47).* Reuben delights in making eccentric exegeses of the Bible. Victor Ramraj says that Reuben's Biblical discussions are characterized by "a raw colloquialism and an ability to apply his interpretation of the Bible to every day situations' (112). His morality talks on "sex and religion" are the hilarious parts of the novel. In his reworking of '*Purim*' from *The Book of Esther* he calls Esther's uncle Mordecai "a real conniver, a suckhole, a very bloodthirsty fella… and certainly the first Jewish pimp" (*JTN 288).* In a mocking parody, he churns out two morals. One is Mordecai's ultimate agenda was personal. The second conclusion is hilariously paradoxical. Reuben finds that there were no complains in the Bible of the Jewess marrying a *goy*, "So, if I interpret the law correctly, you are not allowed to marry out of the faith unless it's into a royal family. Interesting, eh?" (*JTN 291*).

Richler attempts another medley of parodies in *Solomon Gursky.* Craniford explains that the novel is a parody of the historical saga genre due to the mythic quality of its eccentric characters and also exploration of the repercussions of greed, revenge and betrayal. Apart from spoofing the World War II graffiti message "Kilroy Was Here", Craniford adds to the list Newman's *Bronfman Dynasty* and A.J.A. Symons *The Quest for Corvo.* The absent

Bronfman third brother is linked to the *Corvo* story thus distancing and recreating the multilayered tale of the booze dynasty.

Richler parodies the Gurskys with his story within story on the Gerstein brothers in chapter five of the novel hinting on the possible murder of Solomon by Bernard, by planting in a bomb. Richler cleverly makes it Barney's detective story. But it is to be noted that the narrator of his next novel is also named Barney who is an unreliable narrator. Richler hints all possible solutions to the mystery that shrouds Solomon's disappearance, but makes suspense a guaranteed end product till the very conclusion.

Craniford writes that Richler has taken his clue for *Barney's Version from* Saul Bellow's *Herzog.* He tackles Bellow's theme of hopelessly mismanaged existence and marriages with boisterous zeal. She further observes that Richler's "own story" is infiltrated with Bellow's "own story" and both are woven into a narrative line that is pure invention (123). Writing a parody of Bellow's story Richler immediately divides Herzog's wife Madeleine into three wives-otherwise known as "Barneys troika". The episode of the disappearance of Boogie, Barney's friend and mentor provides a magnificent example of how Richler can take a line from another writer's work, and put his own spin on it. Richler replays his courtship of Florence and winning of her love with the situation played in the reverse in the Barney-Miriam encounter.

Richler not only alludes to other works but also of his own writings. Craniford observes that Noah in *Smaller Hero* hopes that he would be a wiser man living in another cottage near a stream with a "less neurotic Miriam" and Richler shadily alludes to this in *Barney's Version.* Noah's "less neurotic Miriam" is Barney "heart's desire Miriam" whom he loses because of his inattention and stupidity. For Barney, Boogie was a writing genius, mentor and a soul-mate. He says, "It was Boogie who introduced me to Goncharov, Huysmans, Celine, and Nathanael West" (*BV 10).* He was a well-read globe trotter who was fluent in German and Hebrew, studied the Zohar the holy book of the Cabbala and once a week was with a *Rabbi* in a synagogue. Craniford observes semblances of Boogie as a "deeply flawed mentor" to Joey Hersh who is Jake's hero. "Boogie is a small, sick version of the shining Horseman: a false moral guide who ends up as a pile of bones and is finally put to rest" (135). Craniford misses out on Solomon who also belongs to this band of vagabonds who fascinated Moses Berger with a larger-than-life image. Isaac the son of Henry is a pursuer of his successful uncle Lionel, leaving behind the ideals of his father in Tulugaqtitut. For a twenty-one-year-old Joshua, on Ibiza Island, Juanito is a mentor. While Joshua is protected by Juanito, Barney and Jake adored their guides but Moses exhausts his youth to solve the Solomon-mystery.

Richler also draws inferences from his personal life while he always denied publically that his works weren't autobiographical. Florence who is Richler's "heart's desire" is the exemplar for Richler's fictional good-wives and home-makers. They include, Nancy the all-supportive wife of Jake Hersh, Pauline, the supportive system that sustained Joshua and shocked him with her absence and who later comes back, the faithful Diana Morgan whom Solomon loved and Miriam the outstanding and long-standing wife of Barney lost by sheer folly. In all these wives overlooking their duration of stay with the men they loved, Richler has nourished them with Florence's abundant love, unconditional care, charming grace and faithfulness. Mordecai's daughter Emma Richler in an E-message stated, "I thought his portrayal and sensitivity towards women characters – as did his descriptions and sensitivity towards landscape – changed drastically with age. This had almost everything to do with my mother".

Irony

Irving Howe claims that Jewish jests flourish with "an irony which measured the distance between pretension and actuality, held it up for public inspection and then made of it the salt of self-ridicule" (19). Ironical twists and statements abound with parody and are embedded in the Richler narratives.

Richler's *Smaller Hero* and *St. Urbain's Horseman* are ironically titled since the smaller hero and the horseman of the titles do not refer to the protagonists of the novels. The smaller hero is not Noah but the "meek, self-effacing father ironically named 'Wolf'" (Craniford 29). The names of the characters are specifically ironic since they suggest characteristics opposite to the characterization. Craniford points out to Melech and Theo. Melech means 'King'. But Noah's grandfather has lost his control over the family as the head. Theo is the Greek name for God. But Theo lacks God-like power to control life and is a helpless, impotent Professor. The unbent Melech's hiding of his love letters beneath the religious artifacts lends poignant irony since it was his religion that forbade his affection for a gentile woman.

The Boy Wonder is the yardstick of success for all St. Urbain Street boys and fathers. For them he was a global success. It's ironical when Duddy comes to know that Mr. Calder one of the powerful men in the city did not know the Boy Wonder. "What, Duddy thought, if the truly powerful people in the city knew nothing about the Wonder? Could it be that the Boy wonder was only famous on St Urbain Street?" (*DK 198).* The irony is the Boy Wonder was much celebrated by the Street people.

Pathetic irony overtakes the final conversations between Uncle Benjy and Duddy. Duddy rebukes his uncle for considering him with contempt like dirt. He says, "I wish I'd made more time for you. God help me but I wish I'd seen what your *zeyda* saw" (*DK 243).* But the irony is, it's too late for Uncle Benjy to understand Duddy. Ironical situation continues when Yvette starts rejecting Duddy whom Duddy was trying to avoid on a life-long relationship. But when she starts walking out of his life because of Virgil's accident, Duddy is pained.

Jake's search for the Horseman and his association with the perverted Harry are ironical given the fact that he has a moral conscience. Brenner notes that his identification with Harry "amounts to his betrayal of the Horseman" (110). The creation of the Horseman is a fine example of ambiguity and irony. Jake believes Joey to be the Horseman of his fantasy where in who fights for Jewish redemption along with Hanna, Joey's mother. But Uncle Abe practically tries to smuggle him out of the thought by factually describing him no less than a cigarette smuggler. Every time Jake pursues Joey he eludes leaving behind debts and women he managed to use. Thus, the Horseman's role in being Jake's moral editor is blatantly ironic because the rest of the world considers him as scandalous and disgraceful. Same is true of Duddy who is encouraged and cheered by Max an ethically-challenged father and Barney who considers Boogie his guru who has misplaced his moral compass. It is ironical that Duddy does not adhere to a morally upright Yvette who acts as a conscience check from time to time. While Jake pursues Joey, Barney continues to uphold Boogie as his moral editor.

Irony runs through the narratives of the concluding chapters of Part IV of *Joshua Then and Now* that include a contrasting study of Uncle Oscar in the 1940's when he is shown thinking up harebrained schemes for becoming a millionaire and in 1970's when as an old man he must drive to make a living. There is also an ironic parallel between the accounts of the past where young Joshua listens to stories of his father's shady, dishonest activities and of the present where the seventy-three-year-old Reuben listened to McMaster's report of Joshua's acts of vandalism.

Barney's Version has irony embedded in its plot, characters and conversations. "Clara, who despised other women, enjoying posthumous fame as a feminist martyr" (*BV 58).* Clara's posthumous fame is an irony as Barney explains, "…the martyred Saint Clara's admirers are legion, and have two things in common: they take me for an abomination and fail to understand that Clara intensely disliked other women, whom she considered rivals for male attention she thrived on" (*BV* 109). Barney the writer of his story is aware of the irony that although he abhorred The Second Mrs. Panofsky's rambling conversation, he on the other hand consumes a lot of pages piled in with digressions deterring away from the main facts that occurred on the seminal Laurentian weekend that destroyed his peace. Seriously interrogated by O'

Hearne, who wouldn't believe in his innocence a frustrated Barney's ironical explanation that he had got Boogie right through the heart and got him buried in the woods is seriously noted by the cop and is reproduced as a statement of confession in the court. Barney in an exasperated tone asks, "Are you a total stranger to irony, O'Hearne?" (*BV* 334).

Saul yells at the hospital staff to find the TV set turned on to Oprah Winfrey and shouted, "This is my father's room, and he doesn't watch such crap" (*BV* 411). Ironically Barney had engaged himself all his life producing crap for television. Richler parodies the celebration of the Passover from a female perspective. Barney ironically gives an account of how The Second Mrs. Panofsky; a militant feminist celebrates a female Passover by joining six other rejected wives for a women's *'Sedar'*. Lifting up the plate with the matzohs, they chant: "This is the Sedar plate. /The plate is flat. Women is flat, like a plate, / flat in the relief of history..." *(BV 204-205).* The tyranny of Barney's trial ends with an ironical twist where a bishop's witness saves his Jew blood.

Close readings of the texts unravel literary and Biblical allusions embedded in conversations. A drunken Friar admits his instable state and calls out to Duddy: "Ah, Kravitz, come to collect your pound of flesh, I suppose" echoing the callous Shylock's nature of Duddy who squeezed the last bit out of dying people. The weak Mr. Friar, the camera man of Duddy's *'Bar mitzvah'* and wedding movies cries out, "I've sold my soul to the Hebrews. Shame on me" *(DK 200).* Friar sounds like the Dr. Faustus with the lost soul, totally under the control of Duddy and the phrase "pound of flesh" echoes Shylock's ruthlessness. On one of the visits to his treasured land around Lac St Pierre Duddy is caught in the wintry snow. Battling his physical hardship and heading for safety to his car, he symbolically alludes to his survival to be a Moses, a champion of Jews but did not want to be denied access to the Promised Land. "His feet burned from the cold... he began to think what in the hell am I doing lost in a blizzard, a Jewish boy? Moses, he recalled from *Biblical Comics,* died without reaching the Promised Land, but *I've* got my future to think of" *(DK 212).* This allusion works out Duddy's obsession with materialistic success and possession.

A brother-bitten Morrie denies that "I'm not Bernard's keeper and he's not mine" (*SG 209)* alluding to Cain's statement, 'Am I my brother's keeper'. Richler parodies Jesus' resurrection in a comical narration of Bernard's funeral. "Mr. Bernard died on a Monday, at the age of seventy-five, his body wasted. He lay in state for two days in the lobby of the Bernard Gursky Tower and, as he failed to rise on the third, he was duly buried" (*SG 253*). Barney notices The Second Mrs. Panofsky at the Ritz and tells Miriam, "Don't look back, ... or you might turn into a pillar of salt" (*BV 143)* alluding to the Biblical Lot's wife. He comically informs that befriending Terry was "a road not taken" alluding to Frost's famous poem. Barney alludes to the mythical characters of the Greek Philemon and Baucis. He dreams that Miriam and he in their nineties would expire simultaneously like their Greek counterparts. He wishes that a beneficent Zeus with a gentle stroke of his caduceus would transmogrify into two trees whose branches would reach out to each other in winter and leaves would intermingle in spring (*BV 217)*.

Although Richler's characters are bound to deceive, transgress and indulge in amoral ways, there is a certain amount of "goodness and grace" that redeems them. This binding of grace with crass makes Richler's plots and characterization distinct from the enormous literary sources he parodies. Linda Hutcheon in *The Canadian Postmodern* notes "intertextuality" is both New Historic and Postmodern in theory where parody is a constant tool of application (9). Richler from the beginning, parodies themes, characters, and incidents from books by writers he admires. Craniford makes an interesting reference to Richler's creation of the Jewish main characters where all Noah, Duddy, Jake, Joshua, Moses and in a sense Solomon, come out more or less intact, except Barney Panofsky. Survival is guaranteed for these characters because of the Biblical names and stories attached to them. Poor Barney, a literary character of Richler's old age alone diminishes. Above all, by using the technique of parody to weave his immense literary material and imagination, Richler parodies himself along with his fictional heroes. It exhibits his ace – technique that he did not just recycle or imitate material but through 'cultural mobility' reinvented stories that would absorb the context of his age into his texts. Richler through allusions and parody negotiates literary boundaries, thus absorbing from his literary space and reworking with the Richler-yarn and twist, to create texts of the hyphenated culture of the mid-twentieth century Jewish Montreal ghetto.

4.4. Richler's Barbs and Caricatures

> "To cope with the anxiety produced by these incongruities, they created a humor in which laughter and trembling were inextricably mingled"
>
> (Sarah Blacher Cohen 2).

A New Historicist study links literature to the idea of constraint that includes cultural reinforcement of boundaries and rules and the 'praise or blame' of it is found in a literary genre such as satire. Magdelene Redekop writes that comedy has a special place in Canada that is hard to separate from the Canadian idea of national literature and presents a catalogue of comic writers which include T.C. Haliburton, Thomas McCulloch, Antonine Maillet, Paul Hiebert, L.M. Montogomery, Robert Kroetsch, Jack Hodgins, Stephen, Leacock, Robertson Davies, Mordecai Richler, Margaret Atwood, Thomas King, Terry Griggs and many more (263).

Richler's works are characterized by sheer wit and gusto. Through caustic satire, Richler emphasizes on the actions or modes of conduct of not only the Jews, but also the non-Jew. For his open ridicule he was even labeled as a 'self-hating Jew' placing him in an ambivalent position. Cohen observes that he is "the doubly alienated minority writer who is forced to be more caustic in his mockery of the majority… What Richler creates then is a Jewish-Canadian comedy of cultural revenge" (12). He was considered a Jew in a gentile literary world and an anti-Semite in a Jewish world. But a reader becomes aware of Richler's morality and an earnest quest to be an honest writer and ridicule was a tool he readily employed wherever he found hypocrisy and greed. David Myers states, "It is also a classical technique of the satirist to mount an ethical attack by mocking his victims with tendentious distortion and simplification" (48).

Cohen observes that Jewish humour was born out of the vast discrepancy between what was to be the "chosen people's" glorious destiny and their desperate straits. She notes that, "Richler's urban comedy, with its unbuttoned candor, schoolboy irreverence and gutter literalness, ridicules the faithful and taunts the squeamish. Uncovering the venal within the venerable, it exposes the earthly fallibility of the seemingly virtuous" (13).

Greenstein in "Mordecai Richler and Jewish-Canadian Humor" states, "Mordecai Richler would probably agree that Jewish-Canadian humor is neither Jewish, nor Canadian, nor humorous" (196). Richler constructs and deconstructs the ghetto walls with his tool of social satire. If his protagonists transgress and moral police hypocrisy; Richler satirizes to expose them.

Eric Wright in his afterword to the novel explains, Comedy begins with a society in disorder, with the wrong people in charge, and it ends, like *Joshua Then and Now*, with an image of the ideal society" (*JTN 371).* He observes that funnier than the WASP satire, is the one on Jewish establishment that has emerged from aping the Westmount they have been competing against because Richler is writing from the inside. "Richler inverts a tradition of anti-Semitic stereotypes into purposeful comedy", states Greenstein. He explains, "Since the displaced person trespasses wherever he steps or runs across the Diaspora's invisible borders, he turns to irony, comic revenge, or heretic humour as a first and last resort" (*TS* 155).

Through black humour he ridicules the Jewish traditions in *Smaller Hero.* Humour is the whip with which Richler strikes the root of hypocrisy. Greenstein observes that Duddy is a comic hero, a caricature of double emergence of a Canadian and a Jew who races and rebels with a rusty spoon in his mouth "all forms of silver-spooned authority" (*Jewish Wry* 198). Scenes of the graduation ceremony at Fletcher's Field school, Duddy's meeting with Aunt Ida and bringing her to Uncle Benjy's home and Cohen's *'Bar mitzvah'* movie are comical masterpieces.

Guy Vanderhaeghe in the Afterword in *St. Urbain's Horseman* notes the peak of hilarity in the passages that deal with the byzantine politics of show biz and notes that by itself is an extension of life itself bared during the Hampstead Heath softball game; Jake's feverish, clowning tell-tale at Ormsby-Fletcher's dinner party and the plot summaries of Doug's socially conscious and stickily earnest radio plays. He adds that, "Uneasy laughter is its natural accompaniment" (464). Jake's indulgence in sexual fancies and reveries like that of Barney's and self-examination of his physic are instances of comical heights that liquefy the demarcating lines between guilt and innocence. Greenstein in his essay notes that these droll situations illustrate "The battle between id and super-ego ends in a confused Yiddish ego, questioning its innocence, sanity, and involvement" (*Jewish Wry* 205). In a collision between nature and culture, Jake's inabilities to align himself with the British pretensions especially in his visit to the Ormsby-Fletcher country home, projected through scatological imagery abound with of hilarity which intends cultural revenge.

Belonging to the urban novels of 1960s and 1970s, Linda Hutcheon notes that Richler's novels exposed his own generation of urban middle-class Jewish professionals and intellectuals in *Joshua Then and Now* without leaving the Protestant establishment unscathed. Richler's two strong contenders for the best comedian are Joshua's parents. While his father Reuben indulges in heretic humour in his decoding of Biblical passages his mother Esther Shapiro strips convention through her strip-tease dance in the *'Bar mitzvah'* that are significant comic interludes. Reuben's jokes with a tinge of cynicism and sharpness strips off "pretentious religious affiliation" of the people. Greenstein remarks that the Jewish jokes help to regain paradise temporarily with instances of laughter that bridges "then" and "now" and retrieves historical loss. He explains that comedy counteracts the Fall and Expulsion and raises the spirit and reintegrates the outsider into society. "Richler employs slapstick, practical jokes, running laughter and running commentary in his marathon" (*TS* 156).

Richler's commentaries on marriage, time and again echo the infidelity that shreds the relationships. He withholds pontification and relieves the uncomfortable tension with his sharp wit. The Senator's unhappy marriage with Madeleine de Gaspe Beirut, a legendary beauty, notoriously unfaithful, a drunkard is stated with Richler's unassuming crafty line, which the Senator's says, "She died in a nursing home, in a state of delirium, even as he held her hand, and she called out another man's name" (*JTN* 129). Richler's recurrent voice is that of the satirist with wicked wits and caustic comedy. Self-deprecating jokes are a part of the Jewish wry.

> "Hey, Stu," Reuben asked, nudging him, "you know why Jews have such
>
> big noses?"
>
> "I bite. Why?"
>
> "Because the air is free." *(JTN 362).*

"As some Jews commit the genetic fallacy of forgetting their humble origins in their drive toward American expansion, Richler's satire serves as a reminder that the past deflates all pretensions to superiority" (Greenstein, *TS* 158).The individual targets range from the crooked cop, Detective McMaster, to the successful Jewish doctors and dentists who have changed their names as they moved up to join the WASPS in Westmount, to the merely ludicrous, compulsive philanderer Seymour Kaplan and Joshua's hopeless Uncle Oscar. If Joshua's vandalizing is a comical revenge on a pseudo-society, powdered with pretense, then his wrongly timed-return to Ibiza is a "comedy of errors".

Richler uses his ace parodying skills with competent humour through Reuben's Biblical interpretations. In a witty explanation of the plague in the Old Testament, Reuben remarks, God "after each one he hardened Pharaoh's heart so he could display his whole bag of tricks" *(JTN 73).* Richler's comedy operates at different levels. From self-deprecating remarks to Biblical satire, he drives into the veins of the morality of his age. In a conversation between Pauline and Joshua, Pauline questions the moral rectitude.

> "Shapiros don't take money from women," Reuben said, appalled.
>
> "I'm not a woman, I'm his wife. How much do we need?"
>
> "You heard my father."
>
> "You mean it's O.K. to rob banks and collect insurance, as you both put it, and break hands and not pay taxes," she said, her voice rising, "but it's immoral to take money from your wife?" (*JTN 254)*

For Richler, humor is not the end but the means. Gurevich affirms, delicious as his putdowns of Jewish bourgeoisie are, his books go beyond mere satire. If self-deprecation is the chief characteristic of Jewish humour, then Mr. Richler has reached the apex with his ruthless, social satire of rich Jews. Herky Hersh's tour of Europe with faithful visits of the continent's urinals display Richler's craftsmanship in *St. Urbain's Horseman.* Be it a six-page description of Bernard Gursky the liquor tycoon's seventy-fifth birthday banquet, featuring elaborate and extravagant arrangements and list of guests or a one-liner, Richler is at his witty peak. In a very funny conversation Bernard Gursky talks to his assistant about who should write his biography:

> "What about Churchill, who wrote his stuff?"
>
> "He did, Mr. Bernard."
>
> "Oh yeah?... Maybe yes and maybe no. Now this Hemingway fella, how much can he earn?"
>
> "He's dead.
>
> "Of course he's dead. You think I don't know? You're getting on my nerves, Harvey. Haven't you any work to do?" (*SG 154*)

Bernard says, "For this job I don't want a Canadian. I want the best" (*SG* 154). In another dialogue, a French Quebec official attending a Gursky wedding scolds his wife for using French the language of the peasantry and to speak Yiddish as the Gurskys. Guervich notes, "Both these jokes are lethally double-edged; as a humorist, Mr. Richler will never waste a stone on just one bird—not when he can get two". He exposes the foolishness of the rich Gurskys. Richler's barbed wires run throughout *Solomon Gursky.* When Lucy, Solomon's daughter in her attempt to become a star wastes money to buy name she decides to showcase a production and invites producers and agents. This Moses thinks is the biggest foolish act as he knows that Lucy has never been an actress nor has taken her lessons. He immediately predicts the fate of the venture and remarks, "I think you should hire an audience as well and pay them to applaud" (*SG 206).*The Hyman Kaplan episode of celebrating the Passover with bleeding *'matzohs'* is a hilarious settling of scores of an avenging Jew, slitting hypocrisy with a comical knife.

Witch-fully satiric, at many instances the Richler-Barney voice blends into one, spurring caustic acid in delineation and description of people, places and events in Barney's Version. Narrating death could be no better than a quip as seen in the reportage of Clara's: "Clara, who now enjoys posthumous fame as a feminist icon, beaten on the anvil of male-chauvinist insentience. My anvil, so they say" (*BV* 2). Richler tears through the skin of hypocrisy with Barney's teeth. The laugh-aloud description and "irreverent satire" of what Greenstein calls "the 'nouveaux riches of Montreal Jewish community' (*CJW* 9) is a direct slam on them. Barney and Richler are inseparable in their laugh aloud commentary on the flippant The Second Mrs. Panofsky. Once Barney remarks that she was the best cook of all his three wives his friend warns him that she strictly wouldn't accept nor appreciate even a compliment from Barney. Barney in a one-liner quip replies, "She still accepts my monthly cheques" (*BV* 86). Richler's hilarity finds its way in delineating characters. Miriam humourously makes an empathizing statement on Barney's "family grievance to nurse", "Some people collect stamps or bookmatch covers, … but you my darling, it's grievances" (*BV* 17-18). The Second Mrs. Panofsky's descriptions are samples of heightened humour. She begins with a line "I've got to be brief, we are just on our way out" *(BV* 223). The brief conversation generously runs to three or four pages of unparagraphed account faithfully sketching out the minutest detail of their trip to Paris with a non-stop grandiose of words that leaves a listener breathless.

Richler armours his sextet men with comedy and wages a battle with "comic revenge" to move from the margins to centre against structures that hinder their progress. His caricatures indulge in what Cohen calls as "a cerebral comedy of errors which showed the limitations of strained thinkers – the circularity of their reasoning, their faulty premises and absurd proofs" (2). Comedy, on one level, is an abdication by the theorist, but the vexing issues remain before us when the laughter dies down (Redekop 266). Richler's jests are characteristic of Jewish humour which Howe remarks "is not humorous" which can provoke an uproarious laughter (19). Richler's satire tends to be more social and cultural. When political it is against Mackenzie and as Woodcock notes its more "local such as Zionism and the lingering Communist echoes of the 1930s" (*IDK* 54). Beneath Richler's wasp-stings of satire and burlesque Greenstein excavates, "a fierce moralism that exposes the hypocrisies of a conservative WASP establishment as well as the foibles of a noveau riche Jewish community that has abandoned its spiritual roots in favour of an illusory security within the Canadian mainstream" (*TS* 206). David Myers identifies Richler's satire to be "light-hearted and farcical in tone, is outrageously explicit on race, religion, and sex, and draws on an apparently inexhaustible supply of contemporary and topical bêtises" (52).

This chapter analyzes how Richler employs literary tools to narrate the belief system of his period. It examines how the systems of social power and the voice of the marginalized as reflected and reinforced in his texts establish a relationship between the aesthetic practices of the literary texts and other social practices. Richler's symbolism unearths the wonder of Jewish-Montreal ghetto which is retrieved in the Greenblatt sense as "a displaced and exotic and idealized image of the cultural mobility" (*MP* 25) of the twentieth century. Thus, Richler through the predominant resonance of the St Urbain Street wonder, Hebraic artifacts, the symbols and metaphors of the raven, salmon, Yiddish inflected discourses, mimetic assumptions of the Jewish Montrealer, representations of the Orthodox-secular Jewish worlds, project the conflicting 'circumambient space' of a hyphenated Jewish-Canadian identity. His sword of satire and barbaric wires of caustic anger evaporates into subtle laughter, exposes the moral standards of the age and maintains an aesthetic distance through ambivalence. Richler's texts supersede market values and stand the test of time with its 'cultural poetics'.

5

The Promised Land

> "Every country gets the foreigners it deserves..." Was I going down the staircase to a strange land? Was I, then, to be a stranger there? But how could I be foreign in the place where my treasure lay? Surely, I was native there, however long I had been absent?
>
> (Robertson Davies, *The Deptford Trilogy 515*)

It is recorded that the Jews in "The Exodus" of *The Holy Bible* took forty years to reach the Promised Land. Their rebellious attitude made a short journey into a long convoluted one. It was arduous and herculean and few reached the Land of milk and honey. Some even wanted to go back to Egypt though it represented oppression in its worst form. Richler's protagonists seethe with rebellion in their youth and deviation seems a likely option. The "Promised Land" for them is a metaphor for transcending the ghetto wall. Chapter V *The Promised Land* analyzes the question whether the protagonists' 'improvisation' results in conforming to the socially given ghetto living or breaking away from their ghetto-mentality or ghetto-mindedness. It examines the roads taken and lands reached by various protagonists and how the culture, stricture, orthodoxy and the towering ghetto wall affects the social formation of the characters and the choices they make.

This chapter summarizes the ideas of previous chapters. It discusses whether the conflicts from the surrounding spaces lead the protagonists in much generalized terms to transgress, transform or transcend the ghetto wall to reach their Promised Land. People who resort to transgression break down rules erected by the ghetto wall. Protagonists who undergo transformation engage in altering the ideology of the 'circumambient space' that raised the ghetto wall and attempt to turn away from a life of transgressions. Some characters through the inner growth that evolves in them transcend and rise above their "victim position". The ghetto wall no longer exists and they accept the established code of conduct. At times the conflicts that rise may never be resolved at the mental level. The individual transcends the physical ghetto wall, wears a mask, but lives within a mental ghetto. The present section also surveys the lands the protagonists reach or aim to arrive at and how the routes they opt in turn affect the family and thereby the society.

The chapter elicits the Co-traveller's response that is the Reader's Response to the select novels. It discusses the impact of the opening and closing lines of the novels in charting the itinerary of the protagonists' journey. It further illuminates the social relevance of the texts in the present context and finally suggests areas for further research and scholarship. This chapter also draws parallels to the present-day situation analyzing that the power play between the surrounding spaces and individuals and the conflict of the protagonists is a universal chaos in a displaced globalized world.

5.1 Trajectory of the Study

The present study traces an intrinsic thematic pattern of moral conflict and transgression that suggests itself in Mordecai Richler's select novels. It proves that surrounding spaces affect Richler's protagonists who indulge in criminal transgressions and possibly in moral policing others by exposing hypocritical families and societies. It examines the effect of the choices they make in their lives.

Chapter I entitled *In the Beginning* introduces the Canadian literary mosaic and the Jewish tessellation of the written word in Canada. It highlights Richler's literary life, works and critical reception. It explicates New Historicism as a textual practice and Greenblatt's major concepts to support the argument of the present work. It differs with the concept of 'Self-Fashioning' that the Self is only a socially-constructed one.

Chapter II on *Surrounding Spaces* discusses the various facets of the 'circumambient space' of the mid-twentieth century Jewish Montreal ghetto which creates cultural constraints that affect the self. It examines Space and 'Social Energy' of post-World War II and Jewish settlement in Montreal that circulates in Richler's select texts. It details the historical context of Jews in Montreal in the mid-twentieth century and traces the presence of the psychological ghetto. Richler knits in the environment and social life which lend to the rich tapestry of the "sights, sounds, seasons" and everyday life which fashioned the ideology and living designs of the ghetto. It discusses Holocaust as the worst form of Jewish victimization which provokes a simmering rage and conflict in the Jewish identity. Kramer observes, "In many ways, Richler's literary reaction against Orthodoxy would be a reaction against the social control that surfaced in such moments" (29) referring to the surrounding space of his age. A study is made on the protagonists' response to Orthodox Jewish observances. Richler's ironic mode and comic vision of the Jew-Gentile world with reference to the novels is also examined.

Chapter III titled *'Self-Fashioning' – Confronting Conflicting Conflicts and Moral Policing* focuses on how the protagonists respond to 'constraints' imposed by the surrounding spaces which includes conflict between the rich and the working-class Jew, Orthodox, Secular and a self-rejecting Jew, Jew and Gentile, self against self, crisis in family and professional life and from being socially non-existent to becoming socially-relevant individual. It also studies how Richler's protagonists resort to varied degrees of transgressions as forms of 'improvisations'. The study differs with Greenblatt's concept of 'Self-fashioning' and discusses that the Self is not a mere social construction. The very act of deviation in Richler's protagonists is an indication of the existence of an innate self. A socially-constructed self would be programmed to conform to the strictures of tradition and culture. An urge to break the ghetto wall, move beyond boundaries is the push for of an individualistic freedom which cannot be restricted to a culture-sculpted self. This indication of deviation and transgression is an outcome of discernment of choice. Noah, Duddy, Jake, Joshua, Moses, Solomon and Barney are characters who are not entirely bound to or free from their environment. But they adequately discern their choice and take charge of the choices and consequent actions. Richler favours an existentialist trope and gives a fictional weight to the notion of free will to his protagonists (Foran 353). The characters arise and evolve out of the conflicts of the surrounding space with an exercise of their discernment of choice and transgress, transform or transcend. Richler's protagonists prove that the Self cannot be fashioned as a mere culture-sculpted self. Thus, there exists an innate existence of freedom be it Jean-Paul Satre's "free will" or Albert Camus' "spontaneous potential of the personality" or Martin Heidegger's *Sorge* (care) or Soren Kierkegard's "soul" (Fowler 81) that drives the Self to respond to conflicts and cultural constraints and evolve a Self of one's own.

Conformity alone shall result in a culture-sculpted self. People either conform to or break the social boundaries. The push in Richler's protagonists to break barriers, inherited social positions and to climb up the social order in paths paved by the self, fall into the "existential trope". Although Richler's men move towards the concept of Benjamin Franklin's "Self-made Men" they deviate from the binding moral foundation of hard work and Frederick Douglas' principles of "honor, integrity and affection" (Wikipedia). Born into a surrounding space which nurtured the idea that material gain is more important, Richler's men are worldly and acquisitive like Lot's wife (*King James Bible* Gen.19.26) and are caught in a spiritual vacuum and web of moral dilemma. On one hand there is particularly deviation as response to conflicts that arise from the 'circumambient space' of multiple restrictions and cultural constraints. On the other hand, the protagonists through transgressions moral police the hypocrisy and greed of a pretentious society. Frank Davey recognizes "pretension" as a major paradigm, "particularly pretention to glamour, power and sophistication" (128). It may be discussed that Richler's men do not fit in Greenblatt's 'Self-fashioning' garments of no-choices within confined ghetto living. They transgress to search, stretch and stitch or steal rich fabric of Westmount and Outremont. This re-fashioning is directed by the existence of the innate self and discernment of choice. As Moss asserts in his Introduction to *The Canadian Novel-Here and Now*, Richler's characters are "...always a matter of choice and will, whatever the social context impinging upon it" (11).

Chapter IV entitled *Textual Relics* touches on the formal aspects of Richler's select novels. Richler's shifting narratives from an objective observer to a moralist, marks his skill as a master story teller and increases the ambivalence of Jewish identity. But evidently, he possesses a distant, dispassionate and non-didactic narrative voice. Writing in the social-realistic tradition he maintains narrative objectivity. Through parody and burlesque Richler unveils the hypocrisy of Orthodox Jews. McSweeney defends criticism on Richler's "certain deconstructive energy" which critics have found to undermine his constructive concerns as a satirist and moralist. He explains, "... Richler's deconstructive energy, however subversive of his constructive intentions as a novelist, is strongly present, the result is the most imaginatively exciting and compelling passages in his fiction" (144). This chapter studies Richler's 'cultural poetics' which reveal an unpretentious mature style with embedded symbolism and integrated imagery. It analyzes how he employs the literary tools to narrate the belief system of his period, the conflicts and transgressions of the protagonists' en route to the Promised Land.

5.2. En route

> L.B. published a story in *Canadian Forum* about a pathetic little Jew, unattractive to women, who had bribed his way out of Siberia, across China, into Japan, and from there to Canada, only to be knocked down and killed by a streetcar on his first day in the next-door place to the promised land. (*SG 127)*

The protagonists' journeys that are lonely or less accompanied indicate the choices they made on one hand and signal a lack of faith in social-human-cooperation that could have accommodated differences and addressed injustice. The journeys have been singular, non-community driven, singled, involved in transgression as a result of the surrounding space of birth and growth, fear of failures and upholding offensive paths to survive and live. En route from ghetto-street-homes to the Promised Land of mansion-living they either transgress, transcend the limiting surrounding spaces or transform self and space.

The quest to be "somebody" in Duddy and "be something" or "serve something" in Noah is an expression of the conundrum of the Jewish cultural memory. In searching to "be something" Noah exclaims "something is missing" (*SH* 38). The memory of a rigid Jewish tradition that wouldn't grow to accommodate the change needed to be a Jewish-Canadian is a point where Richler makes Noah and Duddy break the illusory walls of tradition and social status. Duddy breaks it with ruthlessness. Noah initially transgresses into the gentile home of Theo and Miriam, but his innate goodness and rightful conscience makes him return home and transcend the web of moral dilemma. With his final leaving of home, he intends to moral police the hypocritical society and transform the surrounding space that induced value conflicts. Arnoldson examines that, "Duddy is, from one point of view (if one assesses the end achieved), a successful Smicha. From another perspective (if we examine the way to that end), he is, of course, a failed Smicha" (93). Duddy transgresses and continues to travel in his so-called rightful path, stating transgression is a way of life.

Jake allows his alter-ego a natural death and from his ashes he raises his real self. The news of Joey's death pulls down the screens of his visual fantasies and clears the fog of doubt and enhances vicinity. But Richler notoriously ambiguous, sparks alive the dying "affirming flame" with Hanna's hope-filled letter that hints Joey may not have been dead. Did the Horseman really exist? Was Joey the Horseman? These are questions Richler does not allow his novel to answer. But towards the end Jake rises as a Horseman with better vicinity, purged as a recovered man, willing to direct Luke's demanding script, living to be a practical husband quite free from isolating bouts of tortured imagination and a more visible father to Sammy, Molly and Ben. He transforms and signals transcendence.

Joshua's path to the Promised Land is tortured with battles. Armouring and at times attacking, Joshua needs to constantly eye his desired destination and keep pushing towards it. He clambers out of his St. Urbain walls, usurps a rich, gentile wife and home in Westmount, taking lifts of transgression to escalate and moral police hypocrisy. In the geographical sense, the Land is his return to Canada to the city Montreal and his cottage around Lake Memphremagog. Metaphorically it is his advancement in career and a settled family life. "In his reunion with Pauline, Richler depicts Joshua as a moral and responsible man who, like Jake Hersh, is ready to pick up the pieces of his life and make an effort to be less self-centered and more accommodating of others" (Ramraj 123). After his physical collapse and Pauline's mental fracture, he transforms, this time transgression-free. From a road of transgression, having paid a near-death penalty, Joshua like Jake seeks to transcend and transform.

It has to be accepted that Solomon had a grace of a king-kind which made people accept him, probably inherited from Ephraim. He had a way with everyone right from Morrie, to the testing Bert and McGraw. Once Solomon helped McGraw to set right a wheel stuck in mud. Immediately McGraw asks Solomon not to muddy himself which he admits that he wouldn't have told anybody else. "No, no," McGraw protested, kneeling in the muck, his own shoulder to the wheel, "you'll only get dirty". Then McGraw turned pale, amazed at himself, because he would not have said such a thing to anybody else in town" (*SG 355).* What Solomon wanted in life was not only money. He sought new lands and fresh experience and has an omniscient presence in the affairs of the world. Although a crook he never shows signs of possessing material wealth, he uses his power to save, protect or surrogate people like Moses, Henry, Lucy and Jewish immigrants. He has a tinge of justice in his ruthless ventures while Bernard and the rest manipulated to be nefarious. Apart from his money-making agenda, he is the much-fantasized Joey, whom Jake pursues in *St. Urbain's Horseman* championing the cause of the Jews. Solomon's transgressions being ambivalent, he transmogrifies.

Barney of all characters has a complete journey, but unfortunately misses out on the last signpost to the Promised Land and deviates into a narrow lane where he loses everything. His is a family journey with the members closely following him at heels. Kramer notes that for everything that is Barney's life be it grace or mishaps "he chose' (353). He transgresses, autocorrects, continues on the long right road, strays in a moment of physical weary, loses love, life, memory and finally transcendence.

Symbolically, the journeys that the protagonists undertake are a quest to resolve their irreconcilable emotional needs. There are a number of aborted journeys as in Noah's short flight into the gentile-Miriam world, Jake's failed trip to New York and ride to Israel in search of the Horseman, Joshua's untimed journey to Spain, Solomon's flight into disappearances and Barney's ride on his "Troika". The journey of life itself is a Pilgrimage. "And Jacob said unto Pharaoh, The days of the years of my pilgrimage..." (Gen. 47.9). For the Jews it was literally a pilgrimage, moving with all their inner and outer baggage of life. Ironically the Jews failed to realize that the concept of the Promised Land was a Pilgrimage through acceptance and surrender and were beyond earthly tents and homelands. They wanted to settle down, own Land and Space. This tension of ownership is peculiar to the Jews and is not the case of all minorities or ghetto people. Most of the African-Americans sought salvation through religion. But the third-generation Canadian Jew did not draw much strength from the Orthodox practices of Judaism, instead sought material success. Arnoldson observes "Whether it is labeled the American dream, the Canadian Dream, or the Jewish Dream, Smicha and Yvette still envision their own version of the dream that drives Duddy, the same old dream of liberation through ownership, of mystical fulfillment through essentially material means" (92).

Lack of inner growth and caught in a flux of material success defines the protagonists' identity. This leads to moral dilemma and affects the choices they make. With a reduced root system as hydrophytes, they float with the currents of economic pressure. Multiply rooted with feathery root hairs that spring out all over, they lack a strong tap root to thrive on. Ironically, inspite of a rich religious tradition, their preoccupation with social and financial escalation makes them opt for transgression and are unaware of the spiritual degeneration. "For I *am* the LORD your God: ye shall therefore sanctify yourselves, and ye shall be holy; for I *am* holy…" (Lev. 11.44). Mary Douglas' commentary on *The Abominations of Leviticus* explains that holiness is exemplified by completeness. She says the words "clean" and "holiness", "requires that individuals shall conform to the class to which they belong" and "keeping distinct the categories of creation" (67). The Jewish protagonists in their quest to escalate social status fail to conform to the spiritual values of their traditions. Their obsession with material success is an outcome of an inherent fear of failures, inherited from their parents and grandparents. Noah fears moral corrosion, Duddy dreads economic failure, Jake, Joshua and Moses are apprehensive about professional disappointments. Also included are Joshua's fancied failures in Ibiza and Barney's fear of losing Miriam. The very act of disappearance through death as in Solomon is an example that he never wants to admit defeat. Their uprooted status contradicts their deep religious strictures. Material aspirations lead to moral corrosion and indulgence in theft, lying, false witness, cheating on the scales, forgery, scandals and finally create a spiritual vacuum.

5.3 Deserts and Pastures

The fictional lives of Richler's crass heroes suffer largely out of mistrust of society and seclude themselves to relative solitude. In the end they either are led into deserts of conflicts or pastures of redemption. Redemption for the protagonists is mostly material success and a few seek moral transformation. Richler recreates a human society which is selfish, materialistic, opinioned with class and prejudice and violent, at the same time suggesting a wistful wish for an egalitarian space. The select six novels indicate a deep restlessness about the past, handicapped by personal, cultural and racial interpretations that have been created prior to the present moments of discomfort. Jews were not only marginalized from time immemorial but as in the Bible and history, they sought isolation themselves with a feeling of exclusiveness as a chosen tribe. Ironically their elected status remains ambiguous. The protagonists transgress to re-align and improvise their lives to become visible to the main stream. They quite often return home in memory or in person, ironically, revisiting the Montreal roots that had grown them and that which they wanted to uproot.

As Frank Birbal Singh states, "Noah's problem is that he feels neither Jewish nor Canadian: the result is that he is spiritually rootless" (102). His penchant for a rooted identity lies in the fact that he has to reconcile to the duality of his existence, one being his Jewishness and the other living as a Canadian. The green pastures for Noah is moral reconstruction of his life and values that he stands for. Duddy on the other hand reveals an ambivalent footing in Jewishness and largely makes money by cheating or out of the foibles of others. An air of ambivalence and ambiguity hovers around Noah and Duddy in being born as a Jew in a Canadian land. Muddled in a maze of moral dilemma and dual identity, Noah leaves home. He departs from the desert of conflicting values from surrounding spaces to greener pastures to frame his system of values that assimilates tradition and individual freedom. As Brian Johnson asserts that Noah's gesture of taking the *Torah* scrolls inscribed by his grandfather "reaffirms his commitment to a form of cosmopolitanism that does not renounce ethnic and family histories…" thereby gesticulating a newer identity (32).

As quoted by Craniford, Duddy battles the French-Canadians who would not let a Jew buy land in their midst. He even surpasses the Boy Wonder in his wild chase of his dreamlands, "Duddy wanted to be a 'somebody'. Another Boy Wonder maybe. Not a loser certainly" (*DK* 62). His confusion between becoming *'macher'* and *'mensch'* results in tragic-comedy. Duddy unlike his blueprint Sammy Glick "is propelled by a need for both material success and respectability… He craves acceptance as much as wealth and influence" (Yanofsky 110). Greenstein in his essay in *Jewish Wry* states, "Like his forefathers, Duddy bargains with a jealous God. The discrepancy between Duddy's future and his religious past, and the discrepancy between a Promised Land and his promises to regain Paradise, reduce the isolated boy on land to a common, recognizable *landsman"* (202). He misinterprets his '*zeyda's'* concept of land and fails to connect with its moral and spiritual regeneration. Dooley prompts that Richler invites a double response, "one which requires us to see Duddy as both victor and victim" (95), Duddy joins the economic rat race, transgresses en route from the ghetto to pastures of the Promised Land of material success and ends in serious human and moral failure. He continues to thrive as a "grating amoral force with a demoralizing psychological datum" a materialist and morally-challenged modern man in his appearances in the latter novels (McSweeney 169).

As for Jake at 37 he had already arrived to the much-sought after green pastures of material success with a well-settled family life, which Duddy wanted in his life. Conflicts surface when he failed to recognize that he had reached his destination and was a little like Oliver Twist asking for more. The 'more' came in the form of trouble and scandal and chasing the Horseman in his wildest dreams and least was he aware that he was in green pastures. The realization needed the news of the physical death of the Horseman so that he could wipe away the foggy fascination and ride down as a real man. For Jake, the journey was a rediscovery of the Promised Land, well in hand.

Eric Wright in his Afterword to *Joshua Then and Now* summarizes,

> The last scene brings together in a tableau Joshua, his wife, his three children, and their two grandfathers, both of whom Joshua loves with a passion, although one still reveres the memory of the "vile" Mackenzie King, and the other breaks fingers for a living. All the revenges have been had, and the yearnings for a place where honour, decency, and love can thrive are satisfied by the coming together of these passionately attached people. The hero has emerged successful in his struggle to create a world as it ought to be, surviving and defeating the forces that have been opposing him. *(371)*

Joshua is similar to Jake who rakes his land of green pastures with his greedy ambitions and mourns its loss in the beginning of the novel. While Jake remains in his London home, Joshua returns to his Montreal roots, to set his home on the mountains overlooking the Streets in which he grew. His Jew-Gentile love story survives a series of serious physical and mental collapses and finally connects the worlds of Westmount and St. Urbain Street. The journey long and arduous, he finally sets his "Garden of Eden" around Lake Memphremagog. Davey opines that he returns to "honest trading…within the bounds of marriage" and the "private garden" (139).

Just as the Jews in the Montreal homes ruminated: "For them Canada is not yet a country but a next-door place. They were still this side of Jordan, in the land of Moab, the political quarterlies as well as the Yiddish newspapers they devoured coming out of New York" *(SG 14)*, Greenstein observes that Moses and Richler long for the Promised Land of letters and recognition on the other side of the border.

The Gursky's leave behind a bloodshed trail and crime-prone deserts and amass wealth to build a Promised Land of gold, pillared with money. Bernard on the other hand led the Gurskys to cross the Red Sea of the ghetto wall. Solomon when questioned about his new identity after the supposedly fatal plane crash, grandly proclaims: "I am that I am" (*SG* 481) which in the Bible is God's answer to Moses from the burning bush. Solomon in comparison to the Biblical Solomon, Craniford notices: "By his wisdom, his wealth, his women, and his literary works, Solomon Gursky is a worthy namesake" (112). Solomon, the all-knowing and all powerful is a surrogate father of Moses Berger. He guides, Richler's Moses Berger to takes up the story of the Gurskys. Individually the Gurskys thrive or fly over their Promised Lands as in Bernard and Solomon. But towards the end of the novel the younger generation of Gurskys, melt the gold and rob the money for personal prosperity, initiating the crumbling of the Gursky Empire.

Barney, like Jake and Joshua lives in a Promised Land in the prime of his life, but unlike them, does not retain the green pastures in his old age. He of all Richler's men, with a guilt-loaded memory, crumbles into grains of sand, lost in the desert of loneliness and mental disintegration. Although his sons, daughter and Miriam, watch over him, he is in the dark of it having succumbed to Alzheimer's disease. His momentary ethical fall, banishes him from the gift of "Garden of Eden' family life. Solomon and Barney completely expand and follow the Duddy prototype of the little *'pusherke'* of money-making skills. Jake and Joshua substitute the business quest with intellectual and professional search. Noah the predecessor sails to explore a system of values befitting for a modern man to live with decent honour.

The select works portray a profound sense of mistrust of social and political patterns and ideology of the age. Although Richler's men originate from community structured families, they are left to manage with their own resources, despaired about polity, restrained from greater companionships and larger circles. They limit themselves to their families and a closed-circuit of friends. The Jewish community whose identity and strength lies in big homes on St. Urbain Street is broken into nuclear homes at the end of the novels. The "Exodus" of the protagonists begin with a large number of people but when they reach their Promised Land are found individually inhabiting the space they cried to create or with a nuclear family to stand by.

A pattern of life-to-death can be traced in the chronological publication of the select novels. The ghetto being the Red-Sea to cross, Noah begins the "Exodus" from Egypt, stands in front of the Red-Sea, safely is supposed to be transported across, by Miriam, but later realizes that he was Jonah, swallowed by the whale and it was dark in the new home. When belched out, Noah returns home only to find himself running back and forth between home and Red Sea. Duddy surprises and shocks the reader with his unscrupulous bargain of his land by bartering morality to exercise new-found freedom. He like Aaron is happily idol-worshipping money and material success. Jake thrills the reader with his tormenting waterslides across the undivided, raving waters, tried and tired returns to follow the New Commandments of his home. Joshua searches for his Promised Land in the far lands of Europe, lives, thrives, falls, untents from Europe, battered emotionally and physically, returns to set up the garden of Eden around lake Memphremagog, alighting the Noah's Ark minus animals with a nuclear family. Moses' quest advances into a long, tedious journey to his land. He is like the first generation of Israelites who came out of Egypt but did not reach Canaan in their quest to reach it. For Moses the arduous journey by itself gives him a sense of reaching the Promised Land. Solomon rises to the omnipresent pedestal, plays God, flies and drowns in the Red Sea, only to rise from his own ashes, living a new life every time. He scripts his death and new life, plays God in many lives, directing them to the Promised Land. Solomon the highest of all Richler's creation is truly human, truly terrible and truly supernatural. Barney finally settles in what could have been Canaan or was Canaan when Miriam was with him. But his youthful promiscuous nature uproots him and turns the Promised Land into a dump yard. Out of St. Urbain's Street, Richler's men, chalk out the pavement, cutting, annihilating, transgressing, transcending the Montreal's invisible ghetto walls. Songs of milk and honey of the land is not an entirely concluding one because of the ways and rugged routes travelled. The open endings of the novels suggest a bend and not an end in the road they travel which is their compromised Promised Land temporarily. The prototypes live a life of conflicts which they confront from time to time and dilemma and conflicts continue as in Barney, shifting between deserts and pastures.

In search of a deeper value system and in response to the conflicts Noah transcends and tends to transform his hypocritical family with his punishing absence. Duddy is a flat-character and transgression is his way of life. Jake and Joshua share similar patterns. They indulge in transgressions, transform and show signs of transcendence. Moses is overshadowed by Solomon's ambivalent transgressions and magically realistic transmogrification. Barney's transformations from transgressing ways do not lead into transcendence. Overlooking the warnings of the angelic Miriam he turns back to the shadowy "night of sin" and crystallizes into a "pillar of salt" (Gen.19.26).

5.4. Co-traveller's Response

It is Montreal's creative fortune that the grandfather of Richler ended up in Montreal and not Chicago, the city to which he was originally ticketed so that the grandson Mordecai would ingeniously place the city on the literary map.

> Richler does not portray another world in his fiction but in chiaroscuro duplicates our own. He establishes a point of view from which we observe the frenetically passing scene. Many readers become annoyed with him for this, because he makes them see their own reality through his eyes, not his reality with theirs. In doing so, he is a threat and a serious satirist. Throughout, Richler explores identity as both quest and burden, always in the glare of moral indignation. Through his protagonist he is judge and victim both. (Moss, "Richler's Horseman" 157)

Richler's profane remarks against self-centered Jewishness and blind observances hold good for any ritual or observance of any tradition, which is followed in word and not in spirit. Although many called him a self-hating Jew, his works reveal that it is not with religion he finds fault but the intolerance and arrogance of void traditions that brings in observance first and humanity next or nowhere.

Greenblatt discusses the need to 'translate signs' in establishing communication between two different cultures. Robson explains that this encounter is a kind of an allegory for the role of a critic. Hence the critic needs to read the signs of the text written in a different period of time, space and culture and has to communicate to reading. As an Indian Reader's Response, Richler is a writer-hero armed with a deep value system. One is awestruck with his extraordinary courage to rip open the hypocrisy and greed of his age. But his expositions on sexual transgressions and extensive passages on physical relationship in his early novels disturb a comfortable reading. This discomfort passes over with the maturing of the novels. Although Richler's novels were criticized for its frank sexuality and social iconoclasm, the public of 1960s applauded his quality. William H. New records, "He repudiated the Canadian middle class, but his books reached exactly that market" (241). His novels written as a young man expose raw passages and as a middle-aged man they tend to reflect more on marital relationships. *Solomon Gursky* moves beyond the family drama and is a classic testimony for the writer's extravagant literary imagination blending geography, history, culture and society, a network carefully designed to assimilate the ideology of his age. *Barney's Version* is the poignant voice of the retiring man, his tryst with truth and value system.

An analysis of the significance of the opening and closing lines of the select novels from a reader's view shall help in mapping the routes of the protagonists' journey. "Noah's room was on the fourth floor. The place had been recommended to him by a taxi driver who worked for the same company as he did" (*SH 13*). The opening lines of *Smaller Hero* subtly introduce Noah's conflicts with home and hints on Noah's home away from home. Nevertheless, the reader realizes the intricacies only with further reading and is not explicit in the opening lines. "Melech didn't protest. He picked up his prayer-book and began to read. And why not? Hadn't the Angel of Death passed over King David because he was at his prayers?" (*SH 205*). The last lines of the novels throw light on the pang in Melech which is representative of all the pains of the family as a result of Noah's leaving home. Noah's action is a silent punishment on the hypocritical family and his society. Since the opening line is on Noah leaving home for the first time and is temporary, the last lines ambiguously point out that the decision this time may or may not be permanent. But a reader is convinced that Noah has left in search of a more binding value system beyond home which never gave him an honest one.

"What with his life so ill these past few weeks and the prospect of three more days of teaching before and the weekend break, Mr. MacPherson felt unusually glum" (*DK 1).* These unassuming first lines of the seminal novel begin with a minor character, MacPherson, Duddy's teacher. He occupies the first few pages of the novel. Richler uses him to expose the crookedness of Duddy and the guilt of being responsible for Mrs. MacPherson's death that will be linked with all his other guilt. MacPherson is a victim of Duddy's cruel pranks and he is followed by Virgil, Yvette and others. Thus, Richler thinks it right to begin his novel with him. Smicha's punishing silence for a brief time leaves Duddy pensive but the last few lines of the novel, by the waiter "Are you the Mr. Kravitz who just bought all land round Lac St Pierre" and offers to take a credit on the bill (*DK* 314). A sober Duddy is soon filled with excitement and understands that he had become 'somebody'. He grabs Max, hugs him and spins him around shouting "You see" in a euphoric gesture. "It is the marvel, the laughter, the innocent hugging of the foolish father that redeem Duddy and the novel" (Arnoldson 102).

One of the most powerful opening lines is in *St. Urbain's Horseman.*

> Sometimes Jake wondered if the *Doktor,* given his declining years, slept with his mouth open, slack, or was it (more characteristically, perhaps) always clamped shut? Doesn't matter. In any event, the Horseman would extract gold fillings from the triangular cleft between his upper front teeth with pliers. Slowly, Jake thought, coming abruptly awake in a sweat. "He's come," Jake proclaimed aloud. (11)

The reader is awakened with the piercing, tortured reverie of Jake that constantly rakes his days and nights. It repeatedly hounds his Jewish blood. While the opening lines unravels the disturbed, troubled psyche of Jake, the closing lines wind up his psycho-somatic, traumatic galloping on the trail of the fantasy world the Horseman's hoof. Jake curls into the realistic world and falls peacefully asleep with the patient Nancy. "Once in his attic aerie, he retrieved the Horseman's journal from the cupboard, found the page where he had written "Died July 20, 1967, in an air crash," crossed it out, and wrote it over, "presumed dead". Then he returned to bed, and fell into a deep sleep, holding Nancy to him" (*SUH* 462). Jake does not want to give up on the self-indulgent dream as Arnoldson notices, "The dream turned into nightmare can be turned back to harmless dream, despite the harm that that dream has done to Jake and his family" (162). Richler sketches the portrait of a mid-twentieth century man caught in various middles. The novel ends where it begins and the ending depicts Jake more peaceful with himself.

An introspective line opens *Joshua Then and Now*, "Look at me now, Joshua thought" (1). The reader for the rest of the "now" has to be deeply engrossed with Joshua and his family, shuttling between his past and present trying to assemble the meaning of his life. His tumultuous journey finally reaches safe harbour with the concluding line, "Joshua wasn't leaning on his cane. Pauline was supporting him. Well, yeah, right, he thought" (370). Frank Davey observes that the novel has its protagonist affirm a small nuclear family in its concluding pages.

A big black bird flies into the novel and perches on the opening lines in *Solomon Gursky*. "One morning-during the record cold spell of 1851-a big menacing black bird, the likes of which had never been seen before, soared over the crude mill town of Magog, swooping low again and again" (*SG* 3). The raven flies many times across the pages symbolizing the tricky and scavenger-attitude of the Gurskys. Richler automates the raven in the last lines of the novel through the mechanized Gypsy Moth airplane that facilitates Solomon's transmogrification. "He watched the bird soar higher and higher, until he lost it in the sun" (*SG* 557). Moses interprets that the raven, Gypsy Moth and Solomon are one.

There are famous first lines of many a classic. But the seemingly unimportant first lines in *Barney's Version*, "TERRY'S THE SPUR. The splinter under my fingernail" (1) is the harbinger of a literary revenge, a self-defensive life explanation and confessions of an aged man. It gains importance as Barney although an unreliable writer promises to write the true account of his "wasted life".

The last line of *Barney's Version* "I picked up the phone, started to dial-stopped-and began to curse. I couldn't remember Miriam's number" (*BV* 403) wrenches the heart of the reader with sympathy for the tragic comedian hero Barney Panofsky. This is the last statement of his true love for Miriam that has stood the test of time and ravages of age. Barney testifies the Shakespearean inflexible strength of love, which does not alter "when it alteration finds". The worst that could happen to Barney than the Alzheimer's disease is to forget Miriam's number. This confirms his intensity of love for Miriam and claims complete sympathy. The reader observes that but for Barney's momentary lapse in all his thirty years of marriage with Miriam, he remains faithful to Miriam. He curtails to renew friendship with Abigail, not even tries to accept Solange as suggested by Saul, after Miriam left. He lives to chant the Miriam mantra and tuned memory to dial her number, while everything is erased off his memory disc, Miriam remains. He protects her from Mr. Disease Alzheimer while Miriam had issued a life-sentence by marrying Blair, although justifiable the last line of the novel makes it difficult to accept. But it is no fault of Miriam, but Richler's skillful engineering of plot and characterization that adds to the poignancy of the novel. Although Richler procures tremendous sympathy for Barney the ethical slant of the writer does not acquit the moral failure of Barney.

The Afterword by Mike Panofsky serves as a narrative experiment and functions primarily to bring in the scattered pieces of the Barney Jig Saw puzzle to find the clue to the lost and found mystery of the Boogie body. Secondly, it serves to correct the factual errors of the unreliable narrator Barney and authenticate his memoirs. Thirdly, it completely serves as a reference point to all Barney empathizers of a belatedly understood a good-at-heart man, erasing accusations of being a wrong man rather than a man wronged in the eyes of the others. If it's Barney who writes the first line of the novel, it is Richler who concludes it.

Richler's opening lines are subtle, less striking but deeply remain as signposts to the routes that the protagonists take. The closing lines are strong, open-ended and create an ambiguous response in the reader. They board and alight off the reader who joins the protagonists' journey of uncertainity and ambivalence and witness transgressions en route their Promised Land.

Ambivalent conclusions of the novels leave the reader to one's own conclusion. In *Solomon Gursky* one is riddled with the question on Solomon's disappearances. Is it a suicide? A man like Solomon cannot admit defeat. The only way out was self-destruction. Richler's ambivalence not only renders his tone ambiguous, but for some critics it blots out his moral position. Brenner observes that while Klein insists on Jewish identity, Cohen suggests assimilation through total dissolution of identity; Layton like Richler hesitates between "poles of assimilation and identity" (18). Moss in "Richler's Horseman" explicates the writer's stand, "He is a moral writer but this is expressed in his fiction by attitude, not a coherent moral system" (164). Richler's moral position and outrage are voiced out not in a didactic tone but most emphatically with his satirical stings. Although ambivalence and inconclusiveness about the Jewish identity is attributed to Richler's writing, his vehement satirical tone and ironic amusement indicates his moral stand.

Richler's ambivalence is not directed to cause confusion but raises questions about moral standards that he doesn't accept. Tom Marshall writes, "It seems to me ambivalence is once again the key word. Richler raises questions that he will not answer" (152). Richler as Woodcock observes is a synthesis of the "rather realistic urban novelist whose subject matter was the Jewish ghetto of his boyhood Montreal and a "fantastic satirist" who mocked the inanities of modern popular culture (As qtd. in Arnoldson 165). It is agreeable as Brian Johnson states that "Richler's ambivalent form of "rooted cosmopolitanism" elevates his novels (as observed by Ramraj) to transcend time, place, and race, and become novels that are at once Jewish, Canadian, and universal (33).

In *Will in the World*, Greenblatt insists that it is important to follow the verbal traces of a writer to understand the writer (Robson 102). Richler did not just recycle the material from his experience or from what he read. He used his imagination, re-fleshed it with dexterity and breathed into it his moral vision revealing it through black comedy, ripping open the festering wounds of a decaying and ambivalent value system with caustic satire and recreating his time and space with dramatic use of imagination and narratives. In a way Richler's imagination simulate a world where he could police it not by penalty or court procedures but by a hearty guffaw with dripping barbed wires of satire. As a new historicist practice the imagination of Richler sets into motion the imagination of the reader, reflecting on the present way of the world. As a reader, one comes to terms with the two different worlds, drawing differences between the political, social and cultural aspect at the same time connecting the doubts, beliefs and ambivalence of the worlds caught in a web of moral dilemma. Thus, employing Greenblatt's "desire to speak with the dead", my desire to speak with Richler engages a literary journey into his world, recreating 'the sights, sounds and smells" of his age. His works are a literary simulation of Montreal life. The novels are literary artifacts of wonder and lead the reader to the resonating depths of his time and space.

No specific work of art, not even history which is not linearly progressive from a new historicist perspective can give a complete view of a particular period or site. Gallagher and Greenblatt accept it can only express or present a literary experience "of a narrow range of the human species" (5). Geertz stresses a study of culture is extremely complex and "intrinsically incomplete" (16) because of the infinite layers of meanings which the author himself would have not grasped completely and also the distance in time and space, between the text and its reader. Hence Richler's works do not guarantee a complete picture of the life and times of mid-twentieth century Montreal ghetto, but nevertheless is a Tessera of literary significance adding value to the grand Canadian literary mosaic. It is an invaluable cultural document of 'symbolic dimension of social action' and certifies his goal to be an honest witness to his time and place, and to write at least one book that would be read after his death. In an interview with Nathan Cohen in 1956, Richler opines,

> There has been a collapse of absolute values… We are living at a time when superficially life seems meaningless, and we have to make value judgments all the time, it seems in relation to nothing… what I am looking for are the values with which in this time a man can live with honour. (qtd. in Brenner 103)

Richler's uncompromising opinions on contemporary Canada easily matched, and sometimes exceeded, the satirical sting of his fiction. Admirers praised Richler for daring to tell uncomfortable truths. Richler to Gibson said, "I feel compelled to be an honest witness to what I do know", "I think it's a moral office" (269, 298). Emma Richler opines, "He had a very fine gift for satire and he was also, for all his wild humour, a deeply moral man, both in his life and work. He is a writer above all, but rare, because unlike so very many novelists, he was full-blooded as well as hugely rigorous in the novels he created". A 2004 oral biography by Michael Posner was aptly entitled *The Last Honest Man*.

End of the Road – A Bend in the Road

The central issue of Greenblatt's work has always been the relationship between works of art and literature and their various histories and contexts. The work traces the relationship between Richler's select novels with Montreal setting and the mid-twentieth century with the various historic contexts. This study is a journey from 'wonder' to 'resonance' where the reader/critic discovers the socio-cultural moments to which it is connected. It can also be said that the prototypes of Noah, Duddy, Jake, Joshua, Solomon and Barney all become artifacts of literary value that connects the reader to Richler's surrounding space.

The select novels of Richler are a powerful testament of the troubled and changing times of his time, space and spirit of the age. *Smaller Hero* testifies the spirit and temper of his age and the debate of identity caught in the flux of the traditional and secular Jewish origin. *Duddy Kravitz* bears witness to the hyphenated struggle to blast the ghetto wall. *St. Urbain Horseman* is entrenched in the mindscape of St. Urbain Street and the aftermath of the Holocaust that affects a character beyond the geographical boundaries. *Joshua Then and Now* is the testimony of the return of the prodigal son to his Montreal home. *Solomon Gursky* is a massive record that ironically maps the horizontal rise of the Jewish booze baron empire and stands as a paradigm of the rich and the powerful Jewish families. *Barney's Version* witnesses the changing times of the old and the new Montreal and a full-lived life of a St. Urbain Street boy.

Richler's texts by themselves are artifacts of wonder of an age characterized by a post-World War II Montreal that was peopled with large Jewish immigrants, where elaborate geography and social history of the Jewish Montreal streets resonate the 'circumambient space' that marked the mid-twentieth century ghetto. Richler in a 1971 interview with Donald Cameron said, "I'm much more interested in criticizing, always, the things I believe in or I'm attached to, which may be a very perverse kind of love. But it's the only kind I'm capable of" (qtd. in Yanofsky 27). He also says, "You really write as a recognition of death. It's an enormous conceit and you hope to leave something, one thing, somewhere that will last. It's an attempt to impose meaning on just being there" (Posner 332). While Richler's Jews are engaged in transgression, transformation, transcendence or even transmogrification, Melina Singer from a Diaspora perspective notes Jews "as having successfully transcended the type of racialized otherness". This viewpoint situates Richler's text as a cultural text, a historical document, "a relic from the past" chronicling an ideology of a particular place and time (22).

Although the present analysis has come to the end of the road, critically it is a bend, where the study halts and hands over the relay baton for future research. Although much has been discussed there is a world of scope to research more on Richler. Broad areas of research interest that could be pursued in Richler's works are:

- *Reading Richler's works from a feminist perspective.*
- *A complete study of the Richler's narratives and stylistics.*
- *A study of the 'fictioned' facts in Richler's works.*
- *An analysis of non-Montreal 'surrounding spaces' in Richler's works.*
- *A comprehensive character analysis of all the ten Richler's heroes.*
- *An evaluative study of Richler's non-fiction and short stories.*
- *A Hermeneutic study of Richler's language.*

- *The dichotomy between the moralist and satirist in Richler's works.*
- *A Postcolonial reading of Richler's Texts.*
- *Hypocrisy and Hilarity in Richler's novels.*
- *Decoding Richler from a contemporary Reader-Response view.*

Parallels between Richler and his protagonists when examined reveal Richler's intense moral values, his perception of his times and observation of the surrounding space that created a Duddy, Noah, Joshua, Jake, Moses, Solomon and Barney. Richler's characters in fiction reflect an inbuilt contradiction of life that assimilate or reconcile and consequently rouse ambivalent responses and attitude in the reader and critic. His ambivalent attitude results in ambivalent responses in absorbing a Jew-Canadian-Gentile world, moral and ruthless, straight and twisted, realistically parodying through biographical observances and fictional expressions.

His World and Ours – Social Relevance

Geertz explains in *Culture as a Text* that on reading the culture of a text or the text as a culture we look into our own selves, ideologies, culture and society. Liu opines, "The goal of cultural interpretation is not for generating universal laws of human behaviors, but is for acquiring deeper understanding of others and thereof ourselves. It is so because, for Geertz, other people's creations can be so utterly their own and so profoundly part of us, and therefore we can always see ourselves amongst others".

Richler, not far off from our times, records the conflicts of his time that are also a deep concern of our time. His predominant tryst with truth and a quest to be an honest chronicler of his times, recreates the sights, sounds and soul of mid-twentieth century Montreal in a literary space. The Jews have a tantalizing history and an unwelcomed reception which constitute their floating social spaces. The conflicts of his time which includes man's morality, perversion, identity and recovery of the self are universal conflicts of our time too.

This conflict and process of improvisation are socially relevant to our times. The idea of self-fashion creates a cultural construction of the self which could be limited to the surrounding space of the character, but it is the Will that drives the character into making the final choice. The cultural and social ambience spreads a menu card of options available at a particular space or time, the Will of the self, primarily influenced by the morality of the age and also includes the strength of the divine communication or the dictates of the conscience, makes or rejects the choices. So to-be-or-not-to-be situations are cultural constructions but to make the choice requires an act of Will. While options galore, discernment of choice informed by the conscience can make a person overcome the constriction of the surrounding space. This choice has to be consciously driven. The protagonists' ironical position of a moral and spiritual vacuum is a siren to the increasing materialistic connection of our age. The will to work on spiritual regeneration and a moral conscience shall facilitate transportation from the wasteland to the Promised Land.

The Jewish-Canadian conflicts from surrounding spaces are representative of all hyphenated identities in a globalized world of ours. At a time when civilization is being cosmopolitan and less and less human, many tribes and races of non-white origin are subjected to prejudice and judgment. It begins with the representation of conflicts that arise as commonly in a domestic space where a girl when married into a home of a different religion, culture, language, nation, to tribal people's journey into civilization from their mountain homes to plains, to people from backward communities groping for equal opportunities with forward classes, to transnational problems found in mass immigrant homes in non-native lands. In all of these circumstances the experience of being transplanted and the process of acclimatization in a new environment, breaking down of a psychological ghetto wall, where one can opt to be confined in a ghetto or allow being ghettoed brings in constant confrontation and altercation.

From a literary perspective, Richler's select novels are relevant to any reader interested in a study of dispossessed people, marginalized voices, hyphenated identities and immigrant living. A certain literary experience of the 'wonder' moments of the texts recreating and resonating the time period with the author's wicked satire is certain.

In accepting the 2012 Nobel Prize for Literature, Chinese Novelist Mo Yan said that the greatest challenge for any writer was writing about difficult social realities. "In writing about the darker aspects of society there is a danger that emotions and anger allows politics to suppress literature" (Vaiju 9*)*. Richler does not get lost in the muddle of complex realities and polity, but handles with dexterity the art of crafting the darker realities of his age without pity or provincial pride but with a scathing satire. He chronicles the transgressions, transformation and signs of transcendence of his generation, breaking the ghetto wall and escalating the Streets of "The Main" to the elite Montreal homes of Outremont and Westmount and Diaspora abodes with a non-didactic voice, thereby moral policing through caustic satire the societies that gave rise to the conflicts.

Greenstein in *Third Solitudes* remarks, "Within one generation, the outsider-turned-insider has made it up from the St Urbain ghetto to the gilded garrison of Westmount – from immigrant marginality to Canadian centrality" (154). The present study examines the protagonists' journey and re-fashioning of lives through conflicts that arises from socially constructed constraints of surrounding spaces and discernment of choices. From a New Historicist perspective, the present analysis marks Richler's works as a powerful testament and literary re-creation of the ideology of the troubled and changing times of space and spirit of the mid-twentieth century Jewish Montreal ghetto.

Appendix I
List of Yiddish Words and References

Aseret Yemai Tushuvah	The ten days of repentance. (*SG* 100)
Bar mitzvah	(Hebrew "son of the commandment"). An important ceremony in a Jewish boy's life who has reached the age of 13 and is thereafter expected to obey the commandments. (Sullivan 8)
Bris	(Hebrew – brit, "covenant"). Colloquial name for the ritual of circumcision, from the Ashkenazi pronunciation of brit. (*GJ*)
Davening	To recite Jewish liturgical prayers. (*JGV)*
Golem	A body without a soul made by Rabbi Judah Ben Bezlal in the sixteenth century to defend the Jews of Prague from a pogrom and who still wanders, turning up whenever a defender is most needed. (*SUH* 252-53)
Goy	(Hebrew – "nation"); Yiddish – "Gentile". (*GJ*)
Goyim	non-Jew (masculine, plural), *goyishe* (adj.). (*GRY*)
Kashrut	Rules concerning which foods may or may not be eaten, and how they should be prepared. (*SULLIVAN* 28) (Hebrew – "fitness"). Jewish dietary laws. (*GJ*)
Kaddish	Jewish prayer for the dead. Prayer proclaiming the greatness of God. Used as the mourners' prayer but also at other points in the liturgy. (*GRY*) (*GJ*)
Kapalah	Skull cap, Disc like head-covering. Also known *'kappel'* or *'kippah'*. (*GJ*)
Kiddush	Jewish prayer on Erev Shabbat. (*GRY)*
Kosher	Anglicized form of kasher (Hebrew, "fit"). Fit for ritual use. Also a verb meaning "to make a food or object fit for ritual use." (*GJ*)

Macher	big shot, important person, literally 'maker'. ("Yiddish Vocabulary")
Matzohs	Also *matzah, matzo* or *mazzah* (Hebrew, "unleavened bread"). Unleavened (non-yeast) bread used during Passover with reference to Exod. 12:39, in which the Israelites fled Egypt with only unleavened bread because they could not wait for the dough to rise. Called the "bread of affliction" based on Deut. 16:3. (*GJ*)
Mensch	refers to a decent or honourable person, a gentleman. (*GRY*)
Mitzvoth	Also *mitzvot,* singular mitzvah; (Hebrew – "commandments"). Religious actions, Commandments (*GJ*). Also refers to duties and good deeds that Jews must fulfill after they have undergone their *Bar mitzvah* ceremony. (Sullivan 28)
Purim	Purim is one of the most joyous and fun holidays on the Jewish calendar. It commemorates a time when the Jewish people living in Persia were saved from extermination. According to the *Book of Esther*, in the Hebrew Bible, Haman, royal vizier to King Ahasuerus (presumed to be Xerxes I of Persia), planned to kill all the Jews in the empire, but his plans were foiled by Mordecai and his adopted daughter Queen Esther. The day of deliverance became a day of feasting and rejoicing. Purim is celebrated on the 14th day of Adar, which is usually in March. The 14th of Adar is the day that Haman chose for the extermination of the Jews. The word "Purim" means "lots" and refers to the lottery that Haman used to choose the date for the massacre. (*JGV*)
Pusherke	Someone pushy and competitive (pejorative). (*GRY*)
Rabbi	(Hebrew-"teacher"). Jewish spiritual leader (*GJ*). An ordained teacher, spiritual leader of his community studies and interprets the *Torah.* (Sullivan 29)
Sabbath	*Shabbat* (*Shabbath*, *Shabbes*, *Shobos*, etc.) is a weekly day of rest, observed from sundown on Friday until the appearance of three stars in the sky on Saturday night. Thirty-nine activities prohibited on *Shabbat* are listed in Tractate *Shabbat* (Talmud). Louis Jacobs explains that the mistress of the house kindles at least two candles before the advent of the Sabbath, one corresponding to "remember the

	Sabbath day" (Ex. 20:8), the other to "observe the Sabbath day" (Deut. 5:12). For each meal two whole loaves of bread are placed on the table, covered by a cloth, to correspond to the double portion of manna for the Sabbath (Ex. 16:22–26). Before the *Kiddush* is recited, the parents bless the children. There is a special order of service for Sabbath in the synagogue. Orthodox Judaism forbids travel by automobile and refrains from the use of electrical appliances on the Sabbath. (*JGV*)
Schlemiel	an inept clumsy person; a bungler; a dolt. (*GJ*)
Schnorrers' day	beggar's day. (*GRY*)
Sedar	A ritual feast that marks the beginning of the Jewish holiday of Passover. (*JGV*)
Siddur	(Hebrew, "order"). Prayer book used in Jewish liturgy. (*GJ*)
Shiva	The customary seven-day mourning period after a death. During this time, the bereaved stay home to receive visitors. (Sullivan 29)
Shetl	a small town with a large Jewish population in pre-Holocaust Europe. (*JGV*)
Shiksa	a young non-Jewish woman. (*GJ*)
Tallith	Also *tallit.* a prayer shawl. (Sullivan 8)
Tefillin	meaning "prayers". (Sullivan 8)
Torah	(Hebrew, "Law"). The first five books of the Jewish Bible. Also known as the Five Books of Moses or the Pentateuch. (*GJ*). Also includes all the teaching that comprises the Jewish tradition as well as methods of inquiry about them. "The Torah remains revelatory to new generations of Jews through time" (Sullivan 29).
Tallis	Rectangular prayer-shawl to whose four corners, fringes are attached. (*JGV*)
Yarmulke	Round cloth head covering worn by observant male Jews. (*GJ*)
Yeshiva	religious school. (*GRY*)
Yom Kippur	The Day of Atonement. On this day Jewish people ask God's forgiveness for whatever wrongs they have done during the year. (Sullivan 29)
Zeyda	Grandfather. (*GRY*)

Appendix II – Portraiture

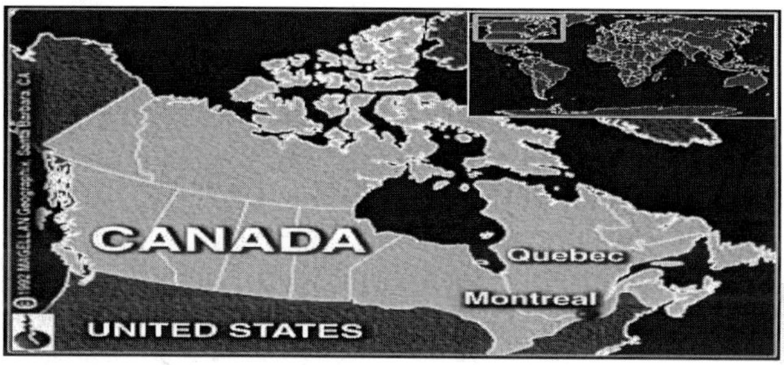

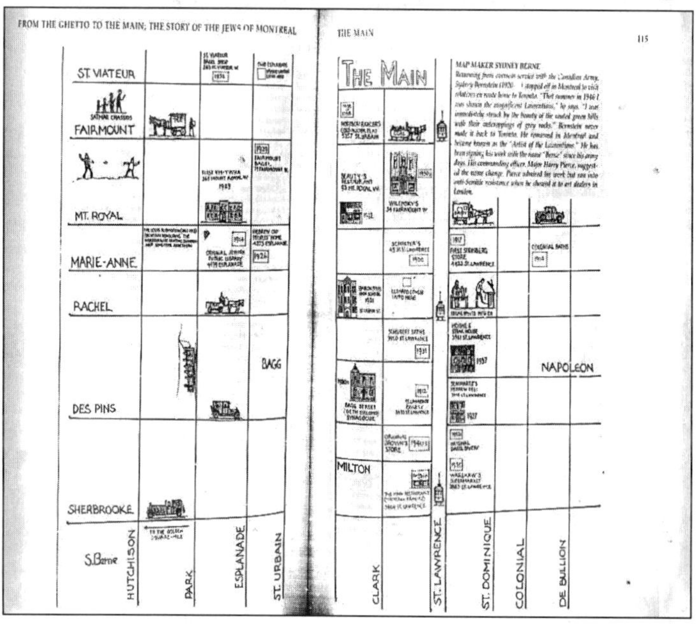

A layout of "The Main" in mid-twentieth century Montreal by map maker Sydney Berne (King 115)

The 19th C Montreal's Jewish community was concentrated around St. Lawrence below Ste. Catherine. Above is a view of Jewish residences on Cadieux Street. The street is now gone. (De Wolf)

The Chevra Cadosha Synagogue on St. Urbain Street in 1914 McCord Museum)

E. corner, Vitre & St. Urbain Streets, Montreal, QC, about 1915 ((McCord Museum)

Mordecai Richler on the steps of a house on St. Urbain Street, Montreal, circa 1970s (Canadian Museum of Civilization

Row houses, St. Urbain Street, Montreal, QC, 1931 (McCord Museum)

St. Urbain Street Now (2011) (A Flickr photo- Source unknown)

Appendix III – The Written Word

E-Mail correspondence with Stephen Greenblatt Cogan University Professor at Harvard University and founding figure of New Historicism

Subject: Re: A voice from the EAST!

From: Greenblatt, Stephen (greenbl@fas.harvard.edu)

To: jayanthimanoj2000@yahoo.com;

Date: Friday, 31 August 2012 9:33 PM

Dear Mary Jayanthi,

Many thanks for your welcome and interesting letter. I think your project sounds exciting, and, though I do not know Richler (apart from the film of Duddy Kravitz) I can easily imagine that he would lend himself to the kind of analysis to which you are drawn. The relationship between a somewhat closed ethnic and religious community and a larger, multi-ethnic world has generated a great deal of powerful 20th century fiction.

With best wishes,

Stephen Greenblatt

Sent from my iPad

On Aug 31, 2012, at 10:09 AM, "Jayanthi Manoj" <jayanthimanoj2000@yahoo.com> wrote:

> Dear Prof. Greenblatt,
> I am indeed happy to write to you and wish that this mail reaches the working mail-inbox of yours and be blessed with the possibility of your time and space to read through.
>
> I am Mary Jayanthi, Assistant Professor of English, Holy Cross College, Trichy, India. My interest in New Historicism deepened with lectures by Prof. PC Kar, a Professor and Critic, who has interacted with you on one of his academic visits to Harvard. This led me to read *Learning to Curse*, *Marvellous Possessions* and other essays on New Historicism.
>
> I am presently working for my Ph.D award and possibly would submit it this December 2012. The title of my thesis is
> **Conflicts from Surrounding Spaces of the mid 20th Century Montreal Ghettos: A New Historicism Approach to Richler's select novels**
> My present work, applies the practice of New Historicism and analysis the select works of Mordecai Richler, the Jewish-Canadian Writer (1931-
> 2001) , focusing on his point of view of time, space, race, religion and history as lived and perceived by the author and the episodes and incidents
> of his childhood and youth. A thesis of intense perception of his period of how people indulge in transgression and moral policing to expose hypocritical societies and families.

Facebook messages with Emma Richler, writer and daughter of Mordecai Richler

Left- My Queries to Emma Richler **Right- Emma Richler's response**

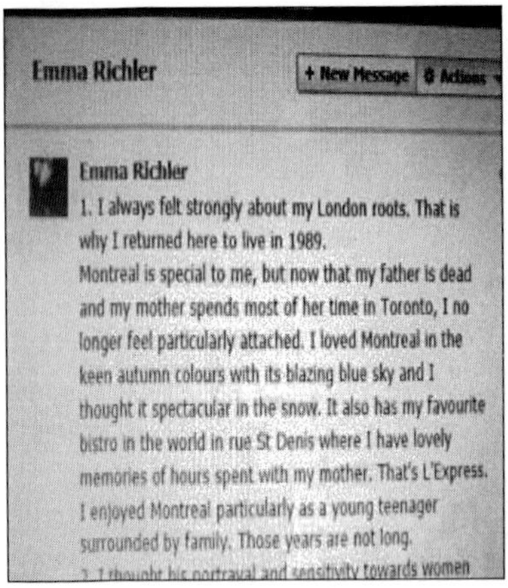

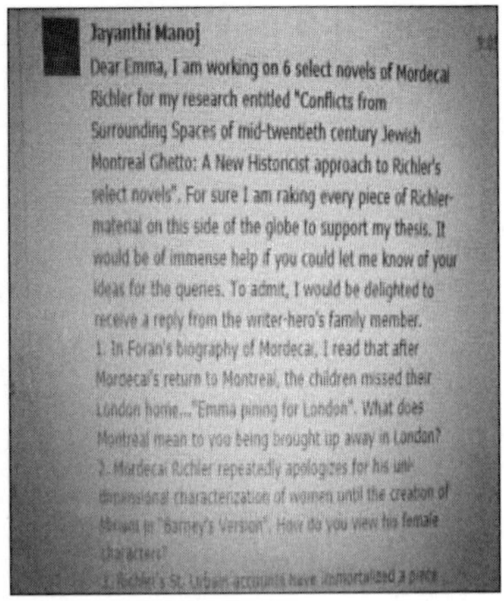

Reprint of parts of the Communication

MJ – Richler repeatedly apologizes for his unidimensional characterization of women until the creation of Miriam in Barney's Version. How do you view his female characters?

ER – I thought his portrayal and sensitivity towards women characters – as did his descriptions and sensitivity towards landscape – changed drastically with age. His had almost everything to do with my mother. Furthermore, there were interesting women in a novel prior to *Barney's Version* and that was *Solomon Gursky was Here.* My mother allowed him to expand as a writer. He wd have developed regardless, but I feel very strongly he wd not have become the same fully fledged artist he became without her inspiration. Quite fascinating.

MJ – Richler's St. Urbain accounts have immortalized a piece of geography in Canadian Literary history. What does St. Urbain mean to you?

ER – St Urbain St does not mean very much to me. I went there. I can't even tell you if that deli Wollensky's he went to as a boy and took us to many years later is in St Urbain St or not. The name is full of my father. So that's largely what it signifies for me. The world of the Jewish ghetto he grew up in was quite special to him. He never imposed it on us as any particular legacy to pay obeisance to.

MJ – According to you is Mr. Mordecai as a writer, a serious moralist or a fantastic satirist?

ER – I don't categorise him at all. He had a very fine gift for satire and he was also, for all his wild humour, a deeply moral man, both in his life and work. He is a writer above all, but rare, because unlike so very many novelists, he was full-blooded as well as hugely rigorous in the novels he created.

MJ – What is Richler's lasting influence on you and which of his writings do you appreciate?

ER – His discipline. His honesty. *Solomon Gursky Was Here* and *Barney's Version* are inspired. I also find his essays remarkable and completely engrossing and stimulating. Just brilliant. He is deeply missed, as a man, as a writer.

E-Mail communication with Charles Foran, Canadian novelist, non-fiction writer and author of Mordecai: His Life and Times

Print Page 1 of 2

Subject: Re: On Reading - Mordecai:His Life and Times

From: charlie@charlesforan.com (charlie@charlesforan.com)

To: jayanthimanoj2000@yahoo.com;

Cc: cforan@hotmail.com;

Date: Friday, 21 September 2012 10:56 PM

Dear Mary,

Thanks for your kind letter, and apologies for this slow reply. Your work on Mordecai Richler sounds remarkable, all the moreso for being done at by an Indian scholar. To answer your questions:

1. The soul-defining moment involved discovering the remarkable letter that Richler wrote to his mother in 1976. On reading it, I realized it was a key to understanding his character, and many of the decisions he had made in his life, and once I thought it through, I realized that the 'narrative' of his terrible relationship with Lily Rosenberg was perhaps one of two key underpinnings to the biography. (The other was his marriage to Florence.)

2. St Urbain Street is maybe the most distinctive, realized, and ardently mapped 'urban' neighbourhood in Canadian literature. It was certainly unusual, given how rural many early Canadian novels were, and it remains an actual 'destination' for admirers of Richler's work, the way people go looking for Joyce's Dublin or Dickens' London. That is very rare, and a testament to how vividly Richler created this world.

3. Richler is best compared with the American-Jewish writers of his generation -- Saul Bellow, Philip Roth, Joseph Heller. The influence of British satirists like Waugh is evident in a couple of his middle period books, and he was always trying to emulate the sensibility of Isaac Babel. That said, like all major writers, his voice, is work, was entirely his own -- a unique vision.

Hope this helps. Good luck with the thesis.

Best wishes,

Charlie F

Quoting Jayanthi Manoj <jayanthimanoj2000@yahoo.com>:

> Dear Charler Foran,
>
> I am Mary Jayanthi, Assistant Professor of English, Holy Cross College, Trichy, India.
> I am greatly happy to write to you after reading your book, Mordecai, The Life and Times, an engaging, evocative, well-reascarched, updated, objective portrait of the honest-writer-hero- Mordecai Richler. The book is a valuable resource for all scholars who cannot make it to the University of Calgary nor Montreal or st. Urbain street but can bring it to their study room on reading your book.
>
> I am presently working for my Ph.D award on Richler's select novels and the title of my thesis is Conflicts from Surrounding Spaces of the mid 20th Century Montreal Ghettos: A New Historicism

http://in.mg5.mail.yahoo.com/neo/launch?.rand=bfeavohp7lfol 9/26/2012

E-mail response from Prof. Prafulla Kar, Director, Centre for Contemporary Theory, MS University of Baroda, India

From: Prafulla Kar <prafullakar@gmail.com>
To: Jayanthi Manoj <jayanthimanoj2000@yahoo.com>
Sent: Tuesday, 28 June 2011 8:39 AM
Subject: Re: Query

Dear Mary:

Thanks for your mail. It's good to know that you are working on Richler's fiction by using New Historicist methodology. The phrase "surrounding spaces" is not used by any specific critic; Greenblatt used the phrase "circumambient space" to suggest that a work of art draws its creative energy from the surrounding space as a cultural artifact. Greenblatt you should use for your work. You may like to look up Catherine Gallagher's work also.
Greenblatt develops his new historicist approach by taking into consideration the works of Bakhtin, Clifford Geertz and Foucault.

All the best,
Yours sincerely,
Prafulla Kar

Works Cited

Abrams. M.H. *The Glossary of Literary Terms.* New Delhi: Macmillan Company, 1978. Print.

Antony, John D. *Mental Disorders Encountered in Counselling.* India: Anugraha Publ., 2006. Print.

Apprenticeship of Duddy Kravitz. by Mordecai Richler. Dir. Ted Kotcheff. Paramount Pictures, 1974. Film.

Atwood, Margaret. *Survival-A Thematic Guide to Canadian Literature.* Toronto: Anansi, 1972. Print.

Barney's Version. By Mordecai Richler. Dir. Richard J. Lewis. Entertainment One, 2010. Film.

Barry, Peter. *Beginning Theory: An introduction to Literary and Cultural theory.* India: T.R. Publ.,1999. Print.

Bethlehem, Louise. *English in Africa.* 27.1 (2000): 140-158. Web. 2 June 2012. <http://www.jstor.org/stable/40238896 >.

Bissell, Claude. "Politics and Literature in the 1960s". *Literary History of Canada.* Ed. Carl F Klinck (et al). Vol 3.Canada: U of Toronto P, 2nd edn, 1976. 3-15. Print.

Brenner, Rachel Feldhay. *Assimilation and Assertion: The Response to the Holocaust in Mordecai Richler's Writing.* NY: Peter Lang Publ., 1989. Print.

Brizee, Allen J. and J. Case Tompkins. "New Historicism, Cultural Studies (1980s-present)". Purdue OWL. Purdue University House.16 March 2012. Web. 28 May 2012. < http://owl.english.purdue.edu/owl/resource/722/09/>.

"Canada". *Encyclopaedia Judaica* – Jewish Virtual Library. The Gale Group, 2008. Web.17 Nov 2009. <http://www.jewishvirtuallibrary.org/jsource/judaica/ejud_ 0002_ 0004_0_03891.html>.

Craniford, Ada. *Mordecai Richler: A life in ten novels.* NY: iUniverse, 2005. Print.

Cross, Michael S. "Canadian History". *Literary History of Canada.* Ed. Carl F Klinck... (etal). Vol. 3. Canada: U of Toronto P, 2nd edn, 1976. 64-83. Print.

Chapman, Gary. *Five Love Languages for Teens.* US: Northfield Publ., 2000. Print.

Chevra Cadosha Synagogue on St. Urbain Street in 1914. Photograph. McCord Museum. Web. 28 Mar. 2013. <*http://www.mccord-museum.qc.ca/en/*>.

Cohen, Sarah Blacher. Introduction. "The Varieties of Jewish Humor". *Jewish Wry – Essays on Jewish Humor.* Ed. Sarah Cohen. Bloomington: Indiana UP., 1987. 1-15. Print.

Das, Bijay Kumar. *Twentieth Century Literary Criticism.* New Delhi: Atlantic Publ. 6th edn, 2010. Print.

Davidson, Arnold E. *Mordecai Richler.* NY: Frederick Ungar Publ. Co.,1983. Print.

Davis, Robertson. *The Deptford Trilogy: The Manticore.* England: Penguin books, 1983. Print.

De Wolf, Christopher. "The 19th C Montreal's Jewish community was concentrated around St. Lawrence ". Photograph. *Yiddishkayt and Soviet Spies: Life on the Main.* 18 Apr. 2007. Web. 27 Mar. 2013. < http://www.urbanphoto.net/blog/ 2007 /04/18 /yiddishkayt-and-soviet-spies-life-on-the-main/>.

Dooley, D.J. "Mordecai Richler and Duddy Kravitz: A Moral Apprenticeship". *Moral Vision in the Canadian Novel.* Toronto: Clarke Irwin Co., 1979. 93-107. Print.

Douglas, Mary. *Purity and Danger.* London: Routledge, 1966. Print.

Davey, Frank. *Post-National Arguments-The Politics of the Anglophone Canadian Novel since 1967.* Toronto: U of Toronto P, 1993. Print.

Deer, Glenn. "Early Richler, *Las Fallas,* and Sacrificing the National Self" *Canadian Literature* 207 (2010): 42-58. Print.

Dvorak, Marta. "Fiction". *The Cambridge Companion to Canadian Literature* Ed. Eva-Marie Kroller. UK: Cambridge UP, 2005. 155-176. Print.

"English Literature – The Figure of the Jew". *Encyclopaedia Judaica* – Jewish Virtual Library. The Gale Group, 2008. Web.17 Nov 2009. <http://www.jewishvirtual library.org/jsource/judaica/ejud_0002_0002_0_01522.html>.

"Every Goy's Guide to Richler: Yiddish phrases & Jewish cultural references in *The Apprenticeship of Duddy Kravitz*" Matt Corks. Web. 20 Feb. 2013. < http://theorem.ca/~mvcorks/yiddish.html>.

Fiamengo, Janice. "Regionalism and Urbanism". *The Cambridge Companion to Canadian Literature* Ed. Eva-Marie Kroller. UK: Cambridge UP, 2005. 241- 262. Print.

Fiddler on the Roof. Dir. Norman Jewison. Untitled Artists, 1971. Film.

Fleras, Augie, and Jean Leonard Elliot. *Multiculturalism in Canada.* Ontario: Nelson Canada, 1992. Print.

Foran, Charles. Interview by Rebecca Brayton. *Mordecai Richler: Bio of Barney's Version Author.* Web. 19 Oct. 2012. <http://watchmojo.com /video/id/9038/>.

.........*Mordecai-The Life and Times.* Toronto: Vintage Canada Edition, 2011.Print.

........."Re: On Reading – Mordecai: His Life and Times." Message to Mary Jayanthi. 21 Sept. 2012. E-mail.

Fowler, Roger. *A Dictionary of Modern Critical Terms.* London: Routledge, 2001. Print.

Gallagher, Catherine, and Stephen Greenblatt. Chicago: U of Chicago P, 2000. Print.

Ganesan, S. "Quest for values in the novels of Mordecai Richler:" Diss. Bharathidasan University, 2006. Print.

Geertz, Clifford. "Thick Description – Toward an Interpretive Theory of Culture". *The Interpretation of Cultures: Selected Essays.* NY: Basic Books, 1973. 3-30. Web.19 Sept.2012. <http://www.sociosite.net/topics/texts/ Geertz_Thick_Description.php>.

Gerson, Carole. "Some Patterns of Exile in Jewish Writing of the Commonwealth". Ariel 13.4 (1982). 103-114. Print.

Gibson, Graeme. *Eleven Canadian Novelists.* Toronto: Anansi, 1973. 265-299. Print.

"Glossary of Judaism". Web. 1 Jan 2012. <http://www.religionfacts.com/ judaism /glossary.htm>.

Golden, Daniel. "Mystical Musing and Comic Confrontations: The Fiction of Saul Bellow and Mordecai Richler." *Essays on Canadian Writing* 22. (1981): 62- 85. Print.

Gore, Al. Teleplay. *An Inconvenient Truth.* Dir. David Guggenheim. Paramount Classics, 2006. Film.

Greenblatt, Stephen, ed. *Cultural Mobility: A Manifesto.* Cambridge: Cambridge UP, 2009. Web. 1 Sept. 2011. <http://www.fas.harvard.edu/~ cardenio/ mobility.html>.

........."Invisible Bullets." *Literary Theory: An Anthology.* Revised edition. Ed.Julie Rivkin and Michael Ryan. Oxford UK: Blackwell, 2002. 787-803. Print.

.........*Learning To Curse: Essays in Early Modern Culture.* NY: Routledge, 1990. Print.

.........*Marvellous Possessions.* Oxford: OUP, 1991. Print.

.........*Renaissance Self-Fashioning: From More to Shakespeare.* Chicago, IL: U of Chicago P, 1980, 2005. Print.

Greenstein, Michael, ed. *Contemporary Jewish Writing in Canada – An Anthology.* Lincoln: U of Nebraska P, 2004. Print.

........."Mordecai Richler and Jewish-Canadian Humor". *Jewish Wry – Essays on Jewish Humor.* Ed. Sarah Cohen. Bloomington: Indiana UP., 1987. 196-215. Print.

.........*Third Solitudes: Tradition and Discontinuity in Jewish-Canadian Literature.* Montreal: McGill: Queen's UP, 1989. Print.

Griffiths, Sian. "Mordecai Richler's Montreal." *Guardian* 11 Jan. 2011. Web. 20 Feb. 2012. <http://www.guardian.co.uk/travel/2011/jan/11/montreal-mordecai richler-literary-guide>.

Gurevich, David. "St. Urbain Revisited". *The New Criterion* 8 (April 1990):72.Web.20 Feb. 2012. <http://www.newcriterion.com/articles.cfm /St Urbain revisited-5662>.

Hall, Donald E. *Literary and Cultural Theory: From Basic Principles to Advanced Applications.* NY: Houghton Mifflin Company, 2001. Print.

Holocaust Encyclopedia. Web. 6 Jan 2013. <http://www.ushmm.org/wlc/en/article. PHP?moduleid=10005059>.

Howe, Irving. "The Nature of Jewish Laughter". *Jewish Wry – Essays on Jewish Humor.* Ed. Sarah Cohen. Bloomington: Indiana UP., 1987. 16-24. Print.

Hutcheon, Linda. *The Canadian Postmodern.* Ontario: Oxford UP,1988. Print.

"The Novel". *Literary History of Canada.* Ed. William H. New... (et al). Vol. 4. Canada: U of Toronto P, 2nd edn, 1990. 73-96. Print.

Humm, Maggie. *The Dictionary of Feminist Theory.* NY: Harvester Wheatsheaf, 1989. Print.

Jacobs, Louis. "The laws and customs of the Sabbath" *Jewish Virtual Library.* The American-Israeli Cooperative Enterprise. 2010. Web. 21 Apr. 2012. <http://www.jewishvirtuallibrary.org/jsource/glossD.html>.

Jewish Family Life and Customs – A Practical Guide. Printed by Linnerlake. Web. 28 Jan. 2010 <http://www.boardofdeputies.org.uk/file/Family Life Customs.pdf>.

"Jewish Glossary" *Jewish Virtual Library.* The American-Israeli Cooperative Enterprise. 2010. Web. 21 Apr. 2012. <http://www.jewishvirtuallibrary.org/jsource/glossD.html>

Johnson, Brian. "Son of a Smaller (Super) Hero: Ethnicity, Comic Books, and Secret identity in Richler's Novels of Apprenticeship". *Canadian Literature* 207 (2010): 26-40. Print.

Kar, Prafulla. "Re: Query." Message to Mary Jayanthi. 28 June 2011. E-mail.

King James Bible. New Jersey: Thomas Nelson Inc., 1970. Print.

King, Joe. *From the Ghetto to the Main: The Story of the Jews of Montreal* .Montreal: The Montreal Jewish Publication Society, 2001. Print.

Kramer, Reinhold. *Mordecai Richler Leaving St Urbain.* Montreal: McGill-Queen's UP, 2008. Print.

Lai, Chung- Hsiung. *Limits and Beyond: Greenblatt, New Historicism and a Feminist Genealogy*, 2006. Web. 17 Nov. 2012. <http://benz.nchu.edu.tw/~intergrams /071-072/071-072-lai.pdf>.

Lakshmi, S. "A Thematic Study of Search for Identity in the novels of Mordecai Richler:" Diss. Bharathidasan University, 2003. Print.

Larson, Thomas. "Review: Solomon Gursky Was Here by Mordecai Richler". *San Diego: Union-Tribune* (May 4, 1990) Web. 8 Oct. 2012. <http://www.thomaslarson.com/publications/criticism/170-solomon-gursky.html>.

Lipset, Seymour Martin. *North American Cultures: Values and Institutions in Canada and the United States.* U.S.A: Borderlands Project-Monographs Series #3, 1990. Print.

Liu, Fei Wen. *Elaborating on Geertz's "Thick Description": From Text to Reading,Narration, and Performance.* Institute of Ethnology, Academia Sinica.Web.6 May 2012. <http://aao.sinica.edu.tw/download/publication_list/en/134.pdf>

Marsh, James H., ed. *The Canadian Encyclopedia.* Edmonton: Hertig, 1988. Print.

Marshall, Tom. "Third Solitude: Canadian as Jew". *The Canadian Novel Here and Now.* Ed. John Moss. Ontario: New Canada Publ. 1978. 147-155. Print.

McSweeney, Kerry. "Mordecai Richler". *Canadian Writers and their Works: Essays on form, context, and development.* Eds. Lecker, David & Quigley. Toronto: ECW Press, 1985.129-179. Print.

Mordecai Richler on the steps of a house on St. Urbain Street, Montreal, circa 1970s Photograph. *Canadian Museum of Civilization.* Web. 28 Mar. 2013. <http:/www.civilization.ca/cmc/exhibitions/hist/biography/biographi240e.shtml>.

Mordecai Richler: The Last of the Wild Jews. Dir. Francine Pelletier, 2010. Film. Web. 19 Oct. 2012. < http://www.youtube.com/watch?v=LyqJpPPwJUM> .

Moss, John. Introduction. *The Canadian Novel-Beginnings.* Ed. John Moss. Vol. II. Ontario: New Canada Publ., 1980. 7-15. Print.

.........Introduction. *The Canadian Novel Here and Now.* Ed. John Moss. Ontario: New Canada Publ. 1978. 7-15. Print.

........."Richler's Horseman". *The Canadian Novel Here and Now.* Ed. John Moss. Ontario: New Canada Publ. 1978. 156-165. Print.

Myers, David. "Mordecai Richler as a Satirist". *Ariel* 4.1 (1973): 47-61. Print.

Myers, D.G. "The New Historicism in Literary Study". *Academic Questions* 2 (1988- 89): 27-36. Web. 29 Mar. 2011. <http://wwwenglish.tamu.edu/pers/fac/myers/historicism.html>.

Myers, Tamara. "On Probation: The Rise and fall of Jewish Women's Antidelinquency

Work in Interwar Montreal". *Negotiating Identities in 19th- and 20th-Century Montreal.* Ed. Bradbury & Myers. Vancouver: UBC Press, 2005. 175-201. Print.

Naravane, Vaiju. "On the art of creating fiction from reality". *Hindu* 15 Dec. 2012: 9 Print.

New, William H. "Fiction". *Literary History of Canada.* Ed. Carl F Klinck... (et al) Vol 3. Canada: U of Toronto P, 2nd edn, 1976. 233-283. Print.

Nobel, Robin. "Heroic Imaginings: Judaism, Masculinity, and Compensation in Richler's *The Apprenticeship of Duddy Kravitz, St. Urbain's Horseman, and Solomon Gursky Was Here". Canadian Literature* 207 (2010): 90-102. Print.

Posner, Michael. *The Last Honest Man – Mordecai Richler – An Oral Biography.* Toronto: McClelland and Stewart Limited, 2004. Print.

"*Purity and Danger by Mary Douglas".* A Report by Victoria Caplan . Web. 20 Feb. 2010. < http://ihome.ust.hk/~lbcaplan/mphil/purity.html>.

Ramraj, Victor J. *Mordecai Richler.* Boston: Twayne Publ., 1983. Print.

.........“Mordecai Richler – Biocritical essay". Sandra Mortensen, comp. Apollonia Steele and Jean F. Tener, eds. *The Mordecai Richler papers: An inventory of the archive at the University of Calgary Libraries.* U of Calgary P, 1987. Web. 8 Oct 2009. <http://www.ucalgary.ca/libold/SpecColl /richlerbioc.htm>.

Ravvin, Norman. *A House of Words.* Montreal: McGill Queen's UP, 1997. Print.

Redekop, Magdalene. "Canadian literary criticism and the idea of a national literature". *The Cambridge Companion to Canadian Literature* Ed. Eva-Marie Kroller. UK: Cambridge UP, 2004. 263-275. Print.

Richler, Emma. Message to Mary Jayanthi. 10 Apr. 2013. E-mail.

Richler, Mordecai. "Coming Home Again". *People of Our Time.* CBC Television. 1 Sept. 1975. CBC Archives. Web. 21 Aug. 2012. <http://www.cbc.ca/archives/ categories/arts-entertainment/literature/ mordecai-richler-was-here/richlers- homecoming.html>.

.........*Home Sweet Home-My Canadian Album.* New York. Knopf. 1984. Print.

.........*Hunting Tigers Under Glass.* London: Panther. 1971. Print.

.........Interview by Reporter: Elaine Grand, Host: J. Frank Willis, Close-Up. CBC Television.5 Nov. 1961.CBC Archives. Web. 28 Jan. 2011. <http://www.cbc. ca/ archives/categories/arts-entertainment/ literature/mordecai-richler>.

.........Interview by Robert Fulford. "Is Mordecai Richler a Jewish anti-Semite?" This is Robert Fulford. CBC Radio. 23 July 1968. CBC Digital

Archives. Web. 28 May 2012. <http://rc-archives.cbc.ca/programs/ 755-4596/page/1/>.

.........*The Street.* Canada: Penguin Books Canada, 1969. Print.

........."Why I Write". Canadian Novelists on Canadian Fiction. Eds. Daymond & Monkman. Ottawa: Borealis Press, 1981. 224-232. Print.

Richler, Mordecai and Robert Fulford. Interview by A. Davidson Dunton. *Room for Argument.* CBC Radio. 5 May 1965. CBC Digital Archives. Web. 22 Aug. 2012. < http://www.cbc.ca/archives/categories/arts-entertainment/ literature/mordecai-richler>.

Robson, Mark. *Stephen Greenblatt.* London: Routledge, 2009. Print.

Rosenberg, Louis. *Canada's Jews: A Social and Economic Study of Jews in Canada in the 1930.* Montreal: Canadian Jewish Congress, 1939. Print.

Row houses, St. Urbain Street, Montreal, QC, 1931. Photograph. McCord

Museum. Web. 28 Mar. 2013. *<http://www.mccord-museum.qc.ca/en/>.*

Ryan, Michael. *Literary Theory: A Practical Introduction.*UK: Blackwell, 2002.Print.

Salat M.F. *The Canadian Novel: A Search for Identity.* Delhi: B.R. Publ.,1993. Print.

S. E. corner, Vitre & St. Urbain Streets, Montreal, QC, *about 1915.* Photograph. McCord Museum. Web. 28 Mar. 2013.< *http://www.mccord museum.qc.ca/en/>*

"Self-Made Men". *Wikipedia.* Web. 21 Apr.2012.

Singer, Melina Baum. ""Is Richler Canadian Content?" – Jewishness, Race, and Diaspora". *Canadian Literature* 207 (2010): 11-24. Print.

Singh, Frank Birbal. "The Early Fiction of Mordecai Richler". *Novels and the Nation.* Toronto: Oxford University Press, 1995. 100-107. Print.

"St. Urbain Street just not St. Urbain enough." *Ottawa Citizen* 21 Oct. 2006. Web. 28 Jan. 2013. <http://www.canada.com/ottawacitizen /news/arts/story.html? >.

Sullivan, Lawrence E. *The Religious Tradition of Judaism.* Philadelphia: Chelsea House, 2000. Print.

"Subversion and Containment". Web. 29 March 2012. <http://en. wikipedia.org/wiki/ Theory_of_Subversion_and_Containment>.

Vanderhaeghe, Guy. Afterword. *St. Urbain's Horseman.* By Mordecai Richler. Toronto: McClelland & Stewart Inc. 1989. Print.

Veeser, Aram H. Introduction. *The New Historicism.* Ed. H. Aram Veeser. New York: Routledge, 1989. ix- xiv. Print.

Weintraub, William. *City Unique: Montreal Days and Nights in the 1940s and '50s.* Toronto: Robin Brass Studio, 2004. Print.

Wohlgelernter, Maurice. *Jewish Writers/Irish Writers: Selected Essays on the Love of Words* New Jersey: Transaction Publishers, 2000. Web. 1 March 2012. <http://books.google.co.in/books?id=X2PvNKDwfUC&pg=PP1&lpg>.

Woodcock, George. Introduction. *Son of a Smaller Hero.* By Mordecai Richler. Toronto: McClelland and Stewart Limited, 1955. Print.

.........*Introducing Mordecai Richler's The Apprenticeship of Duddy Kravitz.* Toronto: ECW Press, 1990. Print.

Wright, Eric. Afterword. *Joshua Then and Now.* By Mordecai Richler. Ontario: McClelland & Stewart Inc. 1980. Print.

Yanofsky, Joel. *Mordecai and Me – An Appreciation of a Kind.* US: Red Deer Press, 2003. Print.

"Yiddish Vocabulary". Web. 1 Mar. 2013. <http://www.pass.to/ glossary/ Default.htm>.

Index

D

E

F

G

H

I

J

K

L

M

Q

R

S

T

W

Y

Z